Archaeology and Digital Communication

Towards Strategies of Public Engagement

Archaeology and Digital Communication

Towards Strategies of Public Engagement

Edited by Chiara Bonacchi

Archetype Publications

First published 2012 by Archetype Publications Ltd

Archetype Publications
6 Fitzroy Square
London W1T 5HJ
www.archetype.co.uk

© Copyright is held jointly among the authors and Archetype Publications Ltd 2012

ISBN 978-1-904982-77-7

British Library Cataloguing in Publication Data
A catalogue record for this book is available from the British Library.

All rights reserved. No part of this publication may be reproduced, stored in a retrieval system, or transmitted, in any form or by any means, electronic, mechanical, photocopying, recording or otherwise, without the prior permission of the publishers.

The views and practices expressed by individual authors are not necessarily those of the editors or the publisher. Publisher's note: Due to the limitations of capturing images from the internet, some of the images in this publication fall below our normal publication standard.

Cover illustrations
Front cover: courtesy of Laboratorio di Archeologia Medievale dell'Università di Firenze
Back cover: © Museum of London

Typeset by A Concept Ltd., London NW1 7EA

Contents

List of contributors	vi
Acknowledgements	vii
Foreword — *Don Henson, Tim Schadla-Hall*	ix
Introduction — *Chiara Bonacchi*	xi
Value, Authority and the Open Society: Some Implications for Digital and Online Archaeology *Andrew Bevan*	1
Twitter and Archaeology: An Archaeological Network in 140 Characters or Less *Lorna Richardson*	15
Wessex Archaeology and the Web: Amesbury Archer to *Archaeocast* *Tom Goskar*	25
Strategy Games and Engagement Strategies *Andrew Gardner*	38
Public Engagement through Online TV Channels: A Way Forward for the Audiovisual Communication of Archaeology? *Chiara Bonacchi, Charles Furneaux, Daniel Pett*	50
Smartphones and Site Interpretation: the Museum of London's *Streetmuseum* Applications *Meriel Jeater*	66
Uses of Social Media within the British Museum and Museum Sector *Daniel Pett*	83
Wikipedia and Blogs: New Fields for Archaeological Research? *Amara Thornton*	103
A Call for Open Scholarship in Archaeology *Brian Hole*	114
Conclusions *Daniel Pett, Chiara Bonacchi*	127
Plates	

List of contributors

Andrew Bevan *(a.bevan@ucl.ac.uk)*
Senior lecturer, Institute of Archaeology, UCL

Chiara Bonacchi *(chiara.bonacchi@gmail.com)*
PhD candidate, Institute of Archaeology, UCL

Charles Furneaux *(charles.furneaux@kaboomtv.co.uk)*
MD, Kaboom Film and Television

Andrew Gardner *(andrew.gardner@ucl.ac.uk)*
Senior lecturer, Institute of Archaeology, UCL

Tom Goskar *(tom@goskar.com)*
Web manager, Wessex Archaeology

Don Henson *(d.henson@ucl.ac.uk)*
Honorary director, Centre for Audio-Visual Study and Practice in Archaeology, UCL

Brian Hole *(b.hole@ucl.ac.uk)*
PhD candidate, Institute of Archaeology, UCL, and Ubiquity Press

Meriel Jeater *(mjeater@museumoflondon.org.uk)*
Curator, Department of Archaeological Collections and Archive, Museum of London

Daniel Pett *(DPETT@britishmuseum.org)*
ICT adviser, The British Museum and Portable Antiquities Scheme

Lorna Richardson *(l.richardson@ucl.ac.uk)*
PhD candidate, Centre for Digital Humanities, UCL

Tim Schadla-Hall *(t.schadla-hall@ucl.ac.uk)*
Reader, Institute of Archaeology, UCL

Amara Thornton *(aalexandrath@gmail.com)*
Honorary research associate, Institute of Archaeology, UCL

Acknowledgements

I am grateful, first and foremost, to the authors of the present volume, who contributed with enthusiasm and commitment on the theme of digital communication in archaeology. I would like to thank Tim Schadla-Hall for his encouragement and support throughout the editing process, and Don Henson, Director of the Centre for Audio-Visual Study and Practice in Archaeology (UCL), for collaborating on the seminar series *Archaeologists and the Digital. Towards Strategies of Engagement* (16 May 2011; Institute of Archaeology, UCL), from which this volume originates. Thank you especially to my friend and colleague, Daniel Pett, whose help and advice has been invaluable and vital to this publication and to the organisation of the seminar series.

For their comments and suggestions and also for help in the review process, I am particularly grateful to Tyler Bell (Factual), Andrew Bevan (UCL), Robert Bewley (Heritage Lottery Fund), James Bradburne (Palazzo Strozzi), Matthew Cock (The British Museum), Enrico Crema (UCL), Eleonora Gandolfi (University of Southampton), Tom Goskar (Wessex Archaeology), Bill Hubbard (University of Nottingham), Leif Isaksen (University of Southampton), Akira Matsuda (University of East Anglia), Gabriel Moshenska (UCL), Jim Mower (Time Team), Daniel Pett (The British Museum), Tim Schadla-Hall (UCL), Jonathan Whitson-Cloud (The British Museum), and Liam Wyatt (Wikimedia Foundation).

Finally, I would like to thank the Publications Committee of the Institute of Archaeology (UCL) and the Portable Antiquities Scheme, for sponsoring this publication and contributing to making it possible.

For your teaching, thank you Guido Vannini. For your love and support, thank you Angela, Mario, Giacomo, Tommaso, and Federico.

Chiara Bonacchi

Foreword

Don Henson and Tim Schadla-Hall

This volume represents the first published fruits of the setting up of CASPAR (the Centre for Audio-Visual Study and Practice in Archaeology) at the UCL Institute of Archaeology, and also a working partnership with ACRN (the Archaeology and Communication Research Network), which in turn led to the organisation of a very successful workshop at the Institute of Archaeology (UCL). The workshop aimed to highlight, review, and examine the potential, as well as the developing role of digital communication in archaeology.

Archaeologists have long relied on communicating their results to a wider public through the most appropriate media available, particularly in the UK. This determination to engage with audiences has involved a close relationship with the dominant medium of the time and, in historical terms, the successful migration from newspapers, through to radio, and subsequently television demonstrates this adeptness to 'follow the medium'. Any history of communication and archaeology will inevitably mention *Chronicle* and *Time Team* and refer to the success of television, but the past is something that we dwell on too much in many ways!

The reasons for both this publication and for the workshop from which it originated was to examine, in what has always been a fast changing world of communication, how archaeology will engage with the public in the digital age. The word 'engagement' (a term often overused and abused) is preferred in this context because the nature of the new medium allows an entirely different relationship – both theoretically and practically – with the public in understanding and exploring the past.

The impact of the digital age is so completely different from what went before – just as we were getting used to the idea of an unlimited number of satellite television channels, with endless possibilities for communication more often, and in a more specialised fashion, the digital revolution, still less than twenty years in development, has yet again changed the dominant form of communication available to us. Access to information and audiences through digital systems has already impacted on all parts of our lives. In the case of archaeology, which has always been so adept at changing medium and techniques and approaches to reach a wider audience, the implications are significant. It was for this reason that the workshop was convened.

In the past, and particularly through the traditional broadcast media, the forms of communication and interaction were very much 'top-down': the archaeologist and programme offering to varying degrees information which the audience could consume – two-way interaction was rarely possible, for example. We now face new potential for engaging with the public in a myriad of ways, so it is critical that this potential and its limitations are closely assessed.

We were both brought up in an age that saw television as the primary communication medium for archaeology, and have then watched the impact of 'the digital' occur, so that it was a revelation and an education to attend the workshop and read the resulting papers. It is clear from the contributions and the discussion that took place that there are a number of issues that need to be addressed and considered – and this apart from the fact that archaeology does not have the resources that either the commercial world or much of the educational world have to make maximum use of the new technologies and to experiment with new forms of media access. This collection of papers not only offers a 'wake-up' insight into how fast the media are changing and into the importance of understanding ongoing changes, but also presents a platform for further work, as the conclusions demonstrate.

The nature of public archaeology is such that engagement with the public is crucial to the future support of archaeological practice. This volume is appearing both in hard copy and as an e-book thus managing to straddle the past – and meet the future! It lays out clearly both the potential, and the canvas and materials that are a challenge for all who want to communicate, engage and make archaeology a genuinely public activity. It is by no means the last word on the subject, but it is a first step towards developing a clearer approach to the study and advancement of this key area.

Introduction

Chiara Bonacchi

The context: new directions for Public Archaeology

The idea for a seminar series entitled *Archaeologists and the Digital. Towards Strategies of Engagement* (16 May 2011; Institute of Archaeology, UCL), which led to this volume, originated from a reflection on the necessity to look more widely at the 'mission' and research directions of Public Archaeology as a field of study.

Since its emergence as an area of academic endeavour, in Britain, in the 1990s, Public Archaeology has examined the plurality of interactions between archaeological research and the public (Schadla-Hall 1999, 2000, 2006; Matsuda 2004; Merriman 2004b). Much of this work focused primarily on discussing ethical issues related to the practice of archaeology, and succeeded in animating debate on archaeologists' actual and desirable code of conduct (for example, repatriation, illicit trade, controversial interpretations of the past) (Ucko 1987; Ascherson 2000). Literature in Public Archaeology often chose provocative tones and, as usually happens to recent research fields, a predominantly case study-based methodology. The reason for this was the pressing need to ensure that archaeologists realised that the study of the implications that their activity had for society at large, and for specific groups particularly, was worthy of more systematic scholarly attention.[1] Such research and debate was clearly essential to justify and ensure a sound foundation for new areas of study, concerned with much more than Cultural Resource Management and education (Schadla-Hall 1999) – the two components that originally characterised and still define Public Archaeology as understood in the USA (McGimsey 1972; Jameson 2004). Developments in the UK widened the scope of Public Archaeology, identifying politics, economics and communication as macro-themes of enquiry, and underlining their interconnectedness (Schadla-Hall 2006: 77), with a subsequent spread of these ideas across the world.[2]

As a result of the previous fifteen years of both research and teaching as well as other changing pressures (not least the current financial climate), archaeologists are now looking for more effective and diverse methods and approaches to reach 'the public'.[3] Therefore, it is time for Public Archaeology to shift its focus from demonstrating the importance of reflecting on the multi-faceted

---

[1] Since its early beginnings, archaeology has dealt with the public, although in different modalities at different times, and the relationship between archaeology and its socio-economic and political context has been the object of scientific investigation also prior to the foundation of Public Archaeology. The original contribution of the UK developments of Public Archaeology is that of having defined, organised and systematised research on the interaction between archaeology and the public within the same framework.

[2] For an overview of the worldwide developments of the UK approach to Public Archaeology, see also some of the contributions contained in the volumes edited by Merriman (2004a) and by Okamura and Matsuda (2011a), in addition to the works cited in Okamura and Matsuda's introduction (2011b: 7), including Bonacchi 2009, for Italy.

[3] The public is here understood in the three separate and related areas of 'state with its institutions', of 'groups of people and communities', and of 'public opinion'. For a discussion of the meanings of the word 'public' in Public Archaeology, see Merriman 2004b, Matsuda 2004, and Carman 2002.

interactions between archaeology and the public, to actually indicating how the positive impact of academic research on society can be developed and maximised. Increasingly a major aim of Public Archaeology should be that of contributing to policy, via systematic programmes of collaborative research designed to develop standards of public engagement and produce guidelines for achieving them, as well as toolkits for monitoring implementation. This seems particularly important in a context where, even more so than in the past, the allocation of public funding is dependent on the provision of robust evidence of public value and relevance,[4] and the diversification of financing sources is vital for the sustainability of the cultural sector (KEA European Affairs 2006: 154; Stanziola 2011). Guidelines are needed in order to respond effectively to the changes that are occurring in the organisational and managerial structures of museums, universities and the private sector. These changes follow the rise of networks and of new forms of partnerships as means of increasing both the economic sustainability and the efficiency of cultural institutions.[5] Such partnerships and networks are facilitated by the (progressively) wider availability of digital technologies, which can significantly strengthen the bonds between cultural and creative industries (Russo 2011; see also Bonacchi *et al.*, Jeater, and Pett, this volume). Unsurprisingly, a knowledge economy built primarily on the continuing growth and application of the digital was highlighted by the Department for Culture, Media and Sports (DCMS) and the Department for Business, Enterprise and Regulatory Reform (BERR) as the path that would lead the United Kingdom out of the current economic crisis that erupted in 2008 (DCMS and BERR 2009: 11).[6]

To pursue the outlined direction of Public Archaeology, a general methodological approach should be adopted comprising robustly conceptualised ideas and a fully thought-through combination of qualitative and quantitative methods. Qualitative methods are useful to formulate questions or to explore causation, and quantitative methods are essential to achieve policy goals, since they allow an assessment of the dimensions of the cultural trends identified. In order to achieve the increasing scale of effort that has been indicated, it is crucial that more practitioners who both recognise and understand the importance of reaching the public engage with Public Archaeology studies, in conjunction with their archaeological research. It is when conducted first and foremost by practicing archaeologists, with their specific archaeological specialisms, that Public Archaeology remains closely linked to the current scope and methods of archaeology, and can fully express its potential. As originally envisaged by McGimsey (1972), archaeologists are 'justified' to step into areas that would normally be the realm of political scientists, economists, or lawyers, based on their deep knowledge of social history reconstructed via material culture. This knowledge allows them to provide a meaningful and unique contribution to a wide variety of debates concerning, for example, the illicit trade of antiquities. The strong links with archaeological theory and practice differentiate Public Archaeology from anthropology, or cultural and heritage studies; yet this difference is not clear to many archaeologists, and such unawareness seems to be one of the strongest reasons for their often limited engagement with Public Archaeology research.

This publication embraces and supports the approach to Public Archaeology that has been described, and responds to demands formulated at policy level, for recommendations to lead practice in and evaluation of digital engagement with archaeology.

---

[4] For an application of this argument to the museum sector, see, for example, Scott 2007 and 2009. For information on the requirements imposed by the new Research Excellence Framework on universities, see HEFCE 2011.

[5] See, for example, KEA European Affairs 2006: 154, particularly Table 16; for an application to the UK creative sector, see Arts Council England 2010: 32–33.

[6] This vision has also been supported in the 2011–2015 *Business Plan* of the Department for Culture, Media and Sports (DCMS 2011: 12). The UK case is underlined because a large number of case studies presented in this publication are concerned with Britain (see Bonacchi *et al.*, Goskar, Jeater, Pett, this volume).

Aim and scope of the volume: digital strategies of public engagement

The primary aim of this volume is to propose digital strategies of public engagement that may be of interest to archaeologists working in various contexts: academics, museum curators and site managers, and the private sector, possibly in collaboration with media professionals and institutions. Contributions identify some of the most promising uses of the digital in different domains of archaeological communication and the benefits they can generate for participants; each use is presented through one or more case studies, highlighting how media experiences were designed and consumed. While providing specific operational recommendations, *Archaeology and Digital Communication: Towards Strategies of Public Engagement* also attempts to chart new potential directions for future research.

Although deriving from a workshop, this publication is not just a collection of developed and refined versions of the papers that were delivered on the day. It is a further step within a larger research project conducted under the aegis of the Centre for Audio-Visual Study and Practice in Archaeology (CASPAR) and the Archaeology and Communication Research Network (ACRN). Thus the volume deliberately maintains 'towards' in the title and concludes with the presentation of research prospects and possible next steps.

Up to this point, the project has been based on predominantly individual, but coordinated research. All the contributions share a broad understanding of public engagement as the maximisation of the impact of scientific research by connecting with the public (see also Bonacchi *et al.*, this volume), but reaching more specific definitions of engagement was considered as an objective to be discussed in the final section of the volume, where the different perspectives presented in the contributions are re-examined.

Under the word 'public', a number of individuals and groups with no formal training in archaeology are represented. Although contributing to the enhancement of intra- and inter-specialist communication (Clôitre and Shinn 1985: 36–51; Clack and Brittain 2007: 31) is not amongst the direct aims of this publication, however, the use of digital technologies applied to inter- and intra-specialist communication is considered. This is because the Internet has significantly eased the accessibility of the results of archaeological research and of data, by means of e-publishing and open access (see Bevan, and Hole, this volume), for example, or even via the websites of archaeological organisations (see Goskar, this volume). Thus, the use that the non-specialist public can make of this material is also discussed, and the continuity between research and public engagement is underlined.[7] Moreover, through digital Open Scholarship, new opportunities can be envisaged for proving the impact of research and guaranteeing the survival of archaeology as a discipline and of public engagement as well (see Hole, this volume).

Consistent with the media ecology view described in detail further on in this introduction, the volume does not concentrate only on entirely new modes of communication, which did not exist prior to the invention of digital technologies. The ways in which 'older' media forms are adapting to the changed environment is also a theme of this collection. The publication, in fact, comprises analyses of Web applications such as Twitter (Richardson, this volume), or Wikipedia (Thornton, this volume), but also of online TV channels (Bonacchi *et al.*, this volume) and of the ways in which smartphone applications and social media are changing the museum communication of archaeology (Jeater, and Pett, this volume).

With different slants, the papers contribute to the advancement of knowledge of four main aspects related to digital engagement with archaeology. These can be identified as: theory; participants; research methods, and the need for policy definition.

---

[7] This approach challenges those such as the one proposed by Copeland (2004), according to which interpretation is conceived as having two sides and 'souls'. In Copeland's analysis, first-phase interpretation is the scientific one, reached by archaeologists through the application of archaeological methods, whereas second-phase interpretation follows the first-phase one and essentially consists of bringing the results of archaeological research to non-specialists.

(1) The theoretical issues at the base of online engagement include themes such as authority and value (important issues to tackle in relation to past as well as contemporary societies; see Bevan, this volume), credibility, accuracy, branding, usability, communication speed, processing of information, and self-expression.
(2) As far as participation is concerned, papers discuss audience composition, perception and experience of digital communication.
(3) They offer a range of possible methods and indicators for researching and evaluating public engagement, while highlighting problematic aspects of data availability, collection and analysis.
(4) Shortcomings are also underlined as regards policy on public engagement, for example in relation to the use of social media by archaeological institutions (see Richardson, this volume).

Finally, the concluding chapter summarises the potential, for archaeologists, to use digital technologies for 'unfiltered' communication with the public, and highlights the strengths, weaknesses and margins of repeatability of the proposed 'strategies'.

The following two sections will offer an explanation of the approach to the study of archaeological communication and of the view over media change and digital communication based on which the scope and structure of the volume have been designed.

The approach to archaeology communication research

Since the 1970s, and even more since the 1990s, there has been a proliferation of scholarly work dealing with the communication of archaeology, as the latter increasingly returned to be a popular media subject (see, for example, Kulik 2007: 121–123). This body of literature, however, has been concerned mainly with content analysis, examining the portrayals of archaeology by the media, and by mass media especially (e.g. Ascherson 2004; Benz and Liedmeier 2007; Gardner 2007; Schadla-Hall and Morris 2003). Furthermore, when discussing presentations of archaeologists and archaeology that were deemed as inaccurate and trivial, researchers have often focused on analysing the negative effects of these narratives on the public (on this, see also Gardner, this volume).[8] There have been few scientific contributions that have tried to examine the cultural processes via which historically accurate interpretations are re-elaborated and turned into inaccurate representations (e.g. Hall 2009, and, with a different approach, Holtorf 2005, 2007b).

The most critical point of all, however, is that virtually no methodologically well-grounded and quantitatively significant audience research has been conducted with the aim of deepening archaeologists' knowledge of their public. It is ironic that, whilst new technologies are entering the media and communication landscape and speeding up its rate of change, the archaeological sector has hardly attempted to grasp the composition, consumption patterns, perceptions, attitudes and experience of the audiences of pre-digital forms of archaeological communication. Two notable exceptions are, firstly, Merriman's survey (1991) of the UK population's practices of and attitudes towards museum visiting and archaeology, and, more recently, Piccini's study of heritage viewers (2007) in Britain.[9] Other research on the public of archaeology usually either has a much smaller scale (e.g. Paynton 2002), or refers to other countries (e.g. Poktylo and Guppy 1999; Ramos and Duganne 2000). Alongside this absence of a sound, evidence-based understanding of audiences is the

---

[8] See, for example, Fowler 2007, or Schadla-Hall 2004, on the discriminatory ideologies embedded in 'alternative archaeologies'.
[9] The study was based on BARB figures and refers to the year between 1 May 2005 and 30 April 2006. Although Piccini investigated the audience of heritage television, she also provided viewing figures for archaeological series and one-off programmes.

lack of defined operational strategies for engaging specific segments of the public.[10]

Archaeology and Digital Communication: Towards Strategies of Public Engagement has addressed the issue of the dearth of audience research and applicable strategies of engagement, also by taking into consideration literature in the field of communication studies, which has often been neglected by archaeologists in the past.

An ecological view of media change and digital communication

Defining strategies of engagement becomes critical in order to better assess the real contribution that the digital realm can offer to archaeology, without suggesting that a new technology may have the power to radically and abruptly subvert previously entrenched practices of communication, and cultural and structural barriers to participation.

Digital technologies are changing the media and communication landscape rapidly and at an increasingly fast pace, by allowing the take-up of two phenomena: new media penetration and convergence. Convergence may be seen as the 'coming together of media economically (through corporate co-operation or merger), technically (through the means of production and distribution of media forms) and aesthetically (through the emergence of new forms of media content)' (Casey *et al.* 2008: 57–58). A similar definition is given by Lister *et al.* (2009: 420), who, however, together with McQuail (2005: 551–552), also specify that convergence occurs through digital technologies. Jenkins (2006: 2) further observes that the drawing together of media causes a 'flow of content across multiple ... platforms' and, consequently, a 'migratory behaviour of ... audiences'. With regards to new media, the novelty of recent years does not consist in their rise or theorization, but in their diffusion. In spite of being used since the 1960s, the expression 'new media' started to be more widely adopted to describe the changes occurring since the 1980s in 'media production, distribution and use' (McQuail 2005: 38; quotation from Lister *et al.* 2009: 13). Particularly, under this umbrella label are concepts such as 'new textual experiences', 'new ways of representing the world', 'new relationships between subjects and media technologies', 'new experiences of the relationship between embodiment, identity and community', 'new conceptions of the biological body's relationship to technological media' and 'new patterns of organization and production' (Lister *et al.* 2009: 12–13). The characteristics shared by new media, according to the same authors, are those of being digital, interactive, hyper textual, virtual, networked and simulated (Lister *et al.* 2009: 13), whilst McQuail (2005: 38) adds that they are ubiquitous and delocated, thus underlining that they do not require the user to be in a specific space. Among new media are social media, a range of 'Web-based platforms, applications and technologies that enable people to socially interact with one another online' (Webopedia 2011). Given their nature, they have the potential of transforming traditionally one-way forms of communication, such as television, into participatory ones. The dimensions of this potential, however, must be carefully assessed. For example, it is not clear whether and how social media allow the attraction of new audiences, or, instead, just help increase the frequency with which existing audiences engage with archaeology (on this topic see, for example, Pett, this volume).

Convergence and new media are radically modifying communication to the point of requiring a review of all its constitutional aspects: theory, policy and regulations, content development, production and delivery, economic models and markets (McQuail 2005; Livingstone and Das 2009). In order to better understand what is occurring, Naughton (2006: 43) has proposed leaving the traditional market-based discourse, and adopting a framework based on the American media theorist

---

[10] For example, Holtorf (2007a, 2007b: 105–129) defines three strategies of public engagement (educational, public-relations, and democratic), yet, however thought-provoking, these are speculative.

Neil Postman's view of 'media ecology', 'the study of media as environments'. This approach sees media as organisms that interact with one another and with the environment, creating a dynamic system (Naughton 2006: 43). This metaphor suggests that any new event introduced into the 'ecosystem' has an impact on all media-organisms and their mutual relationships, thus breaking the state of equilibrium (Naughton 2006: 43). The latter is reached again through 'ecological adaptations'. In such a framework, the possibility of 'wipe-out scenarios' is minimal and older media tend to adjust and survive next to newer ones (Naughton 2006: 43–44; Mackay and Ivey 2004: 92). For example, Buonanno (2008: 22) has noted that, in the evolution of the televisual medium, earlier stages usually overlap with later ones, especially when more recent phases raise the medium's threshold of accessibility. So, developing the previous example, there are two main reasons why it is probable that broadcast television will survive next to online TV. The first is connected with contents (some are more suited for broadcast mass communication); the second with accessibility thresholds (i.e. accessing broadcast television is easier). Notably, Thinkbox (2011) discovered that on-demand television has consolidated viewers' loyalty and boosted linear programming.

Since media ecology has its root in McLuhan's technological determinism (McLuhan 1962), the whole framework is based on the assumption that society is an organism that is fed by the media environment and modified by it (Naughton 2006; Postman 2000). This aspect needs to be nuanced. As highlighted by Livingstone (2002: 17), media are 'embedded in a social landscape, which precedes, shapes, contextualizes and continues after any specific technological innovation'. Such innovations cannot be considered as the products of another sphere of reality (Livingstone 2002: 18), because they are the result of questions posed by scientists within society and are preceded and followed by a process of design and development,

by the creation of a need and the identification of a market. Moreover, technological advancements are much more rapid than changes of identity, labour, social organisation etc. (Livingstone 2003: 4). The positions of technological and cultural determinism appear extreme and partial at the same time, but there is a path between the two apparent extremes that is potentially more convincing.

Whatever the causal links, there is enough evidence to suppose that the relationship between media and society is readjusting in a way that opens up new opportunities for engaging the public with archaeology (Lister *et al.* 2009: 11; DCMS and BERR 2009). This is suggested by Anderson's Long Tail model (2004; 2006), according to which the new economy will be based on selling less of more, as opposed to much of few. Thanks to digital technologies two main constraints of the 20th century media market may be overcome: the necessity to find a local market and the actual physical nature of media. The first, for instance, used to require a cinema to screen only those films that would be likely to attract large audiences within a maximum distance of ten miles. The second constraint is illustrated by the possibility to display only a limited number of CDs on the shelf of a music store, or of films in a rental shop, imposing the selection of products that will sell among a geographically well defined community. Digital technologies are, instead, progressively transforming a 'world of scarcity' into one of 'saturation', where space is no more an issue, as information is represented by binary numeric sequences and, through the Internet environment, audiences may be global.[11]

In this context, archaeology, which has largely been considered as a niche subject (e.g. by broadcasters), can more easily have a market next to the latest Hollywood blockbuster movie. Moreover, the Long Tail activates a virtuous circle that slowly changes the demand, since the possibility of exploring alternatives is leading the

---

[11] Anderson (2004) continues his argument by underlining that 'virtually anything can be made available online and companies such as Amazon are realising that a hit and a miss are on equal economic footing, both just entries in a database called up on demand, both equally worthy of being carried'. Although Anderson's overall argument has been reviewed by cultural economists such as Hjorth-Andersen (2007) as pointing towards a direction that is worth deepening, the details of his (journalistic) economic analysis have been criticised for not being entirely accurate.

public to discover that their tastes are not always so mainstream (Anderson 2004). This phenomenon reflects the wider social point described by Willman-Iivarinen (2009: 62), who suggested that people, today, have greater possibilities of choosing the groups to which to belong, as opposed to belonging to those in which they were born and definable in terms of social class, family, etc. As a consequence, they are driven to acquire that specific knowledge that goes along with the groups they have opted for. Audiences are multiplying and diversifying. Each is becoming less numerous, more homogeneous (McQuail 2005: 447) and primarily recruited on the basis of taste and lifestyle (McQuail 2005: 447). On one hand, then, the social landscape has characteristics that feed narrowcasting (in the marketing meaning of the term), while, on the other, new media and convergence contribute to the re-shaping of mass communication audiences, to the point of challenging the very existence of that notion.

The way in which the media landscape is changing is calling for a holistic re-evaluation of archaeological communication, based on data rather than supposition and faith. This publication is offered as an initial set of potential approaches to tackle these challenges and to develop a clear way forward.

References

Anderson C., 2004. The Long Tail. *Wired* 12.10 [online] October 2004. Available at: http://www.wired.com/wired/archive/12.10/tail.html?pg=1&topic=tail&topic_set (accessed 01 September 2011).

Anderson C., 2006. *The Long Tail. Why the Future of Business is Selling Less of More.* New York: Hyperion.

Anderson C. and Wolff M., 2010. The Web is Dead. Long Live the Internet. *Wired* 18.8 [online] 17 August 2010. Available at: http://www.wired.com/magazine/2010/08/ff_webrip/all/1 (accessed 01 September 2011).

Arts Council England, 2010. *Achieving Great Art for Everyone. A Strategic Framework for the Arts* [online]. Available at: http://www.artscouncil.org.uk/media/uploads/achieving_great_art_for_everyone.pdf (accessed 11 September 2011).

Ascherson N., 2000. Editorial. *Public Archaeology* 1 (1), pp. 1–4.

Ascherson N., 2004. Archaeology and the British Media. In Merriman N. ed., 2004. *Public Archaeology.* London: Routledge, pp. 145–158.

Benz M. and Liedmeier A., 2007. Archaeology and the German Press. In Clack T. and Brittain M. eds, 2007. *Archaeology and the Media.* Walnut Creek: Left Coast Press, pp. 154–173 .

Bonacchi C., 2009. Archeologia Pubblica in Italia. Origini e prospettive di un 'nuovo' settore disciplinare. *Ricerche Storiche* XXXIX (2–3), pp. 329–350.

Buonanno M., 2008. *The age of television: experiences and theories.* Bristol and Chicago: Intellect.

Carman J., 2002. *Archaeology and Heritage. An Introduction.* London: Continuum.

Casey N., Casey B., Lewis J., Calvert B., and French L., 2008. *Television studies: the key concepts.* London: Routledge.

Clack T. and Brittain M., 2007. Introduction. In Clack T. and Brittain M. eds, 2007. *Archaeology and the Media.* Walnut Creek: Left Coast Press, pp. 11–65.

Clôitre M. and Shinn T., 1985. Expository Practice: Social, Cognitive and Epistemological Linkage. In Shinn T. and Whitley R. eds, 1985. *Expositing Science: Forms and Functions of Popularization.* Dordrecht: Reidel, pp. 31–60.

Copeland T., 2004. Presenting archaeology to the public. Constructing insights on-site. In Merriman N. ed., 2004. *Public Archaeology.* London: Routledge, pp. 132–144.

DCMS (Department for Culture, Media and Sport), 2011. *Business Plan 2011–2015. Department for Culture, Media and Sport* [online] May 2011. Available at: http://www.number10.gov.uk/wp-content/uploads/DCMS-Business-Plan1.pdf (accessed 30 September 2011).

DCMS and BERR (Department for Culture, Media and Sport and Department for Business, Enterprise and Regulatory Reform), 2009. *Digital Britain. The interim report* [online] June 2009. Available at: http://www.culture.gov.uk/what_we_do/broadcasting/5631.aspx (accessed 30 September 2009).

Fowler P., 2007. Not Archaeology and the Media. In Clack T. and Brittain M. eds, 2007. *Archaeology and the Media.* Walnut Creek: Left Coast Press, pp. 89–107.

Gardner A., 2007. The Past as Playground: The Ancient World in Video Game Representation. In Clack T. and Brittain M. eds, 2007. *Archaeology and the Media.* Walnut Creek: Left Coast Press, pp. 255–272.

Hall M., 2009. Making the Past Present: Cinematic Narratives of the Middle Ages. In Gilchrist R. and Reynolds A. eds, 2009. *Refections: 50 Years of Medieval Archae-

ology. Society for Medieval Archaeology Monograph Series. Leeds: Maney Publishing, pp. 489–511.

HEFCE (Higher Education Funding Council for England), 2011. Research Excellence Framework [online]. Available at: http://www.hefce.ac.uk/research/ref/ (accessed 30 September 2011).

Hjorth-Andersen C., 2007. Book Review: Chris Anderson, The Long Tail: How Endless Choice is Creating Unlimited Demand. The New Economics of Culture and Commerce. *Journal of Cultural Economics* 31, pp. 235–237.

Holtorf C., 2005. *From Stonehenge to Las Vegas: Archaeology as Popular Culture*. Walnut Creek: AltaMira Press.

Holtorf C., 2007a. Can You Hear Me at the Back? Archaeology, Communication and Society. *European Journal of Archaeology* 10 (2/3), pp. 149–165.

Holtorf C., 2007b. *Archaeology is a Brand! The Meaning of Archaeology in Contemporary Popular Culture*. Walnut Creek: AltaMira Press.

Jameson J., 2004. Public Archaeology in the United States. In Merriman N. ed., 2004. *Public Archaeology*. London: Routledge, pp. 21–58.

Jenkins H., 2006. *Convergence culture: where old and new media collide*. New York: New York University Press.

KEA European Affairs, 2006. *The Economy of Culture in Europe* [online]. Available at: http://ec.europa.eu/culture/key-documents/economy-of-culture-in-europe_en.html (accessed 11 September 2011).

Kulik K., 2007. A Short History of Archaeological Communication. In Clack T. and Brittain M. eds, 2007. *Archaeology and the Media*. Walnut Creek: Left Coast Press, pp. 111–124.

Lister M., Dovey J., Giddings S., Grant I., and Kelly K., 2009. *New media: a critical introduction*. New York: Routledge.

Livingstone S., 2002. Introduction. In Lievrouw L. and Livingstone S. eds, 2002. *Handbook of New Media*. London: SAGE, pp.17–21.

Livingstone S., 2003. The changing nature of audiences: from the mass audience to the interactive media user. In Valdivia A. ed., 2003. *Companion to media studies. Blackwell companions in cultural studies* (6). Oxford: Blackwell Publishing, pp. 337–359.

Livingstone S. and Das R., 2009. The end of audiences: theoretical echoes of reception amidst the uncertainties of use. *Transforming Audiences* 2. London, 3–4 September 2009 [online]. Available at: http://eprints.lse.ac.uk/25116/ (accessed 01 September 2011).

Mackay H. and Ivey D., 2004. *Modern Media in the Home. An Ethnographic Study*. Rome: John Libbey Publishing

Matsuda A. 2004. The concept of 'the Public' and the aims of Public Archaeology. *Papers from the Institute of Archaeology* 15, pp. 66–76.

McGimsey C., 1972. *Public Archaeology*. New York and London: Seminar Press.

McLuhan M., 1962. *The Gutenberg Galaxy*. Toronto: University of Toronto Press.

McQuail D., 2005. *McQuail's Mass Communication Theory*. London: SAGE.

Merriman N., 1991. *Beyond the Glass Case: The Past, the Heritage and the Public in Britain*. Leicester, Leicester University Press.

Merriman N. ed., 2004a. *Public Archaeology*. London: Routledge.

Merriman N., 2004b. Introduction: Diversity and dissonance in public archaeology. In Merriman N. ed., 2004. *Public Archaeology*. London: Routledge, pp. 1–17.

Naughton J. 2006. Our changing media ecosystem. In Richards E., Foster R. and Kiedrowski T., 2006. *Communication – The Next Decade. Section 1 – Trends and challenges* [online]. Available at: http://www.ofcom.org.uk/research/commsdecade/ (accessed 14 January 2010), pp. 41–50.

Okamura K. and Matsuda A. eds, 2011a. *New Perspectives in Global Public Archaeology*. New York: Springer.

Okamura K. and Matsuda A., 2011b. Introduction: New Perspectives in Global Public Archaeology. In Okamura K. and Matsuda A. eds, 2011. *New Perspectives in Global Public Archaeology*. New York: Springer, pp. 1–18.

Paynton C., 2002. Public Perception and 'Pop Archaeology': A Survey of Current Attitudes Toward Televised Archaeology. *The SAA Archaeological Record. The magazine of the society for American archaeology* 2 (2), pp. 33–36.

Piccini A., 2007. *A survey of heritage television viewing figures* [online] June 2007. Available at: http://www.britarch.ac.uk/publications/bulletin/piccini_full.html (accessed 22 October 2011).

Pokotylo D. and Guppy N., 1999. Public opinion and archaeological heritage: views from outside the profession. *American Antiquity* 64 (3), pp. 400–416.

Postman N., 2000. The Humanism of Media Ecology [online]. *Proceedings of the Media Ecology Association* 1 (2000). New York, 16–17 June 2000. Available at: http://www.media-ecology.org/publications/MEA_proceedings/v1/postman01.pdf (accessed 15 October 2011).

Ramos M. and Duganne D., 2000. *Exploring Public Perceptions and Attitudes About Archaeology* [online] February 2000. Society for American Archaeology. Available at: http://www.saa.org/Portals/0/SAA/pubedu/nrptdraft4.pdf (accessed 31 January 2010).

Russo A., 2011. Transformations in Cultural Communication: Social Media, Cultural Exchange, and Creative Connections. *Curator* 54 (3), pp. 327–346.

Schadla-Hall T., 1999. Editorial: Public Archaeology. *European Journal of Archaeology* 2 (2), pp. 147–158.

Schadla-Hall T., 2000. Commentary: Archaeology as a public activity. *Cultural Trends* 39, pp. 33–38.

Schadla-Hall T., 2004. The Comforts of Unreason: the Importance and Relevance of Alternative Archaeology. In Merriman N. ed., 2004. *Public Archaeology*. London: Routledge, pp. 255–271.

Schadla-Hall T., 2006. Public Archaeology in the Twenty-First Century. In Layton R. and Stone P. eds, 2006. *A Future for Archaeology: The Past in the Present*. London: UCL Press/Cavendish Publishing, pp. 75–82.

Schadla-Hall T. and Morris G., 2003. Ancient Egypt on the Small Screen – from Fact to Fiction in the UK. In MacDonald S. and Rice M. eds, 2003. *Consuming Ancient Egypt*. London: UCL Press, pp. 195–214.

Scott C., 2007. Advocating the value of museums. Presented to *INTERCOM/ICOM*, Vienna, 20 August 2007 [online]. Available at: http://www.intercom.museum/documents/CarolScott.pdf (accessed 17 September 2011).

Scott C., 2009. Exploring the evidence base for museum value. *Museum Management and Curatorship* 24 (3), pp. 195–213.

Stanziola J., 2011. Some more unequal than others: alternative financing for museums, libraries and archives in England. *Cultural Trends* 20 (2), pp. 113–140.

Thinkbox, 2011. The drive to live: on-demand strengthens appeal of live TV [online]. Available at: http://www.thinkbox.tv/server/show/ConWebDoc.2603 (accessed 01 October 2011).

Ucko P., 1987. *Academic Freedom and Apartheid. The Story of the World Archaeological Congress*. London: Duckworth.

Webopedia, 2011. Social media [online]. Available at: http://www.webopedia.com/TERM/S/social_media.html (accessed 15 September 2011).

Willman-Iivarinen H., 2009. Changing Demand for Media Products. In Koskela M. and Vinnari M. eds, 2009. *Future of the Consumer Society*. Tampere: Finland Futures Research Centre, Turku School of Economics [online]. Available at: http://ffrc.utu.fi/julkaisut/e-julkaisuja/eTutu_2009-7.pdf (accessed 22 October 2011).

Value, Authority and the Open Society: Some Implications for Digital and Online Archaeology

Andrew Bevan

Abstract

This paper argues that two major related trends – the now substantial circulation of digital archaeological datasets and the increasing number of ways in which people engage with archaeology via online media – should encourage us to reassess what value we and others wish to place on the past, how we share archaeological information and what kinds of archaeological communities we wish to promote. One useful approach to these questions is via social anthropological theory that addresses valuation, authority and the structuring of inter-personal relationships. Understanding the degree to which these features of social life are, or are not, transformed by new digital communication technologies also helps us to re-conceptualise archaeological communication with new priorities and opportunities in mind. This paper explores these ideas further via two case studies involving the sharing of spatial or spatio-temporal knowledge: (a) open data and open source software for spatial analysis, and (b) neogeography and geocaching.

Introduction

Conventionally, archaeologists are seen as detectives and analysts, connoisseurs and enthusiasts, or guardians and interpreters of past human culture. These are often complementary but occasionally conflicting roles that have always demanded some pretty deft costume changes, but the altered realities of the modern digital and online world now expose them to renewed scrutiny. This paper argues that two major related trends – the now substantial circulation of digital archaeological datasets and the similarly substantial presence of archaeology online – should prompt us to revisit questions such as what value we and others wish to place on the past, how we share archaeological information and what kinds of archaeological communities we wish to promote. One useful approach to these questions is via bodies of social anthropological theory that addresses valuation, authority and the structuring of inter-personal relationships. Elsewhere, I have argued that archaeologists can benefit from paying greater attention to how such concepts operate in different ways in different past societies, but the discussion below focuses on the fact that they also have relevance to public archaeology in the present. The mass uptake of digital technologies in general, and the Internet in particular, have been touted as marking a hugely transformative threshold in which traditional hierarchies are subverted, value systems turned upside down, and social relationships enhanced or degraded, depending on your point of view. Whether or not these claims are strictly true is something worth reconsidering below, but regardless, there clearly remains a pressing need for us to re-conceptualise archaeological communication with new priorities and opportunities in mind. The section that follows therefore begins by theorising about concepts of value and authority, with particular attention to the relevance of these concepts for archaeological communication, as well as how this relevance is altered by digital technologies and online interaction. The next section then focuses on inter-personal relationships and questions of individual and group agency, particularly in terms of how these are affected by new forms of physically-remote interaction and collaboration. Finally, I will consider two useful case studies involving the sharing of spatial or spatio-temporal knowledge that have important consequences in archaeology: (a) open data and open source software for spatial analysis, and (b) 'neogeography'.

Value and authority

Value is an ambivalent concept that we ascribe both to tangible and intangible things. It is something we sometimes pretend is objective or innate, but which in fact is not, and something that we can promote as either ethically-progressive or ethically-bankrupt. In fact, it is part of a wider moral economy and English terms such as 'value(s)', 'taste', 'free' and 'worth' carry just this kind of semantic flexibility and moral overtone, as do equivalents in several other languages (Simmel 1900; Bourdieu 1994; Miller 2008; see also Bevan 2007: 8–18, 2010; Graeber 2001). Archaeologists grapple with the term value from a variety of different perspectives. We discuss the value ascribed to objects and landscapes in the past and the degree to which: (a) their character can be understood in terms of the impetus of profit, supply, demand, social signalling, etc., (b) they reflect ethno-taxonomies or particular societal norms, and (c) they are transformed by major changes in technical know-how (e.g. from stone to metal tools). Likewise, museum staff and cultural heritage managers in particular are often asked to pronounce on the relative value of an archaeological site (e.g. for management or conservation purposes) or the commercial value of an archaeological object (e.g. in the ethically fraught context of antiquities trading). In the latter world of cultural heritage management and public archaeology, assessments of value in the present sometimes involve declaring, from a position of perceived authority, that X is a priceless cultural relic and worth saving for the nation, regardless of effort and cost. At other times, an assessment of equivalence (we have X number of equivalent artefacts in our collection or know about X number of similar type sites and hence further focus on them is not currently necessary) or alternatively of relative ranking is involved (e.g. this locality is worthy of being a World Heritage Site, while this other one is not). Sometimes we can measure such value in more flexible and market-driven ways (e.g. through visitor numbers, revenue, etc.). The degree to which these different approaches reflect some prevailing ways in which human beings organise their social relationships with one another is returned to in the next section.

In any case, archaeology often retains a strong traditional sense of expert intervention. In the media, our discipline has to some degree always thrived on its ability to usher forward one or more antiquarian gurus who can pronounce definitively on the material and historical value of the past. In a sense its popularity has therefore been underwritten by a strong sense of intellectual authority, from Mortimer Wheeler's appearances on *Animal, Vegetable, Mineral* onwards. For the public at large, antiquarian connoisseurship (authority-over-old objects) is the archaeologist's super-power but also often a way for socially aspiring groups to express perceived refinement and social taste, to make claims to powerful lineage or indeed to assert a kind of moral superiority. Furthermore, authority in general (i.e. rarefied responsibility, knowledge and/or power over something or someone), like value, is a powerful but ambivalent term. It possesses an ultimately nebulous and fleeting quality despite society's best efforts to institutionalise it, and is typically something that people both love and hate in equal measure. Individuals claim such authority in a variety of curious ways, via big hats, impressive certificates, fancy badges, appropriate dress, choreographed coronations, etc., and groups have equally innovative authority signalling mechanisms (imposing architecture, ranked uniforms, official affiliation networks, branded product marks, etc.).

Of particular interest for the discussion below is the way in which value and authority are affected by the kinds of mass interaction and mass collaborative creations that are made possible by the Internet. For example, there have been real teething problems associated with how we express value in this brave new online world. The combination of rapidly developing, low-cost, freely shared or illegally pirated creative outputs (including data), have been very unsettling for existing value regimes. For different kinds of commercial venture, the challenge has been how to develop a viable long-term business model, for which a range of advertising-led, pay-for-content, pay-for-service, 'freemium', 'Street Performer Protocols' and/or personal data harvesting strategies have been advanced (Anderson 2009a, and for the ensuing debate Gladwell 2009, Anderson 2009b; see also Kelsey and Schneier 1998). For those less interested in, or sometimes just delaying, the goal of commercial profit (e.g. public sector institutions, charities, academics), the challenge of measuring the relative value or impact of their digital and online efforts (e.g. blogging, webpages, data archives, etc.) versus more traditional outputs has been addressed by adopting specialised digital metrics based on 'nano-endorsements' such as hit counters, hyperlink networks, click-throughs, cloud-sourced reviews, shares, 'likes', retweets and citation indices (Morozov 2011: 99, see also Richardson, this volume; Pett, this volume).

Signalling and agreeing on what constitutes authority in an online and data-centric world has raised some interesting challenges and equally innovative solutions. Traditional ideas of authority often evoke a sense of near-blind trust whether this is with regard to secular power, economic decision-making or sources of information (e.g. Divine Right of Kings, the Bank of England, the Oxford English Dictionary, etc.). Authoritative brands of information in particular often drew their traditional strength from a perceived longevity of use (e.g. Encyclopaedia Britannica), but this is now sometimes undermined both by the existence of widely shared digital data and by the structure of human interactions online. Certain equivalent kinds of information loyalty are slowly emerging online, but nonetheless remain harder to pin down given a wider propensity for cloud-sourced knowledge (i.e. information produced by the collaborative offerings and amendments of multiple authors, many of whom are hard to trace as people with trustworthy pedigrees in that particular domain of knowledge). The uncertainty over how best to exploit and be critical about Wikipedia[1] as an information resource is a good example (e.g. Magnus 2009; also Thornton, this volume). Further ways in which online authority is preserved and conveyed are through user badges, community standards, compliance certificates and institutionally-explicit URLs.

Digital data offerings (e.g. spreadsheets, databases, spatial coordinates, photo archives, video) also suffer from similar problems of authority. For example, there is not always as clear-cut an end product and various versions can happily circulate for long periods – in theory the latest one is often supposed the be the most authoritative, but the experience is often unsettling for those who are used to the physically-imposed and hence transparent versioning of hard copy publication. Second, even when there is a clear-cut final digital dataset, the latter can thereafter be transformed and used in a wildly imaginative set of new ways, with the original producer potentially having very little control over the results. For some this is a freeing experience and immensely creative if properly enabled (e.g. by appropriate metadata, proper open licensing and transparent primary publication), but for others it is a fear- and legislation-inducing problem.

---

[1] http://www.wikipedia.org/ (accessed 02 September 2011).

What relevance do these insights have for archaeology? As mentioned above, the authoritative pronouncements of an expert are often something we expect as part of outreach in archaeology. Indeed, they are also built into our recording systems and our academic publication structure. While we might use new media to break these hierarchies down, from the trowel's edge onwards (Hodder 1997), there will probably always remain a creative tension, as our efforts at multilateral engagement can only ever be piecemeal and, if we are honest, often conceal a desire to retain some control over the final consensus or narrative. The next section comes back to how we might approach such issues with regard to digital archaeological data and archaeological communication online.

Agency and social relationships

All of these issues to do with value and authority reflect the wider social context of human relationships both online and offline. The simple challenge behind any relationship involving two or more people is how to establish some predictable ground rules for how to behave in a given social situation. People use a wide range of contingent cultural cues – involving objects, dress, language, spoken inflection, spatial and temporal context – to make sure everyone can coordinate their behaviour appropriately. When these cues fail and people's behavioural rules and relational expectations conflict, they become offended and/or are disapproving (see also Appadurai 1986: 14–16; Kopytoff 1986; McGraw and Tetlock 2005; Pinker *et al.* 2008; Tuk *et al.* 2009). So, for instance, the monetising of objects originally acquired as significant personal gifts involves actions and actors that often frowned upon (e.g. pawning a wedding ring or a family heirloom). When such an act does occur, it is at best assumed to be personally traumatic for the seller or at worst greeted with outrage. This takes us back to the semantic flexibility of words such as value(s), taste, free and worth that convey a subtle combination of economic, social and moral messages.

The different conceptual models which people use to coordinate their inter-personal relationships has been the subject of anthropological enquiry for over a hundred years at least (e.g. see some of the classifications advanced by Douglas, Mauss, Piaget, Ricoeur, Sahlins, and Weber amongst others: Whitehead 1993: 11–12). In particular, Alan Fiske's suggestion (1991, 2004) of four main structuring models for human relationships is a useful starting point for thinking about archaeologists' interactions with each and with the wider public. Depending on the context, people can agree to interact via: a) undifferentiated relationships of inclusion or exclusion (what Fiske terms 'communal sharing'), b) ordered relationships of unequal status ('authority ranking'), c) peer-to-peer relationships ('equality matching'), or d) certain very flexible kinds of metrical relationship ('market pricing'). Different kinds of human communities clearly prioritise these in different ways and give them culturally-relative shapes, but there are good

Figure 1. A Noise to Signal cartoon (riffing on Stewart Brand's well-known aphorism 'information wants to be free') that nicely captures the fraught relationship between value, authority, information flow and the structure of social relationships (with the kind permission of Rob Cottingham; available at: http://robcottingham.ca/cartoon [accessed 02 September 2011]).

reasons to think that they also reflect some innate human proclivities (e.g. Haslam 2004).

It is fair to say that prevailing wisdom (and some of the commentary in the previous section) sees the Internet as an environment that heavily promotes relationships coordinated via the first of these four social logics ('community sharing'), sometimes at the expense of relationships that were previously modelled via the other three. Web-based technologies (collaborative information, search engines, blogs, social networking, discussion groups, etc.) are often seen through a very cyber-utopian lens (Morozov 2011: xiii), as things that promote democracy of action, subvert traditional hierarchies, undermine existing commercial regimes and encourage new virtual tribes (see also the next section). A useful question however to raise in passing is whether all of this represents a truly different configuration of social relations or has simply been an unusually free-spirited pioneer episode, prior to the re-establishment (or disembling the continuing operation) of a wider set of traditional social mores (see especially Barbrook 1998; O'Neil 2009; Lanier 2010)?

In answer to the above question, it is first worth re-emphasising that there undoubtedly are certain technological features of the Internet as we have it today that promote acts of sharing and broadly egalitarian interaction. One is the very low costs and largely unrestricted character of online information flow, at least in western countries. Related to this is also the massive reduction of many of the traditional tyrannies of geographical distance, at least for certain individuals in certain favoured social and economic contexts (e.g. Castells 2000). Another is the fact that online interaction, as currently configured, can easily dissolve or disrupt traditional, physically-embodied forms of human agency in favour of new or different online forms. Not only are there instances of character impersonation (with both positive and negative consequences), but also of companies tweeting as individuals, individuals fronting as companies and 'communities' without any physical coherence or geographic proximity (e.g. ones of shared experience, endeavour or culture). As ever in cases of surprisingly intense social interaction and ambivalent identity, the fallback behavioural model is that people often emphasise neighbourliness and the politics of the small village (for a similar choreography of long-distance elite contacts in the Bronze Age Mediterranean, see Bevan 2010: 44–5, with further references). This hyper-local thinking, whether the topic is in fact large or small, is arguably something that archaeology could foster more aggressively.

In any case, of additional relevance to archaeologists is the increased degree of agency that can adhere to virtual archaeological artefacts online – a picture or 3D model of a decorated pot, can for example, often tell you information about itself, can interact with the online user in a variety of ways, can have a pseudo-physical presence in one or more online worlds, can have a Facebook page, can be tagged and monitored via location-based services, etc. We should see these newly empowered archaeological objects as an enormous opportunity: just as tangible culture in the physical world is often used by people to promote certain views of themselves and cue for certain kinds of relationships with others, so online objects have the potential to do something similar. If we can produce sufficiently attractive online avatars for archaeological objects (or enable others to create their own) then there is no reason that they will not be invoked by the public as part of their online social personas, just as photos, video, page styles, group or campaign memberships and topical experiences already are on sites such as Facebook.[2]

While the above technological affordances are indeed responsible for the communal sharing ethos pervading many interactions online today, they do not necessarily reflect a hard-wired feature of digital technologies in general or even of the Internet in particular. Digital technologies can, of course, also foster very hierarchical forms of surveillance (e.g. via remote sensing, video, location-based services) as well as very extreme forms of market pricing (e.g. the automated and semi-automated exchanges that make up an increasingly

---

[2] http://facebook.com/ (accessed 02 September 2011).

large slice of the commodities trading market). Untrammelled online access still relies on infrastructure that can be controlled, with effects that could also promote one or more of the other relational logics discussed above. Likewise, it is clear that a more diverse range of social relational models are emerging online or have been there all along but have gone little-noticed (see the excellent, O'Neil 2009). Certain online relationships require careful tit-for-tat and/or reciprocal ('equivalence matching') behaviours to build trust (e.g. Steinmueller 2005). People gain ranked forms of status over one another in all sorts of ways online: for example they can receive extra permissions, earn user badges, become the 'mayor' or 'sheriff' of a physical location in a virtual space, if they are popular among other users, flag/moderate inappropriate comments in a list, visit a location regularly, or buy premium levels of functionality. All of these lead to a sharper hierarchy of users, on top of the fact that there already exists a geographically and economically skewed hierarchy due to different speeds of, and limitations on, Internet access worldwide. Rightly or wrongly, 'sharing' is a concept whose social boundaries online are also now being redefined legally, with strong calls in some quarters for greater restriction (e.g. via digital rights/restrictions management; e.g. Stallman 2010 for a strongly opposed position). As the range of business models for the monetisation of online spaces and products has developed, various forms of market led transactional relationship have also become more common, and virtual worlds such as Second Life[3], if anything, have been more rather than less commercial in ethos. It is thus highly likely that the same sense of outrage about mis-communicated relational intentions will also become an ever more common feature of online life.

The relevance of these sociological insights for archaeology should hopefully become clearer still in the case studies below, but a general point to make at this stage is that it would be short-sighted to assume that archaeological communication online will grapple with anything less than the full suite of relationships and agendas. The value and authority of archaeological data in digital form or of online archaeological outreach initiatives is something to be argued over just as it is in real life, and the key is an explicit understanding of the kinds of academic and public cooperation (in short, the kind of social relationships) that we might wish to foster.

Open communities, open data and open source

With these broader issues of value, authority and social relationships in mind, it is worth having a look at the first of two case studies that consider some spatial or spatio-temporal resources that are increasingly relevant to archaeologists. At the moment, there is a huge emphasise on 'openness' in various areas of public and private life, engendered in part by the community sharing norms that currently prevail online. Hence we can talk about initiatives that promote 'open societies' (e.g. fostering democracy and greater communication) or open access (e.g. to academic publications in archaeology, see Carver 2007), open software and data exchange, etc. In particular, I want to focus here on two sub-themes of the open digital society and archaeology's role in it: a) a growing emphasis on the dissemination of digital datasets under very liberal use licenses, and b) the sharply increasing importance of software distributed under similarly generous licensing and for which the source code is visible to, and modifiable by, everyone.

In academic archaeology, as in many other disciplines, it is fair to say that the publication of 'data' remains the afterthought and the very poor cousin of more discursive publications, despite the clear interpretative and design input involved in generating the former (i.e. 'raw data' is usually a misleading term). This situation is, I would argue, very likely to change to a more balanced emphasis in the near future (see Hole, this volume). At any rate, open archaeological data can be thought of as part of a wider realm of well-documented and largely unrestricted knowledge ('from sonnets to statistics, genes to geodata' as one major advocacy

---

[3] http://www.secondlife.com/ (accessed 02 September 2011).

group styles it[4]), and there is by now a substantial move towards making archaeological data freely available in this manner, and several initiatives to promote good practice.[5] One particular driver for open data in general is the growing assertion of a citizen's democratic right to access, re-use and re-distribute digital data collected partly or wholly with public tax money. Hence government bodies increasingly now release spatial (and other) datasets free of charge and with very limited use restrictions, while academic funding bodies often insist on a clear plan for digital archiving in a suitable repository. Making data available under Creative Commons[6] or Open Data Commons[7] licenses (that offer a range of generous options for onward use, often stipulate no restrictions, or only the requirement of proper attribution) is now very popular as is the use of a range of international, national and subject-specific data archives (e.g. the UK Archaeology Data Service;[8] also Kansa and Kansa 2011; Richards *et al*. 2011).

Moral and practical arguments about property underpin most perspectives on data dissemination and the debate is often ideologically framed in the context of resource rights, and particularly the idea of resources held by everyone versus those controlled by a few. The historical and archaeological point of reference is typically the shift from 'commons' land to enclosed land in Medieval England and one frequently-invoked morality tale is that of the 'tragedy of the commons' in which individuals acting in their own self-interest gradually exhaust a finite shared resource, even when it might be in everyone's longer-term interest to husband it more carefully. Open data, access and software initiatives emphasise the continuing value of resources held in common (and hence are in step with other concerns about shared resources such as those associated with the global environment), and seek to develop communities whose ethos, amongst other things, avoids or manages tragedy-of-the-commons situations. One important point is that data is for all intents and purposes an infinite resource and hence not something whose sharing poses the same risks as a plot of land. It is useful to also think of a tragedy of the anti-commons (Heller 1998), where notions of private ownership over a resource are dominant, but where these individual rights of use are so disaggregated into a host of small permissions that they are inadequate on their own to facilitate practical use of a resource (e.g. due to an over-proliferation of licensing restrictions) and stifle all forms of coordination (see also Yakowitz in press).

Archaeology is a discipline that produces substantial amounts of data with a very clear spatio-temporal quality (i.e. typically with dates of production, deposition, and/or recovery, as well as locations). While the particular qualities of temporal data in archaeology offer their own important academic challenges (Crema *et al*. 2010), it is the spatial aspect of these datasets that pose the most challenging problems for those who espouse (as I do) a very open approach to dissemination. One of the well-known fears of complete sharing of georeferenced archaeological datasets is that they will promote some kind of spatially-enhanced looting (e.g. Ur 2006: 37–8; Parcak 2009: 224).[9] This gets especially tricky of course when our open data efforts cross modern political borders: consider, for example, the now regular practice of international research projects publishing fairly high resolution mappings of archaeological sites in a different country. The unrestricted publication of the project's digital results and the retention of the physical archaeology in-country goes some way to addressing a traditional 'colonial' problem of the expropriation

---

[4] http://okfn.org/ (accessed 02 September 2011).
[5] e.g. The Open Knowledge Foundation Archaeology Working Group, http://archaeology.okfn.org/ (accessed 02 September 2011).
[6] http://creativecommons.org/ (accessed 02 September 2011).
[7] http://opendatacommons.org/ (accessed 02 September 2011).
[8] http://archaeologydataservice.ac.uk/ (accessed 02 September 2011).
[9] It is ironic that, while there are a whole range of non-spatial datasets such as material science analyses, radiocarbon dates, artefact databases etc., that do not raise any looting concerns over any spatial component, initially these were perhaps more rarely made available under open licenses than spatial datasets.

of national heritage. However, a different kind of digital plunder arguably persists if we fail to consult with local heritage authorities about how untrammelled access to spatial data might facilitate forms of accurate looting that they are ill-equipped to counteract. Behind such conundrums is a much older and wider archaeological problem linked to the sociology of property rights: who gets to decide how to restrict or share archaeological information (or indeed artefacts)? Is it done for the good of the individual, the community, the state or the world and what happens when these interests collide?

One sensible interim way to handle the problem is to degrade the spatial locations made available with open datasets (i.e. round-off the precision to, for example, the nearest kilometre), but allow affiliated academics and other vetted users access to full spatial resolution data upon request (e.g. the approach adopted by the UK's Portable Antiquities Scheme[10]). While the creation of two- or more tiers of access is not ideal from an information-should-be-free point of view and could conceivably lead to unfortunate kinds of gate-keeping, at least it responds decisively to the issue, rather than using it as an excuse for locking the information away in a cupboard. More broadly, the problem of spatial precision in open archaeological data recapitulates in small-scale, wider privacy and protection debates about holding back certain categories of personal, military, state or diplomatic information from full public disclosure (e.g. the challenge posed by Wikileaks[11]). What is clearly missing but very necessary for the dissemination of spatial data in archaeology is a careful risk-utility analysis (a good model is recently conducted risk-utility study of how to release data which respects the anonymity of individuals but does not aggregate or blur the data so heavily that it loses all analytical potential; Yakowitz 2011). In fact, the widespread fear amongst archaeologists that greater looting will result from freely available spatial data (i.e. of cases where looters have used the digital data of archaeologists as a superior guide to their looting than local knowledge) is at present a largely theoretical argument in need of further documentation and too often simply invoked as a plausible-sounding reason not to making any data available whatsoever. To reiterate, we may conceivably risk much by making precise archaeological locations widely available, but the magnitude of this risk is at present wholly unknown, and we also stand to lose a great deal by imposing too many spatial restrictions. Furthermore, in many cases, the issue is slowly being taken out of our hands by the fact that site visitors with cameras, hikers with GPS, metal detectorists, locals promoting their community heritage, and the enthusiastic uploads of archaeological fieldwork participants can now contribute fairly precise locations of cultural heritage finds and sites to Google Earth, etc.

Another important aspect of open knowledge in a computing environment is the right not only to use computer software without a fee, but also to inspect the source code from which it was built, alter such code and pass on in either modified or unmodified versions without any licensing restrictions. Under various names, open source software has been popular amongst certain groups of computer scientists for a long time, but has only become better known amongst the public at large over the last decade or so. In fact, arguments about the semantics of the term itself evoke just the same moral and practical ambiguity discussed above: the software has been called 'Free', 'Open Source' or 'Free/Libre and Open Source' (with acronyms such as FOSS, FLOSS, F/LOSS): one characterisation of such software is that is akin to 'free speech' not 'free beer' (i.e. a basic right rather than a giveaway; e.g. Stallman 2009; also Berry 2008). Open source software explicitly contrasts itself with closed source and/or proprietary software, in terms of its code development, testing procedures and dissemination practices (e.g. Raymond 1998). Two major bugbears for those promoting open source software are the 'black boxes' produced by commercial closed source alternatives (where the exact working software algorithms are not visible to the end-user) and 'vendor lock-in' practices (where it becomes

---

[10] http://finds.org.uk/ (accessed 02 September 2011).

[11] http://wikileaks.org/ (accessed 02 September 2011).

difficult for users to switch to other software once they have bought into one company's solution, e.g. by promotional licenses, proprietary formats, etc.).

The peculiar collaborative communities behind open source software are arguably part of the broader set of digital sharing economies mentioned above (what von Hippel 2005 calls a 'free revealing' strategy). Overall, open source projects have been variously likened to a gift and homesteading economies (Raymond 1998: 65–111; albeit unlike the Maussian reciprocal gifting familiar to many anthropologists), guild systems (Coleman 2001), 'cooking pot' economics (Ghosh 1998) or a kinship system (Zeitlyn 2003). Regardless of these distinctions, the normative view is they are or should be largely volunteerist, meritocratic and driven by reputation-based competition, community-minded but sometimes tribal, democratic but with a strong sense of mentoring relationships and intellectual lineage (see also Berdou 2011). Most projects therefore fall very comfortably into Fiske's model of 'community sharing' (see above). People who relate to one another in this general way often emphasise membership of a carefully defined in-group (e.g. the family or the small village providing a common metaphor for the way these relations are framed). Members of the community are often prepared to perform altruistic acts and possessions may often be shared at need without any perceived accounting, specific taboo behaviours are sometimes present that reinforce group cohesion, and ostracism is a common mechanism for dealing with conflict situations.

While the above description is both the ideal- and the stereotype of open source communities, real projects are often more complicated and increasingly so (see O'Neil 2009: 93–168). First of all there is usually a clear hierarchy of decision makers (with lead developers, other developers, code testers, translators, users, etc.). Second, certain groups have so far been underrepresented in open source projects: for example, several studies have suggested that an unusually small fraction of participants are female, particularly amongst the actual programmers (and fewer proportionally, it seems, than female in commercial programming roles: Nafus *et al.* 2006). Likewise, there are, in fact, a variety of F/LOSS forms, including some initiatives that are promoted and largely developed within corporations, and others primarily driven by non-commercial cooperatives. While these two spheres can produce quite different authority structures and exchange mechanisms, they lead to examples of hybridisation in either direction (Söderberg 2008: 137–55; Berdou 2011). There have also been efforts to incentivise open source development via either money offered by companies for the best solution to one of their problems (e.g. the GNOME Bounty Hunt, which led to discontent within that particular community over the way workflows were being distorted: Berdou 2011: 61–66) or sponsored mass coding initiatives (e.g. Google Summer of Code[12]).

The above should make clear that open source software communities are more complicated in practice than they initially seem. Yet the opportunity presented by open source remains hugely important for archaeology. Currently, while there are archaeological contributors to a range of major open source projects (e.g. GRASS,[13] gvSIG-CE,[14] R, RePast[15]), the vast majority of archaeological practitioners use commercial software (for the GIS preferences of UK sites and monuments records, see Bevan and Bell 2004), which means that it has been comparatively difficult for them to tailor methods to explicitly archaeological research questions (for a discussion of this issue, see Lake *et al.* 1998) or use more advanced techniques in poorly-resourced countries without major institutional support to cover licensing. Put simply, archaeology is a niche market. If we considered a hypothetical frequency distribution of spatial software users by their net financial outlay on licences, archaeologists would be very much on the 'long tail' of very

---

[12] http://code.google.com/soc/ (accessed 02 September 2011).
[13] http://grass.osgeo.org/ (accessed 02 September 2011).
[14] http://gvsigce.sourceforge.net/ (accessed 02 September 2011).
[15] http://repast.sourceforge.net/ (accessed 02 September 2011).

small-scale consumers (for the latter concept in Internet-enabled economics, see Anderson 2006). We therefore need to engage with open source solutions as much as possible, as the code availability and development structures of such projects are far better suited to (occasionally) fostering the specific scientific needs of our discipline.

Place, reinvented and recolonised

The second case study considered here addresses the implications for archaeologists of a different, looser kind of openness, which has been promoted by the cloud-sourcing of geographic knowledge and the geo-social networking of modern online individuals. The former practice is often now called 'neogeography' and refers to various kinds of locational information created by individuals or communities who are typically neither paid for it, nor experts. It is an approach to mapping and publishing rich location-based content that is very much enabled by so-called Web 2.0 technologies and has taken an especially dramatic turn with the emergence of virtual globes or earth viewers (e.g. Google Earth,[16] Nasa Worldwind[17]) over the last seven years or so. More generally, there has been a flurry of 'geotagging' (giving locational information datasets such as digital photographs or video that is otherwise not map-like in character) and 'georeferencing' (situating a map or aerial photo in correct absolute 2D space), as well as the emergence of a host of other automated or semi-automated ways in which geographic information is captured and made available online.

Neogeography, as Michael Goodchild points out (2009: 82), implies a quite different way of learning about spatial phenomena and promotes a kind of citizen science in which simple to moderately specialised recording and observation (counting, coarse-scale georeferencing, etc.) can be contributed by individuals without formal training. In some ways, neogeography poses a challenge to the traditional one-to-many, 'authoritative' outputs of the professional cartographer and is thus another example of an emancipatory, community-sharing ethos online. However, in other ways, it is merely part of a more widely diminishing distinction between the producer and consumer of goods (in this case, of maps) in present-day commerce and capitalism (Thrift 2006). For archaeologists, Google Earth dramatically lowers the costs of landscape research design and rapid public engagement, but it also is becoming a way of producing quick and easy coordinate data on the location of archaeological sites. In fact, the latter is a highly problematic practice, not because of the 10–30 m absolute positional inaccuracies often present in even the higher resolution imagery, but because these base datasets remain under strict copyright, as do the polygons and placemarks produced by users from them.[18] The onward use of such spatial data, outside of the original software and for commercial or academic purposes, may often be hard to identify (and thus likely to continue), but it is still technically in breach of current copyright law. This is also a relational *faux pas*, between the happily egalitarian consumer and various rights-aware producer, that is unfortunately just waiting for its day in court.

In any case, a related example of new location-based activity with which archaeology will need to engage enthusiastically but carefully in the future is geocaching (e.g. in archaeology and museums: Gray 2008; Witcher 2010). Geocachers use GPS to record the location of small boxes of items that they have placed somewhere out there in the physical world. They then upload the resulting coordinates of the cache, and allow others to search for and rediscover it via similar methods. Often, the token objects in the cache are taken and replaced by others of equivalent minor value. People log their rediscoveries both in a physical notebook kept with the cache and thereafter also online and an online community develops around both this

---

[16] http://earth.google.co.uk/ (accessed 02 September 2011).

[17] http://worldwind.arc.nasa.gov/ (accessed 02 September 2011).

[18] Google Maps/Google Earth APIs Terms of Service 2011, section 10.3.1.
http://code.google.com/intl/en/apis/maps/terms.html (accessed 02 September 2011).

direct experience and the wider one that often involves an individual, family and/or group on an outdoor hike or day-trip. At the time of writing, one of the main geocaching websites claims that there are 1.5 million active caches and over five million registered geocachers worldwide, with five million logs of rediscovered caches in the last month alone.[19]

At present there is no consistent link between geocaching and archaeology, but the fact that the activity can be described by the above same website as 'a high-tech treasure hunting game played throughout the world by adventure seekers'[20] nonetheless implies a risk that it will morph into the search and discovery of antiquities as well. For example one recent geocache was located on some Mesolithic timbers on the Thames foreshore in London, with the label 'London's Oldest Structure' (GC2MD1B), and interestingly, is now only available to 'premium', paying members of the site. While this is potentially harmless and undoubtedly informative as a destination for visitors, there remains a risk that unregulated visitation, caching and re-caching (whether or not it actually involved excavation of the soil) will be damaging to this kind of fragile archaeological site.

A more positive view is that geocaching also exhibits a very strong turn-taking, reciprocal character that belongs to what Alan Fiske's might term an 'equivalence matching' logic. Such a logic is a generically effective way, in a whole host of social circumstances, to build up trust amongst comparative strangers, and the role of the cache itself, continually replenished by reciprocal gifts, anchors this trust in the physical world. Geocaching also currently has a strong ecologically-aware ethic, so if we can get the formula right, then there are useful ways in which to foster greater archaeological stewardship through such pastimes despite their superficial 'treasure-hunting' association. A recent initiative by the Museum of London involving a 'Captain Kidd' geocache[21] on the waterfront in London is a step in the right direction, but further projects might want to exploit the trust-building structure of such practices to tackle more sensitive archaeological topics that are of importance to professionals, well-informed enthusiasts and the wider public.

In any case, geocaching uses spatial information as a good excuse of an adventurous trip, and its online forums enable discussion before and after the event. At present, it is not however an activity that harnesses location-aware mobile services so remains slightly different from the kinds of activity now involved in 'geo-social networks' (e.g. the act of checking into certain locations via mobile phone, on sites such as FourSquare[22]). For some, the latter kind of total surveillance is a gross violation of personal privacy (e.g. Stallman 2010), for others it is a natural extension of the kinds of location-agnostic online socialising that is already so popular. The opportunities for monetising geo-social life online are huge, with possible rewards of greater advertising money, greater investment or simply greater commercial throughput for more visibly popular destinations. Likewise, there are certainly incentives for archaeologists and museums to fine-tune both their non-commercial (e.g. improved conservation and circulation as a result of location aware visitor studies) and money-spinning activities (e.g. better sponsorship tie-ins based on being able to demonstrate the time-space links between visits to museums/sites and to nearby commercial venues).

A final way in which archaeology is increasingly harnessing location-aware services is through 'augmented reality' (AR), in which direct or indirect sensory experience of a real environment is enriched by the addition of computer-generated input via a mobile device (e.g. Jeater, this volume).[23] At present, such an approach is still very much in the traditional top-down mould of 'authoritative'

---

[19] http://www.geocaching.com/ (accessed 02 September 2011).
[20] http://www.geocaching.com/ (accessed 02 September 2011).
[21] http://www.museumoflondon.org.uk/Docklands/Whats-on/Events/FeaturedEvents/Geocache.htm (accessed 02 September 2011).
[22] https://foursquare.com/ (accessed 02 September 2011).
[23] See also http://www.dead-mens-eyes.org/ (accessed 02 September 2011).

digital reconstructions and other institutionally vetted materials that augment the learning experience of the wider public. While this is undeniably powerful outreach method, there are also clearly opportunities to foster wholly freeform community interactions in AR, reciprocal or turn-taking archaeological reconstructions of the same location (e.g. rival interpretations) and/or various kinds of wholly monetised (or simply impact-tallying) AR venture.

Brief final thoughts

The above discussion has explored some recent trends in digital, spatial and online archaeology via broader questions of value, authority and sociality. It has sought to provide this wider context in order to debunk ideas that archaeological engagement online will inevitably become wholly egalitarian, even if aspects of this vision remain very attractive. In any case, with its visual and data-rich content, its overlap between the humanities and sciences, and its fundamental need for both expert knowledge and public participation, archaeology is well-placed to offer a very distinctive contribution to the evolution of 'open' and online communities. We gain much however from carefully thinking through the structure of the social relationships that we wish to foster in these arenas.

Acknowledgements

My thanks to Chiara Bonacchi and Tim Schadla-Hall, for organising two very fruitful seminar series hosted by Centre for Audio-Visual Study and Practice in Archaeology (CASPAR) at the UCL Institute of Archaeology in early 2011. Thanks also to both of them, Don Henson and Stefano Costa for cajoling me into discussing some aspects of spatial and digital archaeology that had not been my focus up to present. Natalie Cohen (Thames Discovery Project) kindly informed me about the geocache linked to the Mesolithic timbers on the Thames foreshore. Thanks also to Lorna Richardson for a variety of useful discussion on the topics mentioned here and for further useful comments from two anonymous reviewers.

References

Anderson C., 2006. *The Long Tail: Why the Future of Business Is Selling Less of More.* New York: Hyperion.

Anderson C., 2009a. *Free: The Future of a Radical Price.* New York: Hyperion.

Anderson C., 2009b. Dear Malcolm: Why so threatened?. *Wired Blog Network* [online]. Available at: http://www.longtail.com/the_long_tail/2009/06/dear-malcolm-why-so-threatened.html (accessed 02 September 2011).

Appadurai A., 1986. Introduction: Commodities and the politics of value. In Appadurai A. ed., 1986. *The Social Life of Things.* Cambridge: Cambridge University Press, pp. 3–63.

Barbrook R., 1998. The Hi-Tech Gift Economy. *First Monday* 3.12 [online]. Available at: http://firstmonday.org/htbin/cgiwrap/bin/ojs/index.php/fm/article/view/631/552 (accessed 02 September 2011).

Bell T. and Bevan, A., 2004. *A Survey of GIS Standards for the English Archaeological Record Community,* Report Commissioned by English Heritage [online]. Available at: http://www.ucl.ac.uk/~tcrnahb/downloads/BellBevan04.pdf (accessed 02 September 2011).

Berdou E., 2011. *Organization in Open Source Communities. At the Crossroads of the Gift and Market Economies.* London: Routledge.

Berry D. M., 2008. *Copy, Rip, Burn. The Politics of Copyleft and Open Source.* London: Pluto Press.

Bevan A., 2007. *Stone Vessels and Values in the Bronze Age Mediterranean.* Cambridge: Cambridge University Press.

Bevan A., 2010. Making and Marking Relationships: Bronze Age Brandings and Mediterranean Commodities. In Bevan A. and Wengrow D. eds, 2010. *Cultures of Commodity Branding.* Walnut Creek: Left Coast Press, pp. 35–85.

Bourdieu P., 1994. *Distinction: A Social Critique of the Judgement of Taste.* London: Routledge.

Carver M., 2007. Archaeology Journals, Academics and Open Access. *European Journal of Archaeology* 10.2–3, pp. 135–148.

Castells M., 2000. *The Rise of the Network Society.* New York: Blackwell.

Coleman E. G., 2001. High-tech guilds in the era of global capital. *Anthropology of Work Review* 22.1, pp. 28–32.

Crema E., Bevan A. and Lake M., 2010. A Probabilistic Framework for Assessing Spatio-temporal Point Patterns in the Archaeological Record. *Journal of Archaeological Science* 37.5, pp. 1118–1130.

Fiske A. P., 1991. *Structures of Social Life: The Four Elementary Forms of Human Relations.* New York: The Free Press.

Fiske A. P., 2004. Four modes of constituting relationships: Consubstantial assimilation; space magnitude, time and force; concrete procedures; abstract symbolism. In Haslam N. ed., 2004. *Relational Models Theory: A Contemporary Overview*. Mahwah, NJ: Erlbaum, pp. 61–146.

Ghosh R., 1998. Cooking Pot Markets: An Economic Model for the Trade in Free Goods and Services on the Internet. *First Monday* 3.3 [online]. Available at: http://dxm.org/fm/cookingpot7 (accessed 17 October 2011).

Gladwell M., 2009. Priced to Sell. Is Free the Future? Book review. *New Yorker Magazine* [online] 06 July 2009. Available at: http://www.newyorker.com/arts/critics/books/2009/07/06/090706crbo_books_gladwell (accessed 02 September 2011).

Goodchild M. F., 2009. NeoGeography and the nature of geographic expertise. *Journal of Location Based Services* 3.2, pp. 82–96.

Graeber D., 2001. *Toward An Anthropological Theory of Value: The False Coin of Our Own Dreams*. New York: Palgrave.

Gray H. R., 2008. Geo-Caching: Place-Based Discovery of Virginia State Parks and Museums. *Journal of Museum Education* 32.3, pp. 285–292.

Haslam N., 2004. Research on relational models: An overview. In Haslam N. ed., 2004. *Relational Models Theory: A Contemporary Overview*. Mahwah, NJ: Erlbaum, pp. 61–146.

Heller M., 1998. The Tragedy of the Anticommons: Property in the Transition from Marx to Markets. *Harvard Law Review* 111.3, pp. 621–668.

Hodder I., 1997. Always momentary, fluid and flexible': towards a reflexive excavation methodology. *Antiquity* 71, pp. 691–700.

Kansa E. C. and Kansa S. W., 2011. Toward A Do-It-Yourself Cyberinfrastructure: Open Data, Incentives, and Reducing Costs and Complexities of Data Sharing. In Kansa E. C., Kansa S. W. and Watrall E. eds, 2011. *Archaeology 2.0: New Approaches to Communication and Collaboration*. Los Angeles: Cotsen Institute of Archaeology, pp. 57–92

Kelsey J. and Schneier B., 1998. Electronic Commerce and the Street Performer Protocol. *The Third USENIX Workshop on Electronic Commerce Proceedings*. USENIX Press [online]. Available at: http://www.schneier.com/paper-street-performer.html (accessed 02 September 2011).

Kopytoff I., 1986. The cultural biography of things: Commoditisation as a process. In Appadurai A. ed., 1986. *The Social Life of Things: Commodities in Cultural Perspective*. Cambridge: Cambridge University Press, pp. 64–91.

Lake M. W., Woodman P. E. and Mithen S. J., 1998. Tailoring GIS Software for Archaeological Applications: an example concerning viewshed analysis. *Journal of Archaeological Science* 25, pp. 27–38.

Lanier J., 2010. *You Are Not a Gadget*. New York: Alfred A. Knopff.

Magnus P. D., 2009. On trusting Wikipedia. *Episteme* 6.1, pp. 74–91.

McGraw A. P. and Tetlock P. E., 2005. Taboo trade-offs, relational framing, and the acceptability of exchanges. *Journal of Consumer Psychology* 15, pp. 2–15.

Miller D., 2008. The uses of value. *Geoforum* 39, pp. 1122–1132.

Morozov E., 2011. *The Net Delusion. The Dark Side of Internet Freedom*. New York: Public Affairs.

Nafus D., Leach J. and Kriege B., 2006. *Free/Libre and Open Source Software Policy Support – Gender: Integrated Report of Findings*. University of Cambridge (European Commission Report) [online]. Available at: http://www.flosspols.org/deliverables/FLOSSPOLS-D16-Gender_Integrated_Report_of_Findings.pdf (accessed 02 September 2011).

O'Neil M., 2009. *Cyber Chiefs: Autonomy and Authority in Online Tribes*. New York: Pluto Press.

Parcak S., 2009. *Satellite Remote Sensing for Archaeology*. London: Routledge.

Pinker S., Nowak M.A. and Lee J. J., 2008. The logic of indirect speech. *Proceedings of the National Academy of Sciences* 105, pp. 833–838.

Raymond E. S., 1998. *The Cathedral and the Bazaar: Musings on Linux and Open Source by an Accidental Revolutionary*. Sebastopol, CA: O'Reilly Media.

Richards J., Jeffrey S., Waller S., Ciravegna F., Chapman S. and Zhang Z., 2011. The Archaeology Data Service and the Archaeotools Project: Faceted Classification and Natural Language Processing. In Kansa E. C., Kansa S. W. and Watrall E. eds, 2011. *Archaeology 2.0: New Approaches to Communication and Collaboration*. Los Angeles: Cotsen Institute of Archaeology, pp. 31–56.

Simmel G., 1900. A chapter in the philosophy of value. *American Journal of Sociology* 5, pp. 179–186.

Söderberg J., 2008. *Hacking Capitalism. The Free and Open Source Software Movement*. New York: Routledge.

Stallman R. M., 2009. Why 'open source' misses the point of free software. *Communications of the ACM* 52.6, pp. 31–33.

Stallman R. M., 2010. Is digital inclusion a good thing? How can we make sure it is? *IEEE Communications Magazine* 48, pp. 112–118.

Steinmueller W. E., 2005. Cyberspace markets, social

capital and trust. In Mansell R. and Collins B. S. eds, 2005. *Trust and Crime in Information Societies*. Cheltenham: Edward Elgar, pp. 431–441.

Thrift N., 2006. Re-inventing invention: new tendencies in capitalist commodification. *Economy and Society* 35.2, pp. 279–306.

Tuk M. A., Verlegh P. W. J., Smidts A. and Wigboldus D. H. J., 2009. Sales and sincerity: The role of relational framing in word-of-mouth marketing. *Journal of Consumer Psychology* 19, pp. 38–47.

Ur J. A., 2006. Google Earth and Archaeology. *The SAA Archaeological Record* 6.3. pp. 35–38.

Von Hippel E., 2005. *Democratising Innovation*. Cambridge MA: MIT Press.

Whitehead H., 1993. Morals, models and motives in a different light: a rumination on Alan P. Fiske's 'Structures of Social Life'. *Ethos* 21.3, pp. 319–356.

Witcher R. E., 2010. The Fabulous Tales of the Common People, Part 2: Encountering Hadrian's Wall. *Public Archaeology* 9.4, pp. 211–238.

Yakowitz J., in press. Tragedy of the Data Commons. *Harvard Journal of Law and Technology* 25 [manuscript]. Available at: http://papers.ssrn.com/sol3/papers.cfm?abstract_id=1789749 (accessed 17 October 2011).

Zeitlyn D., 2003. Gift economies in the development of open source software: anthropological reflections. *Research Policy* 32, pp. 1287–1291.

Twitter and Archaeology: An Archaeological Network in 140 Characters or Less

Lorna Richardson

Abstract

This paper discusses the use that the archaeological community currently makes of Twitter, based on a survey of archaeological tweeters conducted by the author in 2011. The survey reveals that this Web-based application is now prevalently an intra-specialist networking tool rather than one of public engagement. Research directions that might help to extend the use of Twitter for communication with non-specialists are offered and theoretical issues such as influence, popularity, authority, accuracy, and credibility are discussed in relation to tweeting. Indicators and modalities for measuring them are proposed. These are intended to offer approaches that may be useful in the future for the evaluation of initiatives in developing public engagement with archaeology that can be supported by the Twitter platform.

Introduction

Twitter is a Web-based application that combines aspects of social networking, instant messaging and blogging into a fast, simple and convenient mode of communication. Twitter enables registered users to post short status updates known as 'tweets' to a Web-based public timeline, or 'microblog'. The site asks users to answer the question 'what's happening?' in 140 characters or less. The disclosure of personal information is pared-down and optional – the emphasis of the Twitter platform is in the present, rather than on detailed back-story such as that found on the social networking platform, Facebook. Twitter describes itself as 'a real-time information network that connects you to the latest information about what you find interesting' (Twitter 2011). Since its creation in 2006, Twitter has developed into a powerful cultural barometer, as a platform for news, commentary and networking.

According to Twitter's own figures, 140 million tweets are sent on average each day (Twitter Blog 2011). Increasingly, Twitter is a widespread method of communication in political debate and political campaigning, as well as in the entertainment, corporate and sports marketing sectors. Many organisations and celebrities have personal Twitter accounts. A significant percentage of these celebrity accounts have many millions of followers; the singer Britney Spears currently has the most followers, at around 7.5 million (Wefollow 2012).

The attraction of the platform may be due in part to its innovation and immediacy. Access to the 'thoughts, intentions and activities of millions of users in real-time' (Phelan *et al.* 2009) has created a powerful channel for understanding the immediate, in-the-moment Web. Rapid development in mobile technology and mobile technology pricing, the increased availability of reliable mobile applications for managing Twitter feeds created by third parties, the rise in the number of Twitter users keen to use mobile technology, and an increase in the use of Twitter as a convenient form of instant social updating and interpersonal interaction will continue to impact upon usage intensity. This ability to foster immediate communication is key for the use of Twitter in archaeology. A small number of live-tweeted excavations have been undertaken during 2011. Conferences are routinely allocated hashtags and tweeted to a wider audience, archaeological problems are 'crowd-sourced', images and maps are shared, and discussions developed. For those archaeologists interested in embracing the possibilities of social and participatory media, especially in the field of public archaeology, Twitter can support both wider public engagement and networking within the discipline. This paper will begin with a discussion of the phenomenon of Twitter and its use and impact in wider society. It will then examine how the platform is currently used by members of the archaeological community, and will discuss potential future developments, based on my research undertaken online during April and May 2011.

So how does Twitter work?
Status updates can be posted and received directly via the Twitter website or its API (Application Programming Interface), through a number of wireless mobile devices such as smartphones or tablets, and through the mobile phone Short Message Service (SMS). The fact that Twitter is easy to use via smartphones makes the application relatively simple to exploit within an archaeological context, such as fieldwork or post-excavation, where it is possible to transmit real-time updates to other users. Twitter users can follow any other accounts, and be followed back, simply with the click of the 'follow' button found below each user profile. Unlike some other social networking platforms there is no complicated social etiquette attached to Twitter use. Reciprocal relationships are not necessary; there are no obligations to follow back, no permission need be granted and no acknowledgement or communication between follower and user is ever required. Users may choose to restrict who can access their profiles by opting for a private account, 'locked' from public view, requiring the approval of new followers. Anyone can choose to block their unwanted or abusive followers, and spam or marketing accounts can be reported and blocked immediately. Tweets from all those accounts followed will appear on an individual's Twitter 'timeline', a stream of real-time tweets from the followed accounts, in reverse chronological order (Twitter 2011).

A number of conventions exist to facilitate sharing, updating and searching. Tweets can be addressed directly from the user to another account holder using the @user syntax (@LornaRichardson, for example). Private messages are passed by a 'DM' (Direct Message). Twitter has its own conventions, slang and abbreviations, which are usually driven by necessity and created by its users, rather than endorsed by the company, although Twitter does provide a limited glossary for newcomers (Twitter Help Center 2011). An informal Twitter lexicon has developed to describe the service, users, and various functions of the service itself, such as the terms 'Tweeps' (followers) or Twettiquette (Twitter etiquette). There are a number of shorthand terms created as a response to the character limitations, such as abt (about), thx (thanks) or nts (note to self), often using terms derived from SMS or live-chat vocabulary (Webopedia 2011).

Participants can share or forward tweets from and to their followers by 'retweeting' information, marked in Twitter shorthand as 'RT'. The most common method is supported by the Twitter platform itself, which provides a retweet option, and uses the shorthand 'RT' to indicate a retweet within the body of the forwarded content. Quoting a tweet is more complicated, and some users may mark these quotes with 'MT' to indicate a modified tweet. A number of mobile Twitter applications allow content to be quoted, rather than retweeted. No truly consistent convention exists for the method by which users can reshare or forward content, and there are many inconsistencies. Users with publicity-seeking objectives will actively seek retweets in order to broaden their audience impact. There are many motivations to perform a RT, including propagation of the topic; visible agreement; demonstration of 'paying attention'; exercising social leverage, or to gain and maintain followers.

Research on the subject of user influence through Twitter by Cha *et al.* (2010) made several important observations, which are especially important to consider in the context of public engagement and archaeology. The work of Cha *et al* focussed on three measures of influence on Twitter: indegree (the number of people who follow a user), the number of retweets and the number of user mentions. They found that whilst the number of followers represents the popularity of the user, it does not necessarily increase the influence of that user. The most important measure of influence can be found in retweets, which represent the value of the name of the Twitter user. Their analysis revealed that the most influential users posted regularly, creatively and with concerted efforts to engage and maintain conversations with their followers. This work is supported by the research undertaken in 2008 by Huberman *et al.* (2009: 6–7) who concluded that the number of followers did not reflect meaningful interaction on a larger scale, and that the number of interactions were restricted to a significantly smaller group of 'friends' within the network of followers.

The lack of a universal convention and syntax for sharing tweets, and restrictions of the 140 character limit has implications for authorship, accuracy and acknowledgement of original content posted on Twitter (boyd *et al.* 2010: 1), and has serious implications for archaeological content, which will be discussed further below. Retweeting may dilute or alter the content of the initial tweet. It is possible that reinterpretation of tweets could lead to the distribution of misinformation, with messages corrupting or modifying as they pass through multiple user accounts. However, research into the use of Twitter during the Chilean earthquake in 2010 by Mendoza *et al.* (2010: 6) noted that 'the propagation of Tweets that correspond to rumors differs from Tweets that spread news because rumors tend to be questioned more than news by the Twitter community', which indicated that, in the Chilean example at least, the Twitter community actively questioned information appearing in their timelines.

Searching Twitter
Access to always-on broadband, the increasing availability of wi-fi in public places and an explosion in mobile smartphone technology has contributed to the habituated use of Twitter around the clock. With over 200 million accounts to follow (Kirkpatrick 2011) Twitter is a source of trivial and banal, as well as useful, information. This creates a need to tune in and out of the Twitter stream and filter useful commentary. Twitter is a simple enough platform for use by people that simply want to publish and broadcast through their status update. However, those seeking specific information have more of a challenge on a platform where status updates are being published at a rate of c. 600 tweets per second. During the revelations of Osama Bin Laden's death by President Obama on 1st May 2011, tweets were being sent at the rate of 5008 per second (Parr 2011).

The solution to this problem grew out the Twitter community itself in 2007, when Twitter user Chris Messina first used a hashtag when he tweeted 'how do you feel about using # (pound) for groups. As in #barcamp [msg]?' (Gannes 2010). The adoption of the hashtag convention allowed users to semi-synchronise conversations and further refine the basic and often inaccurate search facilities on Twitter. The hashtag is indicated by the use of the # (hash) symbol, which is placed before words within the text of the tweet (**Figure 2**). The hash symbol is used to create unique tags that can be used to annotate and cluster relevant tweets around themes, subjects, people, organisations and sentiments. Two common archaeological hashtags are #archaeology or #commarch (community archaeology). These hashtags allow users to collect, identify, and categorise their tweets by including one or more hashtags within the text of their posts. Then, anyone using a public account can search for and view any post by any user including these specific hashtags when using Twitter.

However, there is no written convention for using hashtags on Twitter and not all of them are used in the same way, if at all. Whilst these are commonly introduced into a community of Twitter users discussing a particular topic or topics, these are, to some extent, a personal choice. Users can prefix anything with the hash symbol to create hashtags, and annotate their tweets at their own discretion, so consistent usage is not guaranteed. As an example, during my research, some archaeological tweets were posted with the hashtag 'archaeology', some used the American-English spelling 'archeology', some were tagged with 'pubarch', for public archaeology, some with 'commarch', for community archaeology, and many archaeology-related tweets, originating in the United States, were tagged with 'anthropology' instead of archaeology.

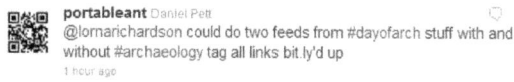

Figure 2. An example of a tweet containing the hashtags 'dayofarch' and 'archaeology'

Information credibility and authenticity

Twitter has been used to break fresh news from world events, political revolutions, and natural disasters. These have been tweeted by official news sources, news agencies and first-person observations from people 'on the ground'. 'Trending topics' are listed on the Twitter site, which represent the most-mentioned keywords and hashtags from emerging news on the whole global or country-wide Twitter timeline. Twitter is highly valued for the ability of this fresh news feed, disseminated in real-time, to rapidly update information and facilitate speedy analysis and interpretation of events far faster even than traditional media websites. Yet, the Twitter timeline can also peddle falsehoods and misinformation, and the issue of establishing credibility within online micro-blogging has been the focus of recent research. Castillo *et al.* (2011: 1), used the example of the 2010 earthquake in Chile, where false rumours circulated through and beyond Twitter via the Internet in the vacuum caused by a lack of news from official sources. Whilst misinformation is not a new Internet phenomenon by any means, the use of a social media platform for political propaganda, marketing, spam and malicious behaviour could seriously damage the credibility of information publicised via Twitter. With the proliferation of pseudo-archaeological websites on the Internet, the possibilities of rapid dissemination of false information via social media should be of concern to any archaeologists that wish to embrace these technologies.

The issue of authority and identity is an important consideration for archaeology on Twitter. The active creation and management of personality and self-expression on social media platforms raise a number of issues around interpersonal perception and controlled identity. The personal information available from a Twitter profile is limited to the user's name, a 160-character biography, the location of the user and the URL of their website (if any) — these last three items are optional. Many account holders prefer to maintain a high degree of anonymity, using nicknames and abstract profile photos. Research into the presentation of self in different mediated contexts has shown that the 'imagined audience' is a key consideration for account holders when using social media (Marwick and boyd 2010: 115). The disconnection between user and audience is important to consider, given the potential reach of the retweet, universal access to all public accounts via search engines, and the likelihood that not every single follower reads every single tweet on their timeline. An audience on Twitter is constructed through the presentation of a suitable user profile, personal relationships built through conversations and managing the balance between one-to-one and one-to-many communications (Marwick and boyd 2010: 130). The contradictions of ambient awareness means that users and followers can experience a relationship on terms negotiated individually and without the other's consent. The limited information available about Twitter users ensures that the development of a deeper sense of trust through personal relationships within the platform is a longer process, if developed at all. Being part of a recognised archaeological authority – a university, museum, company – would appear to add weight to the content of the user profile, beyond the content of the associated tweets.

Lurking and listening
Twitter supports communication, as individual-to-individual, and to a broader individual-to-public basis – a 'broadcast' or announcement to the time line audience. However, research undertaken by website-monitoring.com in April 2010 showed that 24% of Twitter users had no followers at all, and 97% of users had less than 100 followers. 41% of Twitter users had never sent a tweet since opening their account (Burcher 2010). The Twitter status update demands both passive readers and active commentators in order to be a worthwhile exercise. As Nonnecke and Preece (2003) point out when studying participation within email discussion lists, 'a case can be made for lurking being normal and public posting being abnormal ... lurkers should be called participants (publicly silent though they may often be)'. Using politicians that use Twitter as an example, Crawford (2009: 530) defines the two most common communication habits: 'reciprocal listening', where the politician will answer questions and respond to comments from their followers, and 'broadcasting', where information and statistics are updated, but direct messages are not answered and dialogue is not pursued. It is increasingly common for organisations to use their communications team, or a public relations consultancy to manage Twitter profiles, what Crawford (2009: 530) describes as 'something akin to ventriloquism'. Archaeologists that use Twitter in the workplace have commented during my research that the practice of using official organisational accounts as a method to only 'broadcast' archaeological information, rather than construct dialogue with the wider tweeting public, has restricted the development of meaningful public engagement.

Archiving tweets
Although the use of Twitter is common as a social tool for news, political debate, branding and entertainment, the surge in the use of the platform as a channel for communication in arenas such as cultural heritage, events, education, research, during natural disasters, civil unrest and political activities, has made a significant case for the preservation of tweets for perpetuity. Tweets reflect 'public reaction and sentiment' (Kelly *et al.* 2010: 2) and can be used for post-event analysis, observation of political debate or to capture a slice of popular sentiment at any given point in the Twitter timeline. In April 2010, the United States Library of Congress announced that Twitter had donated the entire back catalogue of all tweets dating back to March 2006. The Library stated 'this information provides detailed evidence about how technology-based social networks form and evolve over time. The collection also documents a remarkable range of social trends. Anyone who wants to understand how an ever-broadening public is using social media to engage in an ongoing debate regarding social and cultural issues will have need of this material' (Library of Congress 2010).

Twitter and archaeology survey 2011
During preliminary research during the winter of 2010/11, it became apparent that the Twitter platform was being used by archaeologists across the globe as a conduit for information sharing, cooperation and discussion. Twitter was used in a very unstructured and informal manner, and was used as a means of transmitting archaeological news amongst peers. The potential of Twitter for the dissemination of information about public archaeology projects and excavations was exciting – but how does the platform work with and for archaeologists now?

An online survey was designed, with 27 questions which concentrated on these central topics: What archaeological information is currently being shared via Twitter? Is Twitter a useful tool for widening public involvement with archaeology? Who uses it within the archaeological sector? What for? How does, and how could, Twitter encourage the development of a useful archaeological online social network for public engagement and information exchange? There was emphasis on the use of the platform within the professional archaeology sector, as initial research demonstrated that the majority of archaeology-related users were academics or working archaeologists. The survey 'went live' in April 2011, and was disseminated via Twitter, reposted daily for 14 days, and shared by numerous fellow tweeters. The tweeted request for participation contained a link to the survey and requests to RT to interested parties. The survey received 167 stored responses, of which, 85 people completed the entire survey.

The original intention for this research was to also use data collected or 'scraped' from the entire Twitter feed during the period of the survey, in order to analyse tweets that included the terms 'archaeology', 'public archaeology', 'archeology' and 'heritage'. However, in March 2011, Twitter announced changes to their terms of service and restrictions to their application programming interface, or API, which governs how external programmes interact with Twitter's servers (Web Ecology Project 2011). This restricts the ability of data collection sites to redistribute content to researchers. The motivation behind Twitter's change of direction may be related to their desire to regain direct control of their data, and exploit this for commercial gain. Twitter encourages researchers instead to subscribe to Twitter's newly-appointed official data reseller, Gnip (Gnip 2011). Gnip aggregates social media data, which includes Twitter. Personal enquiry to Charles Ince (2011), a sales manager at Gnip, showed that access to the most basic data streams, 10% of all tweets at any one time, for academic use (a discount on full-price) would costs $2000 per month. This price puts access to the real-time Twitter stream out of the reach of most academic researchers and institutions.

Discussion

The results from the survey demonstrated that archaeological communities worldwide are embracing the Twitter platform for the same reasons as everyone else – to broadcast, listen and network with others in their field, but also to share and benefit from current archaeological research and discuss professional issues. This boundary-crossing global network lies both within and outside archaeological specialisms, and provides collaboration and contact that could only otherwise be facilitated by geographical proximity, synchronous research fields or conference attendance, organisational membership or personal acquaintance. Indeed, the majority of users have already met in person, or plan to meet in person those archaeological acquaintances made through Twitter. Archaeological tweeters are active, with the majority regularly posting content on archaeologically-related topics each week. The survey respondents were certainly enthusiastic about sharing their subject: tweeting frequency on archaeological topics does not depend on whether they have an official work account or one for personal use, and the use of archaeology-related lists to filter and manage information is common.

The survey showed a growing sense of 'belonging' to a distinct archaeological community. The survey participants especially valued the way in which Twitter facilitated small-group interaction across archaeological disciplines and the opportunity to learn from new, unpublished research and 'listen' and comment during tweeted conferences. However, there are barriers that exist on the Twitter platform that prevent a deeper sense of archaeological community. Some felt there are low numbers of archaeological Twitter users, and highlighted a concern that infrequent participation, or the adoption of a passive role, would fail to establish a meaningful sense of belonging, as an individual, in a larger archaeological network. Although social media offer a variety of platforms on which to communicate, the unique functionality of Twitter that provides a simple, informal networking channel and access to immediate news would be sorely missed should it fold, and similar experiences would be sought out using other Web tools. The survey noted that the use of Twitter in communication with the non-archaeological public could create friction with organisational policy and structure. There is a notable lack of organisational guidance for the use of Twitter, and indeed other forms of the social Web. This absence of policies for social media use appears to be widespread within archaeological organisations. However, the scant information from the survey regarding organisational use could also be due to the prevalence of the use of the platform for personal opinion, news and dialogue, using non-work devices, as highlighted by the number of mobile phones used to tweet, rather than any form of prescriptive organisational broadcasting.

The extent of influence on Twitter that can be seen exercised through the act of retweeting has a number of implications for the use of social media for dissemination of information and publicity. It is important for archaeology projects that wish to communicate through this medium to consider issues of authority, influence and reach through retweeted content – the currency of news can last longer than expected. During the period of research for this paper, an international news item was circulated via Twitter that covered the discovery of a so-called 'Gay Caveman' during an archaeological excavation in the Czech Republic. This sensationalist story, first reported in *The Daily Telegraph* (Anon. 2011) in the UK and the *Daily Mail* (Daily Mail Reporter 2011) on the 6th and 8th of April respectively, was swiftly spread via global media platforms. The newspaper articles included information about the identification of the sexual orientation of an individual in a Copper Age burial, dating to around 5,000 years ago. This biological male had been interred with an 'unusual' grave assemblage and orientation, previously only found in burials found in the region that had been identified as belonging to biological females. There was much conjecture in the press and online about the transsexualism and homosexuality of the human interred in the unusual burial, often in disparaging terms; the *Daily Mail* referred to the individual as 'The Oldest Gay in the Village' in the article headlines (Daily Mail Reporter 2011).

The reactions to this news by the archaeological community during this period varied. Many of the archaeological Twitter news accounts simply retweeted this information as a news item, without critical analysis. A small but vocal number of archaeologists met the news with increasing anger and derision both on Twitter and in the blogosphere (Killgrove 2011; Hawks 2011; Joyce 2011), and attempts were made to bring some archaeological critique to an otherwise inflammatory and inaccurate tabloid story. However, the 'Gay Caveman' story as a Twitter phenomenon did not simply disappear in the face of these denunciations by high profile archaeological experts. The most recent of this story was on the 28th September 2011, when user @dermonx tweeted a link to the *Daily Mail* article and wrote: 'Gay caveman: 5,000-year-old male skeleton 'outed' by way he was buried'. The story has yet to fade from view and is an interesting development of the mythology and history of homosexuality. A useful warning about the potential 'long-tail' of inaccurately interpreted archaeological stories from global media.

The search for authority and influence, alongside issues of accuracy and trustworthiness are important considerations for the survey respondents. One response emphasised the need for a sense of responsibility from archaeological Twitter users as a representation of the discipline in a public arena, and highlighted the need to prevent the distribution of inaccurate archaeological information, with the comment, 'we inform such twitter users that they are doing archaeology a disservice'. To some extent, the perception of influence on the platform depends on a Twitter user's standing in the 'real' archaeological community, alongside organisational links, quantity and quality of information and geographical location. The methods with which users determine authority in other archaeological users reflect both the limited size of the archaeological network on Twitter and the 'real-life' archaeological community in general. Again, personal reputation, personal acquaintance and organisational affiliation are used in the assessment of tweeted information, and, as perhaps could be expected from archaeologists used to the critical examination of source material, the primary source outside Twitter is researched and critiqued thoroughly before being commented on, or redistributed. This has some interesting ramifications for the potential ease of involvement for less 'institutional', less familiar, non-academic community and amateur archaeology groups and individuals, who may wish to exploit the medium to promote their work via Twitter.

Credibility and authenticity are critical issues when dealing with the public dissemination of archaeological news and information. Many, if not most, archaeological Twitter users are professional archaeologists; many work in the academic field, and the authenticity and validity of archaeological news is an emotive subject. An interesting addition to this research is demonstrated by the results of the Twitter and archaeology survey. Results from the survey suggested that the limitations of the account profile mean that *what* you say on Twitter, *how often* and *to whom* is of far greater importance for how other archaeologists perceive a user's tweeted life and influence, than a simple assessment of the contents of the short biography and accompanying profile image. Personal and professional reputation, perceived reliability, influence in 'real life' and biographical information found elsewhere online is pivotal to the perceived trustworthiness of information shared through Twitter. Twitter followers in archaeological circles will actively search for more information about a person or status update, via search engines, to ascertain the reliability of the information provided.

A slim majority of the archaeological tweeters questioned were seasoned users, and 43% of respondents had joined the platform since 2010. This reflects the wider increase in uptake of the service globally during 2010 and 2011. Those archaeologists using Twitter are a mobile and technologically-forward looking group; laptops, smartphones and tablet devices facilitate nearly 74% of all respondents' access to Twitter. The majority of status updates were made through third-party clients or mobile phone applications, suggesting perhaps an industry-specific need for portability, the desire for 'always on' access to the social Web, or perhaps that the use of Twitter is restricted on workplace equipment. Most respondents were active social networkers, with websites, blogs, photo-sharing, email lists and the use of Facebook the most frequently used sources of information and methods of communication for archaeological topics besides Twitter, although the majority of respondents did not link their accounts directly to other services. The question of archiving highlights the lack of perceived need to take responsibility for the long-term preservation of their tweets amongst the survey respondents. Their comments suggest that the existing methods available for archiving tweets are either not considered at all or are frequently misunderstood, and responsibility for the long-term safeguard of this information is seen to belong to the Twitter platform, rather than the user themselves.

The results of the Twitter and archaeology survey have established that the platform plays an important role in the communications tool kit of the digitally-minded archaeologist. The growth in use, and a growing sense of belonging to an archaeological network or community bode well for the adoption of the platform for public engagement with archaeology in the future. However, the number of archaeologists using the platform remains small and unrepresentative, with, roughly, around 1,000 archaeological users, heavily concentrated in the UK and USA, and predominately from desk-bound work in commercial archaeology companies, museums and academia. The development of the platform as an archaeological outreach tool depends on more participation within the sector, or it will remain a niche tool for intra-archaeological networking. More archaeologists need to be encouraged to join the Twitter conversation, and institutions need to encourage their staff to engage with the public, and their peers through the platform. This will need some careful consideration: the information shared and broadcast will need to be accessible to the layperson, and organisations and researchers will need to consider carefully how to manage that process. The types of archaeological activity that can be shared need experimentation, and an understanding of what kind of archaeological information members of the public would like to access through tweets would also be useful. Further research into the reasons why individuals and organisations in the archaeological world choose *not* to use Twitter would complement this study and perhaps allay some of the fears attached to this medium of communication. Access to the full Twitter feed would be the gold standard for research, and would enable a true understanding of what type of archaeological information is being shared and discussed on Twitter, when and how – unfortunately, given Twitter's understandable desire to exploit its surging popularity as a source of commercial revenue, this looks difficult at present.

Acknowledgments

Thanks are due to my supervisors Dan Pett, Tim Schadla-Hall, Melissa Terras, and Claire Warwick. I am very grateful to all my Twitter followers and retweeters that helped spread the word about my work, and to the anonymous Twitter users that responded to my survey: #thanks.

References

Anon., 2011. First Homosexual Caveman Found. *The Daily Telegraph* [online] 06 April 2011. Available at: http://www.telegraph.co.uk/news/newstopics/howaboutthat/8433527/First-homosexual-caveman-found.html (accessed 04 June 2011).

Boyd d., Golder S. and Lotan G., 2010. Tweet, Tweet, ReTweet: Conversational Aspects of ReTweeting on Twitter [online]. *Proceedings of 43rd Hawaii International Conference on System Sciences 2010*. 1–10. Available at: http://research.microsoft.com/pubs/102168/TweetTweetRetweet.pdf (accessed 13 April 2011).

Burcher N., 2010. Twitter Facts and Figures – latest Twitter statistics users, countries, demographics, timelines etc. *Nick Burcher: Personal Thoughts on the Evolution of Media and Advertising* [online] 13 May 2010. Available at: http://www.nickburcher.com/2010/05/twitter-facts-and-figures-latest.html (accessed 15 May 2011).

Castillo C., Mendoza M. and Poblete B., 2011. Information Credibility on Twitter [online]. *WWW '11 Proceedings of the 20th International Conference on World Wide Web*. Available at: http://research.yahoo.com/node/3475 (accessed 13 April 2011).

Cha M., Haddadi H., Benevenuto F. and Gummadi K. P., 2010. Measuring user influence in Twitter: The million follower fallacy [online]. *Proceedings of International AAAI Conference on Weblogs and Social Media*. Available at: http://www.mpi-sws.org/~gummadi/papers/icwsm2010_cha.pdf (accessed 13 April 2011).

Crawford K., 2009. Following you: Disciplines of listening in social media. *Continuum: Journal of Media & Cultural Studies* 23 (4), pp. 525–535.

Daily Mail Reporter, 2011. The oldest gay in the village: 5,000-year-old is 'outed' by the way he was buried. *Daily Mail* [online] 08 April 2011. Available at: http://www.dailymail.co.uk/sciencetech/article-1374060/Gay-caveman-5-000-year-old-male-skeleton-outed-way-buried.html (accessed 06 June 2011).

Gannes L., 2010. The Short and Illustrious History of Twitter #Hashtags [online]. Available at: http://gigaom.com/2010/04/30/the-short-and-illustrious-history-of-twitter-hashtags/ (accessed 15 June 2011).

Gnip: The Social Media API, 2011 [online]. Available at: http://gnip.com/ (accessed 30 April 2011).

Hawks J., 2011. The 'Gay Caveman'. *John Hawks* [online] 07 April 2011. Available at: http://johnhawks.net/weblog/topics/meta/communication/gay-caveman-prague-2011.html (accessed 06 June 2011).

Huberman B. A., Romero D. M. and Wu F., 2009. Social networks that matter: Twitter under the microscope. *First Monday* 14 (1) [online]. Available at: http://firstmonday.org/htbin/cgiwrap/bin/ojs/index.php/fm/article/view/2317/2063 (accessed 13 April 2011).

Ince C., 2011. *Gnip*. (Personal Communication, 29 June 2011).

Joyce A., 2011. Gay Cavemen Wrecking a Perfectly Good Story. *Ancient Bodies, Ancient Lives* [online] 07 April 2011. Available at: http://ancientbodies.wordpress.com/2011/04/07/gay-caveman-wrecking-a-perfectly-good-story/ (accessed 06 June 2011).

Kelly B., Hawksey M., O'Brien J., Guy M. and Rowe M., 2010. Twitter Archiving Using Twapper Keeper: Technical and Policy Challenges [online]. *Proceedings of the 7th International Conference on Preservation of Digital Objects 2010*. Available at: http://opus.bath.ac.uk (accessed 15 May 2011).

Killgrove K., 2011. Gay Caveman! ZOMFG! *Powered by Osteons* [online] 06 April 2011. Available at: http://www.poweredbyosteons.org/2011/04/gay-caveman-zomfg.html (accessed 06 June 2011).

Kirkpatrick M., 2011. Twitter Confirms It Has Passed 200 Million Accounts, 70% of Traffic Now International [online] 29 April 2011. Available at: http://www.readwriteweb.com/archives/twitter_confirms_it_has_passed_200_million_account.php (01 May 2011).

Library of Congress, 2010. Twitter Donates Entire Tweet Archive to Library of Congress [online] 15 April 2010. Available at: http://www.loc.gov/today/pr/2010/10-081.html (accessed 15 April 2011).

Marwick A. E. and boyd d., 2010. I tweet honesty, I tweet passionately: Twitter users, context collapse, and the imagined audience. *New Media & Society* 13 (1), pp. 114–133.

Mendoza M., Poblete B. and Castillo C., 2010. Twitter Under Crisis: Can we trust what we RT? [online]. *Proceedings of the First Workshop on Social Media Analytics KDD '10*. Available at: http://research.yahoo.com/pub/3255 (accessed 06 June 2011).

Nonnecke B. and Preece J., 2003. Silent participants: Getting to know lurkers better. In Fisher D. and Lueg

C. eds, 2003. *From Usenet to Co Webs: Interacting with social information spaces.* London: Springer-Verlag, pp. 110–132.

Parr B., 2011. Bin Laden's Death Sparks Record 12.4 Million Tweets Per Hour [online]. Available at: http://mashable.com/2011/05/02/bin-laden-death-twitter/ (accessed 02 May 2011).

Phelan O., McCarthy K. and Smyth B., 2009. Using Twitter to recommend Real-Time Topical News. *Proceedings of the Third ACM Conference on Recommender Systems.* DOI: http://doi.acm.org/10.1145/1639714.1639794.

Twitter, 2011. About [online]. Available at: http://twitter.com/about (accessed 13 April 2011).

Twitter Blog, 2011 [online]. Available at: http://blog.twitter.com/2011/03/numbers.html (accessed 30 October 2011).

Twitter Help Center, 2011. The Twitter Glossary [online]. Available at: https://support.twitter.com/articles/166337-the-twitter-glossary (accessed 30 October 2011).

Web Ecology Project, 2011. 140 Kit [online]. Available at: http://140kit.com/documents/Regarding_API_Change.pdf (accessed 13 April 2011).

Webopedia, 2011. Twitter Dictionary: a Guide to Understanding Twitter Chat [online]. Available at: http://www.webopedia.com/quick_ref/Twitter_Dictionary_Guide.asp (accessed 06 June 2011).

Wefollow, 2012. Top Twitter Users [online]. Available at: http://wefollow.com/top (accessed 24 January 2012).

Wessex Archaeology and the Web: Amesbury Archer to *Archaeocast*

Tom Goskar

Abstract

Wessex Archaeology (WA) is a non-profit charitable company which maintains one of the largest interpretive archaeological websites in the UK. As of July 2011, the website contains over 4,000 pages of content and attracts an average of 12,000 unique visitors per month, but statistics have recorded close to that in one day during periods where new discoveries and announcements have attracted popular media coverage. This essay is a retrospective account of the last ten years, highlighting specific turning points that influenced the direction of WA's Web practices, such as the opportunity presented by the discovery of the Amesbury Archer and the experiment of *Archaeocast*, at a time when concepts of Web 2.0 were firmly in the domain of technophiles. How the WA website has impacted on the practice of communicating archaeological information to the global village more generally will also be considered, in addition to highlighting some of the challenges of ensuring that online engagement remains a central and sustainable function of the organisation and of archaeology.

First steps

WA was established in May 1979 as the Wessex Archaeological Committee based in Salisbury, and, in 1983, it became the non-profit charitable company that it remains today. Its charitable objects are 'to promote the advancement of the education of the public in the subjects of culture, arts, heritage and science through the pursuit of archaeology' (CharitiesDirect 2011). Currently (2011), the company employs around two hundred people, with offices in Salisbury, Rochester, Sheffield, and Edinburgh. It undertakes commercial archaeology projects to fund its remit to educate the public about its work, and about archaeology in general. WA conducts about five hundred projects each year, and had a turnover of over £6 million in 2009–2010.

WA started disseminating its work online at www.wessexarch.co.uk in 2001. The simple brochure-style site was designed by the company's Drawing Office, using desktop publishing (DTP) software Claris Works. It comprised nine pages listing the name, address, company overview, and the main seven commercial services offered (Wessex Archaeology 2001). At this time, senior management primarily saw the Web as a 'shop window' advertising that Wessex Archaeology existed to the world. Its wider potential, particularly for public engagement, was unrecognised.

The main outreach activities undertaken by WA before this time included school visits, lectures to local societies, national institutions and students; the publication of articles and summaries in county and national archaeology journals and the popular press, the publication of monographs, the deposition of site reports in Historic Environment Records (HERs), volunteering in local archaeology society and museum events, community digs, and assisting the press and media with their enquiries. This is the traditional fare of archaeological outreach in the UK and many WA archaeologists continue to be involved in these activities today. In spite of the growing ubiquity of Web access over the last ten years, not everyone in the office is comfortable with, or understands the Web's potential to improve access to archaeological information. Voluntary contribution to Web content has been, and remains, the biggest challenge to the future growth of WA's online identity.

The discovery of the Amesbury Archer and the re-launch of WA online

By April 2002 a new website was being developed, using Macromedia (now Adobe) Dreamweaver and static HTML; the website was hosted on a Web server within Portway House, WA's head office. However, there was uncertainty about how to proceed with developing content and how much resource to allocate. The website developed within specific confines, separate from the organisation's main activities; it was seen as an 'IT project' rather than a global communication tool that would represent the company, its services and fulfil its charitable goals; but external events forced a change in attitudes.

In May 2002 Wessex Archaeology discovered the grave of a man dating to around 2,300 BC, three miles from Stonehenge on the edge of Amesbury (Wiltshire). The burial contained an extensive array of grave goods, including the oldest examples of gold yet found in Britain. The discovery was the catalyst to finish and launch the new website. WA anticipated unprecedented media coverage, so the website had to be finished quickly and contain a good summary of what we knew at the time, as well as a press release and related imagery (Wessex Archaeology 2002). The new website was launched on 13 May 2002 (**Figure 3**), a day before the formal press release, and was an immediate success, taking the news about this newly discovered Bronze Age archer's burial global. A measure of its impact is demonstrated in how the moniker 'Amesbury Archer', first used to give an identity to the Web content – and not mentioned in the original press release – was repeated in TV and newspaper headlines and has since lent its name to the primary school built on the site[1]. It allowed the archaeologists to tell the story of the discovery in their own words, rather than just relying upon the variable interpretation provided by journalists and based on the press release (Wessex Archaeology 2002).

The decision to devote resources to creating high-quality publically available information on the Amesbury Archer on the WA website was also vindicated in a very practical sense. Media interest in the discovery exceeded expectations and without any communications staff, the organisation was grateful to be able to point people to the website to download the relevant information and images.

During that first week of the re-launch, some 63,912 unique visits were made to the WA website

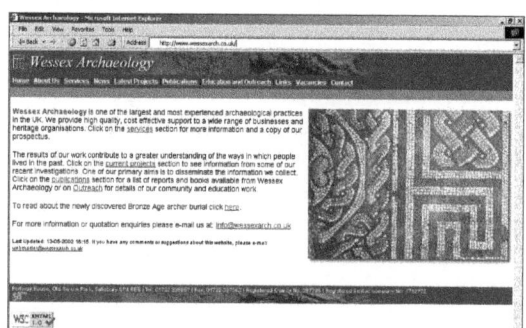

Figure 3. Wessex Archaeology website at the launch on 13 May 2002 (see Plate 1).

---

[1] http://www.amesburyarcher.wilts.sch.uk/ (accessed 18 October 2011).

by people from over thirty countries; the site almost became a victim of its own success as it was quickly knocked offline by the sheer number of visits. At the time, the website was hosted on free Web space offered by our Internet Service Provider, who quickly and politely recommended that a more professional hosting arrangement was found. Alternative arrangements were sought and the website moved to a dedicated hosting company.

By the summer of 2002, Wessex Archaeology's opinion of how and what the Web could be used for had been changed forever. The website was seen to be a tool which the company could use for a large number of purposes, from a media hub, to educational and commercial uses. Indeed, media attention encouraged the company to appoint their first Head of Communications, with a background in journalism, and, more crucially, a new role was created in the IT department for an Archaeological Multimedia Developer who had special responsibility for Web development, in addition to providing other archaeological computing services.

Challenges to development

In spite of the obvious success of exploiting WA's online presence to promote discoveries of world significance, public engagement still tended to take place away from the Web, and educational materials would take even a few years to find their way online. The speed at which new content could be commissioned and published online was frustratingly slow, in an era when other heritage and cultural institutions were devoting significant time and resources to improve their Web presence and access to their institution's information and collections.

This was partially caused by the approval process which demanded that all new content had to be authorised by the Senior Management Group. Owing to the demands of commercial archaeology projects, it was not surprising that their attentions were often turned to other, more urgent priorities. More generally, there was an anxiety amongst staff of writing in an accessible style and some were very vocal about what was perceived as the 'dumbing down' of information. Web publication was viewed as very much secondary to traditional scholarly print media publications or technical reports. It was rare for any of the several hundreds of projects undertaken annually to have any form of presence on the website. Those that did generate new content did so because they were personally enthusiastic about increasing online access.

During the first three years, the website underwent several redesigns and represented a learning curve for the company as a whole. However, the impetus for keeping WA's online image fresh and developing a site that was fit for purpose came from the IT department, and remained siloed as a concern for computing rather than the organisation as a whole. Once again, it was the Amesbury Archer site that led growth and in June 2003 it delivered high resolution versions of the press photographs to alleviate the burden of frequent requests. At this time visitor traffic again increased significantly because of a new discovery and we served 18GB of data in just one week. This followed the announcement of the discovery of the Boscombe Bowmen, a Bronze Age grave containing seven individuals that had possible links to the construction of Stonehenge (Wessex Archaeology 2008). While there is no doubting the special draw of any story related to Stonehenge, it demonstrated again the appetite for high quality archaeological stories and the ability to sate it through online dissemination.

2003 marked a golden year for the attention that WA received because of its online communication of headline projects. Later in the year a standalone website was launched for a joint project which involved laser scanning at Stonehenge[2]. The interest in the project again caught the IT team at WA off guard and their Web hosting company immediately suspended the account for violating 'fair use' terms. This forced the website offline for forty-eight hours before a new hosting company was found; the episode stretched the technical know-how of the IT team to its limits and much that was learnt informed WA's future expansion online.

---

[2] http://www.stonehengelaserscan.org (accessed 18 October 2011).

The first Head of Communications left in 2005 and his responsibilities were assigned to an archaeologist already in WA's employ, but one with extensive experience of the media and outreach, as well as of project management. This combination of skills and experience meant that Web content could now be authorised at this level, finally removing the perceived blockage caused by the previous arrangement for authorising new content.

Despite these procedural and technical challenges, and attempts to encourage a cultural change within the organisation that was more favourable to online publication and outreach, WA's website soon became a popular destination for interesting archaeological news and information. The discovery of the Amesbury Archer had catapulted WA into a global spotlight; this highlighted the need to maintain a dynamism that would retain audiences and expand them. As relatively low numbers of projects continued to be published online, it was clear that the attitudes towards Web publication within the organisation needed to be improved, if WA was to continue its role as a leading archaeological website. New trends in Web publishing and broadcasting from 2004 onwards began to demonstrate the need to innovate and explore new avenues of content creation.

Going social: Web 2.0 and democratising archaeology

The term 'Web 2.0' was coined by publisher and technologist Tim O'Reilly in 2004 as part of a conference session and, by October of that year, the Web 2.0 Conference was born (O'Reilly 2005). The basic premise was that there was a turning point in the way the Web was being used, and that, in essence, Web 2.0 was a new way of thinking about what people could do online. It responded to the increasing use that millions of people made of the Internet and how people interacted with organisations and individuals online. In mid 2005, the Wikipedia article on this subject changed on a daily basis as people argued over the multitude of meanings it could imply.[3]

Some of the most notable aspects of Web 2.0 showed promise for archaeology. The concept of immediate publishing and syndication through blogs, of sharing photos through socially enabled Web applications such as Flickr, and broadcasting audio documentaries through podcasting, all held unimaginable potential for democratising and spreading knowledge – potential that has still to be fully realised. Nevertheless, resource-impoverished archaeologists could now more speedily publish information on excavations, finds and community work in these new online spaces, and audiences could respond directly. Archaeologists could provide their own media.

The use of technologies such as AJAX (Asynchronous JavaScript and XML) enabled websites such as Flickr to have a user interface that felt less like a website and more like a desktop application[4]. Webpages did not need to reload just to edit a title or add some tags; they were easier and quicker to use. Blogging systems and RSS (Really Simple Syndication) allowed content to be syndicated to other websites. Times were definitely changing, and the pace at which information could be published was picking up speed. This whirlwind was in stark contrast to the normal experience of excavations and reports being published sometimes many decades after the event.

Blogs: instant broadcasting

Blogs, websites which can be easily updated with time-stamped entries, or 'posts', were the first Web 2.0 applications to be adopted by WA. They are best suited to content that is time specific and of the moment, akin to a diary, and so the idea for using two blogs, one for news and one for events such as excavation diaries, was proposed. The news and events blogs were set up in December 2004. The blogging platform WordPress[5] was

---

[3] http://en.wikipedia.org/wiki/Web_2.0 (accessed 18 October 2011).

[4] http://www.flickr.com/photos/wessexarchaeology (accessed 18 October 2011).

[5] http://www.wordpress.org (accessed 18 October 2011).

used, then at version 1.2. Whilst our main website continued to be updated using desktop software (Dreamweaver), WordPress could be updated live online. Publication could be as quick as sending an email, in most cases; it was the easiest form of Web publication that we had come across, and our first introduction to a content management system (CMS).

It was hoped that the ease of publishing via WordPress would encourage more contributions, as we could create accounts for other authors. Unfortunately, this idea did not come to fruition immediately, due to a continuing reluctance by staff to find the time to write content, build that time into contract tenders or even check with clients to see if they would consent to updates being posted online.

There was also scepticism about allowing visitors to interact with the posts directly by leaving comments, asking a question, or linking to posts from their own blogs. The decision to enable the comments facility had to be considered carefully. How many people would comment? Would replying become an obligation? How much time would be required to respond? These were all unknowns, and the new Head of Communications allowed a trial period which resulted in the function being instituted permanently as comments that required response or monitoring were rarely left, allaying many of the fears previously held and converting the WA blogs into solid broadcasting mechanisms. Content could also be syndicated by others via RSS feeds, increasing global visibility. A number of websites republish WA news headlines, including the Council for British Archaeology.[6]

Today, WA maintains 14 separate blogs as internal attitudes towards their impact on the organisation are slowly becoming more positive. The original news and events blogs still exist, and have been followed by content-specific blogs such as 'Splash', run by WA's Coastal and Marine section, and others on terrestrial geophysics and archaeological computing. Project-specific blogs such as 'Time Travelling by Water' and 'Explore the Seafloor' have been central to WA education and outreach projects[7]. Although many of these blogs are infrequently updated, the information they have now permanently made available online has demonstrated the importance of them to communicating archaeology.

Podcasting and the industry's first *Archaeocast*

The term 'podcast' was first used in 2004, and is a *portmanteau* of the terms 'iPod' and 'broadcast' (Hammersley 2004). A podcast can best be described as a pre-recorded radio programme that is delivered to subscribers automatically over the Internet, each time a new episode is released. Listeners can find appropriate podcasts, under several categories, via directories such as Apple Inc.'s iTunes Music Store, and directly via software like iTunes or Google Listen, and, more recently, even through software applications ('apps') designed for mobile devices.

Podcasting, when it first became popular in 2005, was seen as another democratising technology. Anybody could start their own radio show, be their own presenter or DJ and potentially gain large audiences online, no longer relying on traditional media to dictate what people could listen to, and without the constraints of schedules. Podcasts emerged on every imaginable topic, but, by summer 2005, despite its popularity in traditional television and radio media, there was still no archaeology podcast.

The comparative lead that WA was taking with other Web 2.0 technologies prompted a trial of podcasting. The concept revolved around series of podcasts that would be recorded live in the field, and see how many people would listen to them. The story of sites could be told from a grass roots perspective, showing all the realities and practicalities of the archaeological process. Initially it was forecasted that listener numbers would be similar to an audience for a public lecture, up

---

[6] http://www.britarch.ac.uk/archaeologylatest (accessed 18 October 2011).

[7] http://www.wessexarch.co.uk/blogs (accessed 18 October 2011).

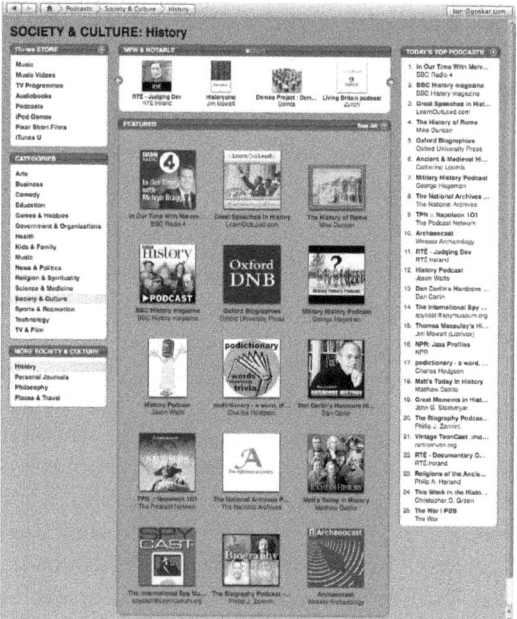

Figure 4. *Archaeocast* in the top 10 History podcasts in the iTunes podcast directory (see Plate 2).

Figure 5. Graphic by Rob Goller (illustrator) used to promote *Archaeocast*; a visual parody of Apple's silhouette adverts for the iPod, 2005.

to approximately 300 people. Time allocated for recording and editing was estimated to match that spent preparing a traditional presentation and slide show. And so *Archaeocast* became the world's first professional archaeology podcast (**Figure 4**).

The first episode of *Archaeocast* was recorded in September 2005, during WA's summer practical archaeology course at Down Farm, in Dorset (Wessex Archaeology 2005). It was recorded by the author on a borrowed MiniDisc recorder with a cheap microphone, and edited on a Mac using Audacity, the open source audio editing software. The podcast was recorded, edited and finished on the same day, and uploaded to the events blog. Within a few weeks, *Archaeocast* had been downloaded many hundreds of times. A second podcast was recorded at Down Farm before the excavation finished. Downloads increased with a speed that was completely unexpected; the original target of 300 listeners had been exceeded by degrees and, by December 2005, downloads of *Archaeocast* were being measured in five figures.

At about the same time, Apple allowed podcasts to be registered on the iTunes Podcast Directory. One of the WA illustrators designed a vibrant logo to communicate the concept of an archaeology broadcast, and *Archaeocast* was quickly listed in iTunes (**Figure 5**). By December 2007 *Archaeocast* was the tenth most popular podcast within the Society and Culture / History category.

In spite of the demonstrated success of the podcast series in terms of downloads, proving the demand for such content, the release of new *Archaeocast* episodes has been rather irregular owing to a combination of factors. The latter have included issues of client confidentiality which in some instances limited the context and timing of a recording, such as not being able to mention the location of a site or if the announcement of an exciting discovery has been embargoed. These are within the usual constraints that commercial archaeology operates, but they often come into conflict with the outreach objectives of the same organisation. Moreover, commercial archaeologists work to extremely tight timescales and can view the recording of a podcast as an unwelcome distraction from the task at hand; others have been shy about being interviewed or filmed. Time poverty to train and be trained has also limited the expansion of the *Archaeocast* series; from a technical point of view, it takes a lot of time to train others in the methodological approach to recording what is essentially a radio programme. A podcast needs to sound good, with decent audio levels and an engaging storyline to be downloaded and shared.

Only 16 podcasts have been recorded to date, but downloads up to July 2011 have totalled an astonishing 211,554 downloads. The potential impact of exploiting this medium has been the least realised by all archaeologists.

Sharing photos on Flickr: galleries of archaeology

In 2005, Flickr was a flagship Web 2.0 website. Full of visual impact, easy to use and easy to share, Flickr enabled users to upload photographs, organise them into sets and submit them to special interest groups that could themselves be set up by registered members. Flickr allowed full participation in a resource that users could control, from leaving comments on individual photographs and sets to participating in group discussions. Networks could be created by adding contacts, and their latest photographs could be easily viewed when updated. All of these features of what is more commonly now known as 'social media' are taken for granted and appear in all sorts of other websites today, but the ability to embrace these functions around a unique collection of images was incredibly novel at the time.

Its application in archaeology was very appealing. Straining under the weight of digital images generated from excavations and surveys, which were now more fulsomely documented than before, Flickr promised a sophisticated, cheap and easy to use online gallery system. Editing titles and descriptions could be done without reloading the page, and it felt much more like desktop software than a website. As well as titles and descriptions, tags (keywords) could be added to photographs, allowing for an extra level of metadata, making images more discoverable, and therefore accessible. Tagging was where what is often referred to as 'crowdsourcing' or 'user-generated content' originated and remains one of the most powerful tools available for improving access to information. Members could tag their own photos and also allow others to tag them too. WA has benefitted from this facility as several hundred of its photographs have had useful tags added to them by other users, with no misuse recorded to date.

WA began to upload photos to Flickr in the summer of 2005,[8] when it was realised that the existing gallery on the main website was proving to be one of the most popular sections, second only to the Amesbury Archer pages. Adopting Flickr was envisaged to bring several benefits. It would enable WA to reach new audiences and contribute to special interest groups. The provision of an API (Application Programming Interface) meant that the WA collections could be easily integrated into the main website (via WordPress), thus reducing duplication of work, and doubling the potential audience. Tagging also offered internal benefits to collections management, as photos could be tagged with their internal project numbers, allowing them to be grouped and linked to corresponding project information on the main WA website. As with the WA blogs the comments facility was enabled; the number of comments WA has received on Flickr outweighs comments left on the blogs by a factor of ten. Time devoted to response, however, still amounts to no more than one hour per month, representing a significant cost-benefit win for the organisation.

Creative Commons licensing of WA's high-resolution photographs was adopted in 2006 and enabled WA to have a positive licence agreement for use in non-commercial contexts. The reuse of WA photos to educational and artistic ends has been very beneficial for meeting the charitable objectives of the company with minimum intervention.

The order of magnitude for the impact that these archaeological images have made through Flickr would have been unimaginable through traditional means. Since 2006, when Flickr began to collect statistics, WA's photos have been viewed nearly 700,000 times; 15% of the collection has received comments, and 32% of the images have been rated as 'favourites' by other members. To date, WA has uploaded over 2,000 photos. Since 2008 visitors have been led directly to the WA

---

[8] http://www.flickr.com/photos/wessexarchaeology (accessed 18 October 2011).

Flickr gallery from the main website's homepage. Flickr is always in the top five traffic sources for the WA site and remains one of the most popular ways in which people discover WA and its work.

Making archaeological grey literature less 'grey'

One of the primary products of archaeological investigations is a final report of one form or another. In commercial archaeology these reports are sent to the client, earning them the name 'client report', and deposited with the local Historic Environment Record (HER). A copy of this report also forms part of the site archive which is usually left with the relevant museum. More recently, a small number of reports have been deposited electronically with the Archaeology Data Service (ADS) as part of the Online Access to the Index of Archaeological Investigations (OASIS) project[9]. A comparatively tiny proportion of projects are disseminated in peer-reviewed publications, in print journals and monographs.

Client reports have come to be known as 'archaeological grey literature' and have been notoriously difficult to access despite the wealth of important archaeological information contained within them (Ford 2010). When the idea of routinely publishing grey literature on the WA website was first suggested, it was doubted that anyone would want to read them. In 2006, a social publishing website called Scribd was launched[10]; it allowed registered members to upload documents which would then be converted into a format easily and attractively viewable online, without the need to download any files. Scribd has been labelled by the high-profile technology blog TechCrunch as the 'YouTube for Documents' (Biggs 2007). There are currently 403 WA documents on Scribd, having first published to the service in March 2007; these can also be accessed on the WA website, using Scribd's embedded document viewer, although a natively hosted PDF copy is always made available for direct download.

Like in similar social media sites, titles, tags and descriptions can be attached to Scribd documents, as well as categories, language information, and license. To add value to these resources WA has taken care to fully describe each uploaded document; this helps readers target content that is of interest to them as well as improving search engine visibility. Anecdotally, it has been found that WA documents can be found via Google within an hour of uploading them to Scribd.

At the time of writing, WA's Scribd account has 18,090 followers (subscribers) and documents have been viewed 741,376 times, comparable to the number of views that WA photos receive on Flickr. Since the 'readcasting' feature was introduced in July 2010, WA documents have been shared 611 times, further increasing awareness of the organisation and the range of its work. Not only do significant numbers seem to want to read archaeological reports, some are enthusiastic enough to share them with their contacts; what is not known is what their motivations are. The use of these reports by students may be high on the list of possibilities and some future work examining citation indexes may be of interest.

However, there have been disadvantages to using such a third-party service. Over the course of the last year, Scribd has started to convert all documents from the proprietary Adobe Flash-based 'iPaper' into HTML5 (Friedman 2010). Although this bold move means that documents will be even easier to find, and available on the increasing numbers of devices which do not support Flash, such as Amazon's Kindle and Apple's iPhone, iPad and iPod Touch, it has given Scribd the opportunity to earn an income from their service by making it possible to embed banner adverts in between every page of each converted document. While users who are logged in and those viewing embedded versions on the WA website do not see the adverts, there is no way to remove these adverts for anonymous users. Should Scribd expand advertising into the embedded documents viewer, the organisation would be compelled to reassess its use

---

[9] http://www.oasis.ac.uk (accessed 18 October 2011).

[10] http://www.scribd.com (accessed 18 October 2011).

of the service and perhaps seek an alternative social publishing solution. But given its huge success in terms of increasing the accessibility and visibility of archaeological grey literature from almost none to hundreds of thousands of views, perhaps the presence of advertising is worth the visual intrusion?

Engaging archaeology in social networks

As demonstrated so far, the importance of social networking through democratising Web technologies for archaeology cannot and should not be underestimated. Our subject has a great popular following, and there can be no doubt that diverse groups of people like to find out the latest discoveries that are made in the course of our work. Communicating that work is the lifeblood of public archaeology, to ensure the profession maintains a strong support base. Online social media provides immensely powerful tools to broadcast and publish archaeological work and new social networking technologies allow countless other people to engage with archaeologists in a way that transcends limits of geography, and potentially culture and language too.

WA is fully engaged in several major social networks where the priority has been to draw increasing numbers of visitors to the information published on the main website. As the Web becomes more crowded it was essential to change course by no longer solely relying on resource discovery through search engines or links, but now trying to push content out into new parts of the Web. This has proven to be a very effective strategy.

There is no exact science to accurately measure engagement or impact via social media, but the statistics showed in **Tables 1–2** provide an impression of how accessible certain content is and where 'hot spots' exist for popular topics. After a recent trial of their most effective position, social sharing icons are now placed above each page on the main WA website, providing an easy and visible way to share content. This trial showed that 12 times more content was shared with an average of 44 pages being shared directly from the site each week.

Table 1 Engagement through social networking sites to August 2011.

Facebook page 'likes'	474	Joined April 2010
Facebook post views	42,632	
Twitter followers	3001	Joined February 2008
Video views on YouTube and Vimeo	208,812	Joined Vimeo: Nov 2007, YouTube: Sept 2006
Document views on Scribd	741,376	Joined October 2007
Photo views on Flickr	748,806	Joined September 2005

Table 2 More 'active' forms of engagement with WA content, via social media, to August 2011.

Website comments	130
Mentions on Twitter (2010–2011)	290
RSS subscribers	581
Photos with comments on Flickr	296
Photos added to favourites on Flickr	440
Derivative creative works using WA photographs	12
Interactions on Facebook (post 'likes', reshares, views)	50,897
Documents shared from Scribd	573
Clicks to WA website via social networks	55,000 (estimate based on Google Analytics data, no data from Scribd visitors)

Confronting content management

The development of WA's participation in Web 2.0 technologies and social networks had a direct bearing on the proliferation of new content published on the main WA website. By 2008, the website consisted of about two thousand HTML pages, and a number of ASP (Active Server Pages), which generated lists of projects against county and period lists. It was becoming increasingly unwieldy to maintain the site in this way with the limited time resources available. WordPress had provided a taste of the benefits of using a basic content management system (CMS), such as speed of publishing new content, more sophisticated facilities to include metadata, features to enhance resource discovery (e.g. tagging and categorisation), and ease of handling images and other media.

After a quick assessment of future time-saving benefits, the decision was made to devote resources to adopting a CMS to deliver existing and new website content. The choice of CMS depended on several factors over and above the ease with the existing website and custom functionality provided by our ASP scripts could be recreated. These included the ability to deliver multiple content groups through a range of templates such as archaeological projects (with associated county and period attributes), 'portal' pages for themed content, unstructured pages, taxonomy pages (which list pages associated with term lists), blog posts, and podcast pages (with in-built audio player), amongst others. The facility to design database queries to generate lists of content in other ways was also a requirement, for example to display a list of periods and administrative areas where content was available, and to filter by content type.

In addition to this kind of flexibility, cost and sustainable support for the system were also major deciding factors. It was therefore a logical step to focus on choosing an open source CMS. A number of systems were evaluated, including Drupal, Joomla, Plone, and Textpattern. Drupal was chosen as the best contender due to the ease of install, scalability, extensibility, and the helpfulness of its developer and user community. A large number of contributed modules were available which would enable WA online to expand into the next five years.

Content migration began in May 2008. A combination of server-based redirects and custom URL paths were set up to ensure that no links were broken in the process. Checks and double-checks were meticulously made to ensure the transition was as smooth as possible and invisible to WA audiences. WA online re-launched for the second time in June 2008. Since this time a slower and more measured set of improvements have been, and continue to be, implemented to improve navigation and expand new sections. The Coastal and Marine website, Splash, which had remained separate, was migrated into Drupal in June 2011, so that its content could be effectively integrated into a new landing page for all WA marine archaeology information.

However, the adoption of Drupal has not been a cure-all and WA continues to maintain a number of WordPress installations for smaller standalone projects where maintaining a dedicated CMS was the better option. These include *Explore the Seafloor*[11], a Heritage Lottery Funded-project to communicate recent scientific studies from seafloor research, and the joint ventures of Framework Archaeology relating to the Heathrow Terminal 5 archaeological investigations[12], and Oxford Wessex Archaeology for the archaeology of the East Kent Access Road[13].

A third content management system, Omeka,[14] is currently being evaluated for a new website dedicated to WA's vast and growing collections of archaeological reports and data downloads. This system provides data gateways and metadata standards, as well as citation links, and formatted bibliographic records; it should prove to be very useful to those studying British archaeology.

---

[11] http://ets.wessexarch.co.uk (accessed 18 October 2011).

[12] http://www.framearch.co.uk/t5 (accessed 18 October 2011).

[13] http://eastkent.owarch.co.uk (accessed 18 October 2011).

[14] http://omeka.org (accessed 18 October 2011).

Conclusion: archaeology online matters

On the homepage of WA's website[15] is a quote from Sue Davies OBE, chief executive: 'Archaeology is all about people: past, present and future. It opens up the past… It contributes to a sense of place, community, identity and pride, and enhances our appreciation of the environment in which we live – of what is important and why' (**Figure 6**). Using the Web to communicate the results of archaeological work, especially because its primary functions are otherwise bound up with the planning process, is absolutely essential. Indeed there is a moral duty to do so.

The Wessex Archaeology website is probably the largest of the commercial archaeology organisations in the UK, at present, and maintains one of the largest interpretive archaeological websites after databases such as the Portable Antiquities Scheme[16] and the Archaeology Data Service[17]. As of July 2011, the WA website contains over 4,000 pages of content. The site attracts an average of 12,000 unique visitors per month, but statistics have recorded close to that in one day during periods where particular stories have attracted popular media coverage. Since 2006, there have been over 2.5 million page views, with the average length of stay on our site of 2.5 minutes. 53% of Web traffic is from search engines, 33% from referring links (URLs), and the remainder from direct traffic. Collaboration with other archaeological institutions has reciprocally improved website traffic further, such as the prominent link to the WA website on Channel 4's *Time Team* homepage[18].

However, given the five hundred projects or so that WA works on each year, more can be done and the forward plan is firmly based on making much more information freely available. To do so, as the limitations of internal resources have almost been reached, the only course of action is to secure external funds. Not only will this benefit the charitable objectives of the organisation and promote

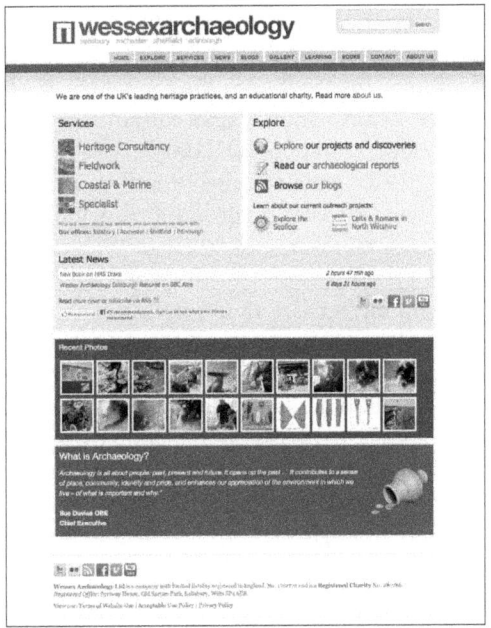

Figure 6. Wessex Archaeology's homepage in July 2011 (see Plate 3).

the company as a responsible corporate citizen, but it will be essential to the continuing campaign to ensure that archaeology as a subject and profession is kept high in the minds of the public, particularly when pressures on funding and income are high.

Since 2002, the growth of WA online's content and social networking has demonstrated the sheer range and wide appeal of archaeology to various audiences, from schools, colleges and universities to *Time Team* fans to potential and existing clients; and some important lessons have been learnt about what kinds of information people want. From the belief that nobody would want to read what were often considered dry archaeological client reports, it has been shown that tens of thousands of people do indeed want to read them, and many of these people have been sufficiently interested to share reports via social networking services. The divi-

---

[15] http://www.wessexarch.co.uk (accessed 18 October 2011).

[16] http://www.finds.org.uk (accessed 18 October 2011).

[17] http://archaeologydataservice.ac.uk (accessed 18 October 2011).

[18] http://www.channel4.com/programmes/time-team (accessed 18 October 2011).

sion between educational activities and the Web has now disappeared from the organisation. Educational material including teacher's packs, SMART Board resources and educational games are developed and published online.

But there remain other hurdles to overcome. Time poverty is still a big issue affecting WA's potential to increase levels of Web content output. Developers pay for the majority of WA's work, and budgets are always tight. Many clients do not wish to draw attention to developments, and perceive archaeology as being akin to other forms of pollution; it costs money to remove and in rare cases it may delay construction work. They would not necessarily wish to pay for Web publication directly, unless contractually obliged to lodge the report through the OASIS scheme. As such, archaeology can be viewed in a financially negative light that requires combatting at a national level to demonstrate how recording and communicating archaeology is a positive, charitable and socially responsible act that promotes local and regional distinctiveness and is an essential part of sustainable economic and social regeneration.

Institutional prejudices and misapprehension about archaeological outreach also need to be overturned; there remains a general assumption that these activities should take place within schools and museums, rather than be made accessible to the much wider audience of the Web. The self-perception of the profession is still largely a scholarly one in which preparing a written report is the primary objective. These things can, and will, change as new archaeologists who embrace the power of the Web in other aspects of their lives enter the profession.

The development of WA online has been an exception rather than a rule of commercial archaeological units, and one that has been emulated by others. The organisation has succeeded in sharing some of its work with the wider world to help people learn about their past and the area in which they live, work or will be developing. Ten years ago the magnitude of WA's online audiences could not have been predicted. New technologies and new external events will surely shape the next decade of WA online's evolution. However, we are now entering a phase of maturity during which Web communication must grow and expand to befit a new world of increasing opportunity in learning, research and entertainment that will be taking place or delivered exclusively online.

Acknowledgements

Thank you to both Professor Andrew Fitzpatrick and Chris Brayne for allowing me to make so many experiments and risks over the years, both technically and in terms of the use of social media. And thanks to Dr Tehmina Goskar for helping me to edit and piece together the chronology and make this paper what it is.

References

Biggs J., 2007. Scribd 'YouTube for Documents' Gets $300K. *TechCrunch* [online] 06 March 2007. Available at: http://techcrunch.com/2007/03/06/scribd-youtube-for-text-gets-300k/ (accessed 03 October 2011).

CharitiesDirect, 2011. Wessex Archaeology Ltd [online]. Available at: http://www.charitiesdirect.com/charities/wessex-archaeology-ltd-287786.html (accessed 03 October 2011).

Ford M., 2010. Archaeology: Hidden treasure. *Nature News* [online] 07 April 2010. Available at: http://www.nature.com/news/2010/100407/full/464826a.html (accessed 03 October 2011).

Friedman J., 2010. The Future of Reading is Open. *The Scribd Blog* [online] 06 May 2010. Available at: http://blog.scribd.com/2010/05/06/the-future-of-reading-is-open/ (accessed 03 October 2011).

Hammersley B., 2004. Audible revolution. *The Guardian* [online] 12 February 2004. Available at: http://www.guardian.co.uk/media/2004/feb/12/broadcasting.digitalmedia (accessed 03 October 2011).

O'Reilly T., 2005. What Is Web 2.0 [online] 30 September 2005. Available at: http://oreilly.com/web2/archive/what-is-web-20.html (accessed 03 October 2011).

Wessex Archaeology, 2001. Wessex Archaeology. *Internet Archive Wayback Machine* [online]. Available at: http://web.archive.org/web/200102020601/http://www.wessexarch.co.uk/ (accessed 03 October 2011).

Wessex Archaeology, 2002. 4000 year old archer with gold earrings [online]. Available at: http://www.wessexarch.co.uk/projects/amesbury/press_original.html (accessed 03 October 2011).

Wessex Archaeology, 2005. Archaeocast: Excavation Podcast [online] 13 September 2005. Available at: http://www.wessexarch.co.uk/blogs/archaeocast/2005/09/13/archaeocast-excavation-podcast (accessed 03 October 2011).

Wessex Archaeology, 2008. The Boscombe Bowmen [online] 30 April 2008. Available at: http://www.wessexarch.co.uk/projects/wiltshire/boscombe/bowmen (accessed 03 October 2011).

Strategy Games and Engagement Strategies

Andrew Gardner

Abstract

The computer and video games industry is an increasingly prominent cultural force in many parts of the world. As with any relatively new medium, popular discussion of games veers between moral panic and optimistic faith in their potential for empowering players. Meanwhile, an emerging academic discipline of 'Game Studies' is directing scholarly attention at many different aspects of the games industry, the content of games, and games players and their communities. A considerable number of commercial games in a range of genres – but particularly strategy games – deal with historical themes, and while some historians have engaged with such products (whether critically or supportively), very rarely have archaeologists done so. This is in spite of the relevance of games to any consideration of popular representation (and simulation) of past material worlds, past cultural entities, and theories about the development of human societies in the long term – all areas of profound archaeological interest. In this paper, I argue that games need to be taken seriously (while never forgetting that they are meant to be fun!) as uniquely interactive visions of the past. Furthermore, I emphasize that while there are grounds to be critical of the ways in which some games propose that human history works (and here *Civilization V* will be used as a case study), the growing propensity of players and fans to actively participate in adapting and modifying games highlights the fact that they offer unprecedented opportunities for thought-provoking public engagement strategies.

Introduction: games and their makers, players and scholars

Computer and video games are increasingly establishing a position as a dominant cultural force in the 21st century. Regularly compared in favourable terms with the commercial health of the movie industry, games are certainly big business (Chatfield 2011: 27–30; McGonigal 2011: 2–4). In the United States, according to figures from the Entertainment Software Association, games sales generated around 16 billion dollars in each of the most recent years for which data is available (2009 and 2010; ESA 2011: 10). Indeed, while data published in 2010 appeared to indicate that games sales were being adversely affected by the global recession (Siwek 2010: 3), in fact the inclusion of figures reflecting the increasing purchase of games via digital download in the 2011 ESA report shows rather that the industry has remained extremely robust (previous data were based on physical sales alone). In the United Kingdom, the picture is similar, with games weathering the recession well and generating 1,940 million pounds of sales in 2010, outstripping music (1,201 million) and coming close to video (2,117 million); for the second year in a row, two of the three top-selling entertainment titles were games (ERA 2011: 18, 32). As part of the entertainment industry, then, games are becoming very difficult to ignore. The proportion of these games which deals with historical subject matter, however, has attracted much less attention than equivalent television programmes or films among scholars interested in the public view of the past (see, for example, Cannadine ed. 2004, Winkler ed. 2004, Clack and Brittain eds 2007, Schablitsky ed. 2007, for volumes concentrating on these latter media). In this paper I will argue that this omission needs to be actively addressed if we are not to fall drastically out of step with a major new vehicle for public engagement with archaeology.

The success of the games industry has of course attracted growing interest from commentators in other media, politicians, and academics in the field of cultural studies. Mainstream newspapers in the United Kingdom regularly feature stories about the effects of games on players. Interestingly, these tend to cleave to the political orientation of individual papers as to whether games are portrayed as positive and educational, in more left-leaning papers (e.g. Jupp 2011 on 'serious games' in *The Independent*), or negative and destructive in those on the right (e.g. Borland 2011 in the *Mail* on the reported health implications of games playing). The latter strand of 'moral panic' has also tended to drive attempted political interventions in the games industry, whether it be the then UK defence secretary Liam Fox calling in 2010 for a ban on a *Medal of Honor* game which allowed players to take the role of the Taliban (BBC 2010), or the 2005 statute in California restricting the sale of games to children, which was struck down by the Supreme Court in 2011 (Hewitt 2011). At this point I should probably declare my position as 'games positive'; as a games player myself I am sceptical that this activity has intrinsically negative effects. In support of this position, I think it is fair to say that research on the deleterious impact of games has generally been inconclusive at best (see, for example, Goldstein 2005). However, this does raise an important logical problem: can one dismiss the idea that games encourage antisocial behaviour and yet still argue, as I will in this paper, that they can be educational (Squire 2002)? Do games affect their players or not? Certainly, considerable effort has been directed by a range of institutions, not to mention games developers, at 'serious games' which have explicit educational content (see, for example, Rockwell and Kee 2011; many such games are available at http://www.gamesforchange. org/). The ways in which they might be effective remain poorly understood, however, and this is a theme I will return to later in this paper, where I argue that the ways in which players engage with games has to be at least as much of a focus of future research as simple critique of game content (cf. Voorhees 2009: 258; Simon 2011). Only then can we begin to capture what makes games a unique element of our culture.

This issue of the distinctive features of games has been one of many that has been taken up in the nascent discipline of Game Studies, as it is crucial to the definition of the discipline. Whether games should be treated within a narrative frame derived from areas such as literary theory or film studies, or from a distinctive 'ludological' perspective, has been one key debate (albeit perhaps exaggerated for polemic effect in some quarters; Voorhees 2009: 256–8). Other issues covered have included aspects of the games industry, sociological or anthropological studies of games players that move significantly beyond the issue of violence to explore themes of identity and community, and critical discussion of some of the political or ideological concepts represented in games themselves (e.g. Wolf ed. 2001; Wark 2007; Egenfeldt-Nielsen *et al.* 2008; Newman 2008; Dyer-Witherford and de Peuter 2009). The latter area particularly overlaps with the theme of this paper, insofar as the historical strategy games which form my core interest (as the type of game which most commonly represents deeper antiquity) have been discussed quite widely as encapsulating very modern ideas about societies, technological progress, and imperialism (e.g. Friedman 1999; Douglas 2002; Poblocki 2002; Schut 2007). More will be said on all of these issues below. Suffice it to say for now, though, that in this paper I will seek to rebut the impact of some of this critique of historical games, by highlighting the ways in which enthusiastic players actively modify game content and potentially subvert even the apparently in-built ideologies of commercial games. The growing phenomenon of players 'modding' games has also attracted attention within Game Studies (e.g. Postigo 2007; Sotamaa 2010), and I want to draw on this literature, as well as some specific material relating to my major case study (the game *Civilization V*), to show two things. The first is that games which deal with archaeological themes are already engaging a whole host of people in thinking about the past – without, so far at least, any direct involvement from archaeologists. This can be seen as both an encouragement and a challenge. Secondly, games are extremely useful in highlighting the very dynamic nature of 'consumption' of ideological concepts which stories about the past may propagate. The study of the 'everyday appropriation' (Thompson 1990: 313) of such outputs offers several lessons for scholars of other media, albeit that these also have their own particular characteristics. Games thus provide very useful material for thinking about strategies of engagement in a range of digital – and indeed analogue – fields.

A case study in playing the past: *Civilization V*
Computer and video games are an extremely diverse form of media, and there are various ways of breaking them down – by technological platform (at the simplest level, 'computer games' are played on a PC or equivalent, 'video games' on a dedicated gaming console), by the kinds of interaction players participate in, or by genre (Egenfeldt-Nielsen *et al.* 2008: 22–44). In terms of the intersection of games with broadly archaeological or historical themes, one can separate out games which portray people in the modern era interacting with past cultural material (sometimes these people are 'archaeologists', sometimes not) from games which allow the player to participate in some version of an ancient culture. The latter category includes games in various genres including action (e.g. *Shadow of Rome*), roleplaying (e.g. the sadly defunct *Roma Victor*) and, representing the majority of titles, strategy. Games in this genre, typically owing quite a lot to the boardgame/wargame tradition, can vary in scale from representing individual historical events (usually battles), to the full sweep of human history, but have in common a detached perspective for the player, who is in control of a range of variables and therefore has the power to 'reshape' the past (Uricchio 2005: 328–31; Voorhees 2009: 262–3). We are therefore here talking more accurately about the 'simulation' of the past than its 'representation' (Uricchio 2005, cf. Fogu 2009), though certainly the graphics of such games do portray material characteristics of different cultures. Strategy games can usually be played either against the computer or other human players (commonly via the Internet), and either operate in 'real time', with continuous gameplay, or on a turn-taking basis. This kind of game is more commonly available for the PC-type segment of the market, and the most recent ESA data reveals that, while the strategy genre made up only 3.8% of video game unit sales in the US in 2010, it comprised 33.6% of computer game sales (ESA 2011: 8). Computer games are a much smaller proportion of the overall game market (0.7 billion dollars in sales in 2010 compared to 9.4 billion for video games; ESA 2011: 10), but a game like *Civilization V* has still sold more than 850,000 copies since its release in September 2010 (gamrReview 2011). This success – *Civilization V* was the fifth top-selling computer game in 2010 (ESA 2011: 9) – is one reason why the game makes a suitable case study to examine in more depth in this paper.

Further reasons are the fairly extensive critical literature surrounding the *Civilization* franchise (including at least one PhD thesis; Squire 2004a), and the large fan communities which have developed around the series, both of which will be examined further below. This interest has flourished not only because the *Civilization* (often simply known as '*Civ*') games are high-profile, successful (over nine million units sold over the lifetime of the series so far; Firaxis Games 2010) and very enjoyable games, but because they have been around for quite some time. The first *Civilization* appeared in 1991, and regular releases of new editions have maintained the series' prominent position over two decades (*Civ II* in 1996, *Civ III* in 2001, *Civ IV* in 2005, and most recently *Civ V* in 2010; there are also several expansion packs to previous editions, and indeed a boardgame version). The essential gameplay has remained the same throughout these iterations, although of course there have been significant developments in the graphics, and several minor modifications to the structure of the game. The purpose of a game of *Civilization* is to steer a particular culture through time from 4,000 BC to AD 2050, managing cities, resources and armies, with the aim of winning by one way or another becoming the leading civilization among the others within the game world. It is quite important to note that there are several ways of achieving victory – the game is not just about military expansion as is the case with many other strategy games. *Civ V* has five types of victory conditions: domination; science; cultural; diplomatic; and a simple points-based calculation when the clock runs out. While the player is nominally represented by a particular historical figure associated with their chosen culture, these are abstractions in the sense that their names do not change, so for example Elizabeth I rules the English civilization throughout the timeline of the game (**Figure 7**). Different cultures and their leaders do have some distinctive characteristics with game effects, but another key feature of the *Civilization* series is that many of the notable cultural and architectural achievements of different historical societies can be built by any civilization in the game. This, along with the ability to play on a range of real or randomly generated maps (**Figure 8**), is a major way in which *Civilization* allows players to in some sense play creatively with the past (cf. Poblocki 2002: 166–8; Uricchio 2005: 335; Schut 2007: 229). What kind of history this generates is a moot point, returned to below.

The gameplay of *Civilization V* in detail need not detain us here; the game is accompanied by a 234-page manual as well as in-game help/background information in the form of a 'Civilopedia'. One or two points, though, will be helpful to inform the subsequent discussion. The player views the action from a disembodied perspective, looking down on the landscape (often leading *Civ* to be characterised as a 'god-game'; Voorhees 2009: 262). There are two main scales of representation of the landscape that the player's civilization occupies and, gradually, explores. The first is a general map-view (**Figure 9**), on which the units that the player controls move. These units include – crucially at first – settlers, who must be used to found the civilization's first city. Subsequently, military units as well as further settlers, workers and resource-gathering units can be developed and moved around the map. As these move into uncharted territory, hitherto dark areas of the map will be revealed, and other civilizations encountered. There are also lurking groups of 'barbarians', who are described in the manual as 'roving bands of villains who hate civilization'

Figure 7. Introductory screen to a game of *Civilization V*, playing as the English (*Civilization V*: 2K Games/Firaxis Games) (see Plate 4).

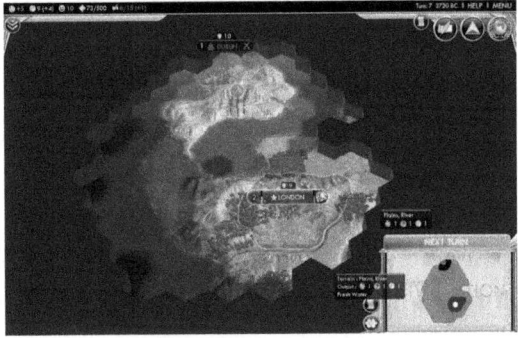

Figure 8. The English empire in 3720 BC, on a randomly-generated map (*Civilization V*: 2K Games/Firaxis Games) (see Plate 5).

(Firaxis/2K 2010: 65). These cause trouble, but their camps, along with 'ancient ruins' in the landscape, can yield game rewards, particularly treasure. Having founded a city, and eventually several, the player can also select a settlement to see a more detailed view of the urban hinterland (**Figure 10**), and information about the buildings and technologies being developed in that location. Effective exploitation of a landscape for resources, which are then invested in steps on the tree of technological development (e.g. 'mining' or 'the wheel'), or the construction of buildings which have military, social or economic benefits, is the key mechanic of the game. In-game help is also provided by advisors who offer suggestions about different priorities (**Figure 11**). As the game progresses, the correspondence of a game-turn to a given amount of time changes, so that activities seem to be completed more quickly; a turn at the beginning of the game is equivalent to 40 years, but to one by the end. Throughout the course of the new history being created there are also set, familiar stages which the player reaches – such as the 'Classical era'. Gameplay is thus a curious and deliberate mixture of traditional historical tropes and this provides much of its pleasure, as well as much food for scholarly thought, as the next section will explore. While not a major feature of *Civilization V* as published, it is also possible to play much more short-term scenarios based around specific events (in the game a Genghis Khan scenario is provided; cf. Graham 2009). There is also extensive support for player modifications, or 'mods', to the game, as will be discussed below.

Figure 9. The English empire in 2200 BC, this time on a real-world map (but with randomised location!). The small icons on the map are different kinds of units (*Civilization V*: 2K Games/Firaxis Games) (see Plate 6).

Figure 10. The city-management screen for London, enabling control of production in the city and its hinterland (*Civilization V*: 2K Games/Firaxis Games) (see Plate 7).

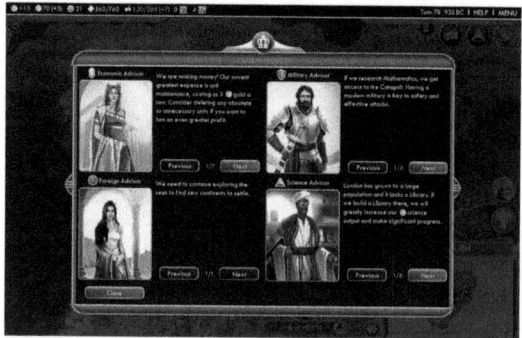

Figure 11. In-game suggestions are provided by the Economic, Military, Foreign and Science advisors (*Civilization V*: 2K Games/Firaxis Games) (see Plate 8).

Critical engagement with games as media: a limiting strategy?

Taking the game as published, though, and as of a piece with previous entries in the *Civilization* franchise, how might we evaluate the way the past is presented in *Civ V*, and consider its potential educational impacts? For a number of years game studies scholars have highlighted problematic elements of ideology implicit in *Civilization*'s gameplay. The emphasis on the expansion of one's civilization, exploitation of the landscape, and technological progress has been seen by a number of commentators as making the logic of western capitalism and globalisation out to be the only logic of history (Friedman 1999; Douglas 2002; Poblocki 2002; Galloway 2006: 85–106; Gardner 2007; Schut 2007; Wark 2007: 51–75). The ability to play the game as one of many cultures, and build different cultural artefacts like the Pyramids or the Great Wall of China, really only reinforces the notion that different cultures are interchangeable within the logic of the game-world; the differences between game cultures are in fact entirely superficial (Bogost 2007: 254). Equally, while the fact that military-led imperialism is not the only way to win does set *Civilization* apart from certain other classic strategy games (like the hugely popular *Age of Empires* series, part II of which alone sold 4.39 million units; gamrReview 2011), cultural or economic imperialism are the major alternatives (Poblocki 2002: 166, 170; King and Krzywinska 2006: 190). On a more profound level, certain mechanisms within the game, like the role of barbarians, encapsulate very 19th century ideas of what 'civilization' is, and is not (Douglas 2002). Ideas of this period are also deeply embedded in the model of technological progress which drives much of the game (Poblocki 2002: 164–5, 173–4). The teleological 'tech-tree' approach to packets of knowledge which are just waiting to be discovered by any culture was rather popular in the social and historical sciences in the 19th century, and to some extent in the mid-20th century, but hardly is so now. Of course this issue provides a direct point of contact with archaeology; essentially, every game in the *Civilization* series puts into practice something like the model of social evolution characteristic of processual archaeology of the late 1960s and 1970s (see, for example, Flannery 1972). Needless to say, that does not make for a very cutting-edge model of society today (cf. e.g. Pauketat 2007). Taken together, then, these points can be seen to damn *Civilization* as representing a classic imperialist ideology, and indeed one which is particularly resonant with some features of United States politics (Douglas 2002: 21–22; Poblocki 2002: 175; King and Krzywinska 2006: 191). As McKenzie Wark writes (2007: 75):

When playing *Civilization III*, it doesn't matter if the civilization you choose to play is Babylon or China, Russia or Zululand, France or India. Whoever wins is America, in that the logic of the game itself is America. America unbound.

If this critique is valid, the next question is: what significance do these problems have? It would be easy for scholars, particularly historians or archaeologists, to add all of this ideological baggage to their reasons for thinking of such games as something very much to avoid (Uricchio 2005: 328). However, noting the widespread popularity of games already discussed, I would argue that this is a very negative and limiting strategy. Rather, we should embrace games and consider the options for how to make use of their positive elements in furthering the engagement of as wide an audience as possible in thinking about the past. One way in which some teachers have attempted to do this is by simply bringing games into the classroom, at a range of levels, and exploiting both the tools for enjoyable simulation activities that they provide, and the flaws in their modelling of societies, for educational gain (Squire 2002, 2004b; Bogost 2007: 252–6; Graham 2009). This is a very worthwhile strategy, although there are constraints on the practical implementation of gaming in the classroom (providing equal access to a game means either everyone needs it installed on their own machine, or the hurdles of site licensing of software in an institution need to be overcome). This also does not reach out particularly widely to all of the people who already play games but aren't formally studying relevant courses.

Another approach, which in my view is rather less fruitful, is to seek to influence the design of future game products. A corollary of the statistics about the games industry cited above is that this is indeed a very commercial industry, and the people making games are mainly concerned with making a successful game, not one which necessarily accurately represents any given ancient culture or social process (even if it could be agreed what such an accurate representation might be). Indeed, the games industry has become such big business, with high development costs for new games, that it has become (arguably like other major entertainment industries) quite conservative (Küchlich 2005). Academic meddling is unlikely to be welcome in such a scenario, and certainly for Sid Meier, the originator of the *Civilization* series, the flavour of history is all that he is interested in (Brake 2002; Uricchio 2005: 330–1; Kumar 2010); the game itself is the top priority (and of course he studiously avoids acknowledging that any of the ideologies discussed above are part of the gameplay; Poblocki 2002: 164). In one recent case where an academic, Niall Ferguson, did get involved in the design of a game (*Making History II*; Zabek 2010), the product received some poor reviews *as a game* (Shannon 2010). The lack of alignment between the interests of the producers of a game and academic critics makes this a very limited strategy, at least if we are considering major commercial titles (the field of more independently-developed 'serious games', noted above, has a different dynamic, which can overlap with academic use of agent-based modelling and simulation[1]).

A third way of developing the use of games as an engagement strategy, and the one which I wish to develop at most length here, is to think of players as *already engaged* with the past through game-play, in ways that may not be entirely constrained by what seem to be the in-built ideologies of titles like *Civilization V*. Game-playing communities could then become arenas which archaeologists can reach out into – not to point out flaws or errors in particular game scenarios, but simply to contribute to discussions among people who have their own visions of the past. Everyone might learn something from such involvement. Establishing the ways in which this might work – examining the nature of existing debates in fan-communities, or the desirability of different kinds of involvement from archaeological professionals – undoubtedly requires further research. The ingredients for such an approach, however, are clearly in place, as my next section will demonstrate. Before discussing these, it is important to emphasise a couple of points about the theoretical underpinnings of such an enterprise, taking us back to the issue of what games actually are. While sharing many characteristics of other media, games are uniquely interactive, not merely in their gameplay but in their open-ness to consumers intervening in the product and actually changing it. To some extent this can be seen as an extension of 'fan culture' that has been studied with reference to film and television (involving, for example, the production of fan-fiction or fan-film; Brooker 2002; Sotamaa 2010: 242–3). However, the combination of the different kinds of interactivity which games offer makes them much more susceptible to appropriation in various ways by players than is the case with consumers of other media (Squire 2002; Schut 2007: 216–8; Voorhees 2009: 258; cf. Thompson 1990: 313–9). As Ted Friedman puts it with respect to *Civ II* (1999: 146): 'If *Civilization II* rests on some questionable ideological premises, the distinct dynamics of computer gaming give the player the chance to transcend those assumptions.' It is vital, therefore, to shift the discourse from 'what games do to players' to 'what players do with games'. As we will see, it is abundantly clear that what many already do is creatively engage with the human past.

Beyond the game: modding, experimentation and authenticity

The notion that games cannot simply be studied as isolated 'texts' (Schut 2007: 216) receives fairly immediate vindication if one looks at some of the websites supporting communities of players of games like *Civilization V*. One of the major fan-sites dedicated to all of the games in the *Civilization* series is *Civilization Fanatics*[2], which was founded in 2000 and currently has 55,795 members listed. Not all of these are necessarily active, of course, but the site is certainly busy; the number of threads in the general discussion forum for *Civ V* alone is 9,772. These deal with all sorts of issues to do with the game, from technical problems and bugs, to effective strategies (cf. Voorhees 2009: 267; Graham 2010), but also discussions

---

[1] See, for example, http://ccl.northwestern.edu/netlogo/ (accessed 12 October 2011).

[2] http://www.civfanatics.com/ (accessed 12 October 2011).

of a historical nature or ones that actively interrogate some of the game elements critiqued above. For example, recent threads include discussions of 'How unique should we make Civs?' (ShahJahanII 27/7/11) and 'Do your social policies reflect your personal beliefs?' (Emperor Giulio 25/7/11). Similar threads can be found on the forums on the general discussion board on the game's official website[3], for example 'Who should be the leader of the Korean civilization?' (RideASpaceCowboy 29/7/11), and a discussion of cultures neglected in the game, 'Underrepresented regions' (Zephyrtr 26/7/11). Certainly, gameplay issues such as play-balance dominate such discussions, but a thread like 'Evolution of civilization' on the 'Civ – Ideas and Suggestions' forum at *Civilization Fanatics* (ArataWata11, 24/1/11), which proposes the idea of civilizations changing their identity over time, clearly shows that players are engaged with how the game relates to 'real-world' historical processes.

Such interest is most evident, though, among those players who create additional material for the game. 'Modding' (a term I will use here as a catch-all for player alterations to what are generally closed-source games, although different forms of modification can have different names; Postigo 2007: 301) is a practice which is arguably descended from the phenomenon of 'hacking' programmes, that has been around as long as computer programmes themselves (Laukkanen 2007: 138–9). In its expansion over the past decade or so, modding perhaps also fits in with wider media trends towards the embracing (or exploiting) of user-generated content, but it has taken on particular significance in the games industry because it has offered a major way of extending the life of games, with minimal investment from their manufacturers (Postigo 2007: 302–8; Küchlich 2005). Modding can take various forms, ranging from adding new levels or maps to a game, or designing new graphics and sounds to depict a different array of characters or objects, right through to 'total conversions' which come close to creating an entirely new game. The activity involved in modding often involves teams of people with different portfolios of computing skills, and with different reasons for undertaking what can be regarded as unpaid labour on behalf of the games industry (Laukkanen 2007: 140–50; Sotamaa 2010: 243–7). Certainly – and not only because of the latter incentive – the games industry has generally supported modding, to the extent of providing tools within games to enable mod-developers to edit them. This practice raises interesting issues to do with the economics and intellectual property aspects of game design (e.g. Laukkanen 2007: 137; Nieborg and van der Graaf 2008), but here our main concern is with the creativity that it makes possible among games players. While games in many different genres have been adapted by their players, strategy games have provided fertile material for modders. Interestingly, many such mods – as with *Rome: Total Realism* (a complete modification package for *Rome: Total War*), or *Age of Chivalry: Hegemony* (a total conversion for *Age of Empires II*) – are inspired by a desire for greater authenticity than the original game, particularly in terms of things like the representation of military units and equipment, or for greater coverage of neglected periods.

This is true for many *Civilization* mods, but there are also a whole range of other ways in which players have altered the game. The *Civilization* series has a well-developed modding scene, encouraged by editorial tools provided with the games from an early stage. In *Civ V*, this is further incorporated into the 'official' game, as there is an in-game menu giving access to mods that players have uploaded (**Figure 12**). Further support for modders and their work is provided on the game's official website[4]. Many other mods are available on the fan-sites. While *Civilization V* does not yet have the number of mods available for previous entries in the series, being a relatively new game, *Civilization Fanatics* is a portal for thousands of mods for *Civ III* and *Civ IV* in particular. These include over 2,500 unit graphics mods for *Civ III* and over 500 more complete modpacks for the same game; for *Civ IV* the equivalent numbers are over

---

[3] http://forums.2kgames.com/forums/forumdisplay.php?74-Civilization-V-General-Discussion (accessed 12 October 2011).

[4] http://forums.2kgames.com/forumdisplay.php?89-Civilization-V-Modding (accessed 12 October 2011).

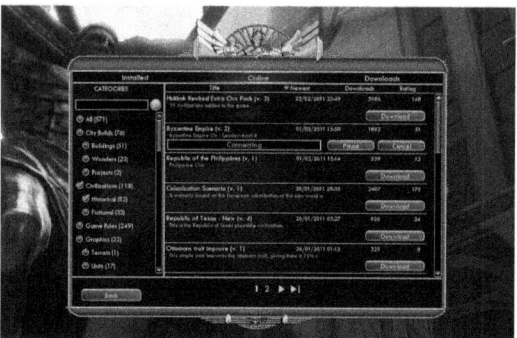

Figure 12. Access to player-created mods is facilitated within the main *Civilization V* programme (*Civilization V*: 2K Games/Firaxis Games) (see Plate 9).

3,700 and 1,000. Many of these adaptations create more specific historical situations and scenarios, or a more detailed historical appearance for different times and places, but there are also mods which allow the gameplay of *Civilization* to take place in fictional worlds drawn from science fiction and fantasy film or literature. Other fan-sites[5] provide further mod portals, while some mods and other adaptations take on something of a life of their own. *Freeciv*[6] is actually more of an independent, open-source version of *Civilization*, allowing greater flexibility with the rules of play. Some historical mods with a specific period of focus have been created as teaching resources (e.g. *History Game Canada*[7], or Graham's 'Year of the Four Emperors' scenario [2009, 2010], which was trialled on *Civilization Fanatics*[8]). Other mods have been created with explicit political content (e.g. the Eastwood – Real Time Strategy Group's own *Civilization V*, modelling corporate capitalism; ISEA 2008), although the game as it stands can also be creatively played with in this way, as an experiment in trying out 'Tea Party' economics has shown (Collazo 2011). Altogether, these cases demonstrate the vibrancy of the community around the *Civilization* games, and this is a community which has considerable longevity (for example, a 'Homeric World' mod for *Civilization III*, a game released in 2001, was posted on *Civilization Fanatics* in 2010; Stico 11/12/10). Successful commercial games can thus be seen to provide rich material for the engagement of many players with the past over the long-term. Within the archaeological community, we need only wonder how we might make more strategic use of this situation.

Conclusion: games as engagement strategies
In this paper, I have argued that commercial computer games are a great source of potential – indeed actual – public engagement in archaeological ideas. The way forward for archaeologists interested in this area seems to me to be more about building bridges with the already vibrant communities of games-players, rather than dismissing games as inaccurate, critiquing them purely as ideological constructs, or trying to design more 'serious' or 'educational' games for what is likely to be rather a small audience (cf. Rockwell and Kee 2011). This process can move forward through pursuit of at least two linked strategies. One is conducting more systematic research on the fan and modding communities, engaging with players and finding out how and why they conduct historical and archaeological research in pursuit of material for game additions – which is something they certainly do (Postigo 2007: 302; Graham 2010; Sotamaa 2010: 247). Secondly, archaeologists themselves can develop mods and try them out in the classroom or on the forums, and see how players react to different ways of structuring history, and there is pioneering work in this vein to be built on (e.g. Graham 2009, 2010; Meyers 2011[9]). While analysing and criticising the ideological content

---

[5] For example, http://www.apolyton.net (accessed 12 October 2011).

[6] http://freeciv.wikia.com/wiki/Main_Page (accessed 12 October 2011).

[7] http://www.historycanadagame.com/ (accessed 12 October 2011).

[8] See also http://electricarchaeologist.wordpress.com/game-mods/ (accessed 12 October 2011).

[9] See also http://www.playthepast.org/ (accessed 12 October 2011).

of games is certainly still necessary, and there are real debates to be had about how games may or may not influence people's thinking about the past and therefore the present (Douglas 2002; Schut 2007: 217–8), I think this only really starts to make sense when twinned with the exploration of game-playing (by all kinds of players, including the public archaeologist) as 'situated practice' (Thompson 1990: 315; Squire 2002). As Sotamaa puts it, with a positive and optimistic emphasis (2010: 242): 'Scrutinizing the practices that surround the playing of games helps to uncover the creative and productive potentials embedded in players.'

There is every indication from the source materials examined above that such strategies will be productive of significant insights about how people engage with the past. One interesting theme to explore, by way of example, will be the apparent tension between the apparent desire of many players for greater authenticity, particularly of graphical (and auditory) representation (very well illustrated by *Rome: Total Realism*; cf. Postigo 2007: 302), and the very counter-factual potentiality embedded in games as interactive simulations. As Uricchio highlights, games offer 'a new means of reflecting upon the past' (2005: 336), treading a path between traditional ideas of historical factual fidelity and post-modern constructivist views of the past's meaning as being always created anew in the present (cf. Fogu 2009). This might bear comparison with other media of public engagement, such as live re-enactment, as manifestations of a distinctive, but now quite widespread, temporal perspective. The development of both study and practice of gaming has thus a great deal to offer. There are certainly obstacles and challenges, including the existence still of some limits to participation in the more active fan-communities (modders of several games are, for example, still predominantly male [Sotamaa 2010: 242, 253], although the demographics of gaming are expanding all the time). Nonetheless, gamers represent a large and growing constituency of people already engaged in the past, and one we absolutely cannot afford to ignore.

Acknowledgements

Thanks to Chiara Bonacchi and Don Henson for inviting me to speak on this subject both at the Archaeology and Communication Research Network/CASPAR workshop, and the CASPAR seminar series in the spring of 2011, and to the anonymous referees for several helpful comments. I am also grateful for fruitful discussions with Felix Ciută (UCL SSEES), particularly concerning the tale of *Making History II*, and Shawn Graham (Carleton University, http://electricarchaeologist.wordpress.com/).

Games

Age of Empires II: The Age of Kings, 1999, Microsoft
Age of Chivalry: Hegemony, 2008–2011, http://aok.heavengames.com/age-of-chivalry (accessed 20 October 2011).
Civilization, 1991. MicroProse.
Civilization II, 1996. MicroProse.
Civilization III, 2001. Infogrames Interactive/Firaxis Games.
Civilization IV, 2005. 2K Games/Firaxis Games.
Civilization V, 2010. 2K Games/Firaxis Games.
Making History II: The War of the World. 2010. Muzzy Lane Software.
Roma Victor, 2001–2011, http://www.roma-victor.com/ (accessed 20 October 2011).
Rome: Total War, 2004, Activision.
Rome: Total Realism, 2005–2011, http://www.rometotalrealism.org/index-2.html (accessed 20 October 2011).
Shadow of Rome, 2005, Capcom.

Forum posts

ArataWata11, 24/1/11, Evolution of civilization, http://forums.civfanatics.com/showthread.php?t=409309 (accessed 20 October 2011).
Emperor Giulio, 25/7/11, Do your social policies reflect your personal beliefs?, http://forums.civfanatics.com/showthread.php?t=432958 (accessed 20 October 2011).
RideASpaceCowboy, 29/7/11, Who should be the leader of the Korean civilization?, http://forums.2kgames.com/showthread.php?111975-Who-should-be-the-leader-of-the-Korean-civilization (accessed 20 October 2011).
ShahJahanII, 27/7/11, How unique should we make Civs?, http://forums.civfanatics.com/showthread.php?t=433179 (accessed 20 October 2011).

Stico, 11/12/10, Homeric World MOD, http://forums.civfanatics.com/showthread.php?t=402382 (accessed 20 October 2011).

Zephyrtr, 26/7/11, Underrepresented regions, http://forums.2kgames.com/showthread.php?111631-Underrepresented-Regions (accessed 20 October 2011).

References

BBC, 2010. Liam Fox defends call for ban of Medal of Honor Game. *BBC online* [online] 23 August 2010. Available at: http://www.bbc.co.uk/news/technology-11056581 (accessed 26 July 2011).

Bogost I., 2007. *Persuasive Games: the expressive power of videogames.* Cambridge: MIT Press.

Borland S., 2011. Playing computer games increases obesity risk in teens by making them hungry. *Mail Online* [online] 21 May 2011. Available at: http://www.dailymail.co.uk (accessed 26 July 2011).

Brake D., 2002. *Civilization* creator Sid Meier: the *Mindjack* interview. *Mindjack* [online]. Available at: http://www.mindjack.com/interviews/sidmeier.html (accessed 29 July 2011).

Brooker W., 2002. *Using the Force: creativity, community and* Star Wars *fans.* New York: Continuum.

Cannadine D. ed., 2004. *History and the Media.* Basingstoke: Palgrave Macmillan.

Chatfield T., 2010. *Fun Inc.: why games are the 21st century's most serious business.* London: Virgin Books.

Clack T. and Brittain M. eds, 2007. *Archaeology and the Media.* Walnut Creek: Left Coast Press.

Collazo G., 2011. Sid Meier's Political Strategist: Civilization V and Tea Party. *Unwinnable* [online]. Available at: http://www.unwinnable.com/2011/02/22/ (accessed 29 July 2011).

Douglas C., 2002. 'You have unleashed a horde of barbarians!': fighting Indians, playing games, forming disciplines. *Postmodern Culture* 13 (1) [online]. Available at: http://muse.jhu.edu/journals/postmodern_culture/v013/13.1douglas.html (accessed 11 July 2011).

Dyer-Witherford N. and de Peuter G., 2009. *Games of Empire: global capitalism and video games.* Minneapolis: University of Minnesota Press.

Egenfeldt-Nielsen S., Smith J. H. and Tosca S. P., 2008. *Understanding Video Games: the essential introduction.* London: Routledge.

ERA, 2011. *ERA Yearbook 2011.* Bournemouth: Entertainment Retailers Association [online]. Available at: http://www.eraltd.org/content/stats.asp (accessed 26 July 2011).

ESA, 2011. *2011 Essential Facts About the Computer and Video Game Industry.* Washington, DC: Entertainment Software Association [online]. Available at: http://www.theesa.com/facts/pdfs/ESA_EF_2011.pdf (accessed 26 July 2011).

Firaxis Games, 2010. *Sid Meier's* Civilization V [online]. Available at: http://www.firaxis.com/games/game_detail.php?gameid=41 (accessed 27 July 2011).

Firaxis/2K, 2010. *Sid Meier's Civilization V Manual.* Sparks/Novato: Firaxis/2K.

Flannery K., 1972. The cultural evolution of civilizations. *Annual Review of Ecology and Systematics* 3, pp. 399–426.

Fogu C., 2009. Digitalizing historical consciousness. *History and Theory* 47, pp. 103–121.

Friedman T., 1999. Civilization and its discontents: simulation, subjectivity, and space. In Smith G. ed., 1999. *On a Silver Platter: CD-ROMs and the promises of a new technology.* New York: New York University Press, pp. 132–50. Also available at: http://www.duke.edu/~tlove/civ.htm (accessed 27 July 2011).

Galloway A. R., 2006. *Gaming: essays on algorithmic culture.* Minneapolis: University of Minnesota Press.

gamrReview, 2011. *Sid Meier's* Civilization V *Sales* [online]. Available at: http://gamrreview.vgchartz.com/sales/43507/sid-meiers-civilization-v/ (accessed 27 July 2011).

Gardner A., 2007. The past as playground: the ancient world in video game representation. In Clack T. and Brittain M. eds, 2007. *Archaeology and the Media.* Walnut Creek: Left Coast Press, pp. 255–272.

Goldstein J., 2005. Violent video games. In Raessens J. and Goldstein J. eds, 2005. *Handbook of Computer Game Studies.* Cambridge: MIT Press, pp. 341–357.

Graham S., 2009. *Re-playing history: the year of the four emperors and Civilization IV.* Subject Centre for History, Classics and Archaeology resource [online]. Available at: http://www.heacademy.ac.uk/hca/resources/detail/re_playing_history (accessed 27 July 2011).

Graham S., 2010. *Rolling your own: on modding commercial games for educational goals* [online]. Available at: http://www.playingwithhistory.com/wp-content/uploads/2010/08/Graham_rolling-your-own-brock-april-2010.doc (accessed 01 August 2011).

Hewitt D., 2011. ESA welcomes sweeping US Supreme Court ruling on constitutional protections for video games [online]. Available at: http://theesa.com/newsroom/release_detail.asp?releaseID=150 (accessed 26 July 2011).

ISEA, 2008. ISEA 2008 Juried Exhibition: Civilization V [online]. Available at: http://www.isea2008singapore.org/exhibitions/air_civilV.html (accessed 29 July 2011).

Jupp E., 2011. Digital hurt locker: 'serious' video games are the first stop for soldiers learning how to find bombs. *The Independent* [online] 22 July 2011. Available at: http://www.independent.co.uk (accessed 26 July 2011).

King G. and Krzywinska T., 2006. *Tomb Raiders and Space Invaders: videogame forms and contexts*. London: I.B. Tauris.

Küchlich J., 2005. Precarious playbour: modders and the digital games industry. *The Fibreculture Journal* 5: FCJ-025 [online]. Available at: http://five.fibreculturejournal.org (accessed 07 July 2011).

Kumar M., 2010. Interview: Sid Meier. *Edge* [online]. Available at: http://www.next-gen.biz/features/interview-sid-meier (accessed 29 July 2011).

Laukkanen T., 2007. Creative gamers: examining the modding culture and its mobile prospects. In Turpeinen M. and Kuikkaniemi K. eds, 2007. *Mobile Content Communities*. Helsinki: Helsinki Institute for Information Technology Publications (2007–1), pp. 137–153.

McGonigal J., 2011. *Reality is Broken: why games make us better and how they can change the world*. London: Jonathan Cape.

Meyers K., 2011. Gaming in archaeology. Post on *Day of Archaeology* 2011 [online]. Available at: http://www.dayofarchaeology.com/author/meyersk/ (accessed 29 July 2011).

Newman J., 2008. *Playing with Videogames*. London: Routledge.

Nieborg D. B. and van der Graaf S., 2008. The mod industries? The industrial logic of non-market game production. *European Journal of Cultural Studies* 11 (2), pp. 177–195.

Pauketat T., 2007. *Chiefdoms and Other Archaeological Delusions*. Lanham: AltaMira.

Poblocki K., 2002. Becoming-state: the bio-cultural imperialism of Sid Meier's Civilization. *Focaal – European Journal of Anthropology* 39, pp. 163–177.

Postigo H., 2007. Of mods and modders: chasing down the value of fan-based digital game modifications. *Games and Culture* 2 (4), p. 300–313.

Rockwell G. M. and Kee K., 2011. The leisure of serious games: a dialogue. *Game Studies* 11 (2) [online]. Available at: http://www.gamestudies.org/1102/articles/geoffrey_rockwell_kevin_kee/ (accessed 11 July 2011).

Schablitsky J. M. ed., 2007. *Box Office Archaeology: refining Hollywood's portrayals of the past*. Walnut Creek: Left Coast Press.

Schut K., 2007. Strategic simulations and our past: the bias of computer games in the presentation of history. *Games and Culture* 2 (3), pp. 213–235.

Shannon D., 2010. *Making History II: the War of the World* review. *Gamespot UK* [online]. Available at: http://uk.gamespot.com/ (accessed 29 July 2011).

Simon B., 2011. Critical theory, political economy and game studies: a review of 'Games of Empire: global capitalism and video games'. *Game Studies* 11 (2) [online]. Available at: http://www.gamestudies.org/1102/articles/simon/ (accessed 04 July 2011).

Siwek S. E., 2010. *Video Games in the 21st Century: the 2010 Report*. Washington, DC: Entertainment Software Association [online]. Available at: http://www.theesa.com/facts/pdfs/VideoGames21stCentury_2010.pdf (accessed 26 July 2011).

Sotamaa O., 2010. When the game is not enough: motivations and practices among computer game modding culture. *Games and Culture* 5 (3), pp. 239–255.

Squire K., 2002. Cultural framing of computer/video games. *Game Studies* 2 (1) [online]. Available at: http://www.gamestudies.org/0102/squire/ (accessed 11 July 2011).

Squire K. D., 2004a. *Replaying History: learning world history through playing* Civilization III. PhD dissertation, Instructional Systems Technology Department, Indiana University [online]. Available at: http://website.education.wisc.edu/kdsquire/dissertation.html (accessed 27 July 2011).

Squire K., 2004b. Review: *Sid Meier's Civilization III*. *Simulation and Gaming* 35 (1), pp. 135–140.

Thompson J. B., 1990. *Ideology and Modern Culture*. Stanford: Stanford University Press.

Uricchio W., 2005. Simulation, history, and computer games. In Raessens J. and Goldstein J. eds, 2005. *Handbook of Computer Game Studies*. Cambridge: MIT Press, pp. 329–338.

Voorhees G. A., 2009. I play therefore I am: *Sid Meier's Civilization*, turn-based strategy games and the cogito. *Games and Culture* 4 (3), pp. 254–275.

Wark M., 2007. *Gamer Theory*. Cambridge: Harvard University Press.

Winkler M. M. ed., 2004. *Gladiator: film and history*. Oxford: Blackwell.

Wolf M. J. P. ed., 2001. *The Medium of the Video Game*. Austin: University of Texas Press.

Zabek J., 2010. *Making History II* – interview with Niall Ferguson. *The Wargamer* [online]. Available at: http://www.wargamer.com/article/2866/making-history-ii-interview-with-niall-ferguson (accessed 29 July 2011).

Public Engagement through Online TV Channels: A Way Forward for the Audiovisual Communication of Archaeology?

Chiara Bonacchi, Charles Furneaux, Daniel Pett

Abstract

This paper assesses the relationship between the public and archaeology within a rapidly evolving world of communication, where the increasingly dominant position of the Internet is changing the role of television.

The first part of the paper examines the ways in which digital technologies have changed the media environment and, in particular, the televisual communication of archaeology, over the past decade, in Britain. The analysis is based on audience figures of archaeology-themed TV series and one-off programmes, and on other statistics regarding the use of digital and online platforms and of mobile technology. It is argued that, in the United Kingdom, opportunities for screening archaeology on both terrestrial and digital channels have diminished. Such opportunities will be likely to decrease even further in the future, due to increasing competition affecting the TV world and diversifying its (once) mass audiences. In this scenario, however, the Internet opens up new possibilities for engagement.

The second section of this paper compares two different forms of online audiovisual communication: 1) that of strongly-branded online TV channels and 2) the one of shorter-term and/or more discontinuous Web-based video communication. The discussion is based on the analysis of specific case studies, investigating the ways in which they have been designed and used.

The conclusion highlights that strongly-branded online TV channels are more visible and effective, not only in terms of public engagement (audience attraction and provision of satisfying experiences), but also of their contribution towards a more sustainable future for the archaeological sector.

Introduction

In her historical synthesis of the relationship between archaeology and the media in Britain, Kulik (2007) identifies five 'ages' of archaeological communication. According to the author (2007: 122), the last age, of 'global communication', spanning from the 1990s to 2007 witnessed an explosion of archaeology on television up to the year 2003 (on this, see also Henson 2006).

In 1994, the television series *Time Team* was aired for the first time (Taylor 1998: 8–15; Mower 2000: 1; Channel 4 2011), and it soon became a brand that would change the UK public's perception and understanding of archaeology (Mower

2000; Hatley 1997: 14, in Kulik 2007).[1] From 1998 to 2002, archaeological documentaries on British terrestrial channels increased by 367% (Kulik 2007: 122). Most programmes were deliberately popular in appeal, relying on entertainment and education to draw their audiences and succeeding in bringing archaeology back to television to an extent that had not been seen since the 1950s–1960s, when *Animal, Vegetable, Mineral* (*AVM*), first, and *Buried Treasure* and *Chronicle*, subsequently, made their appearance on the small screen (see Daniel 1978; Jordan 1981; Schadla-Hall and Morris 2003: 199–200; West 2004: 114–115). For example, on 20 October 2003,[2] in a certainly much more competitive televisual and, more generally, media environment, the programme *Pompeii* doubled the five million viewers of *AVM* (Kulik 2007: 118),[3] with a share of 38%.[4]

In 2004, however, the trend started to change radically and the number of programmes about archaeology on terrestrial television dropped (Kulik 2007: 123). In considering possible future developments of this scenario, Kulik (2007: 123) underlines that the take-up of narrowcasting could lead to archaeology moving to more niche channels, like BBC4, and that such a change might also allow higher quality programming, tailored for smaller and interested segments of the public.

Although convincing at the time of publication (2007), Kulik's analysis needs to be reviewed, by retracing the evolution of the television world since the beginning of the 21st century and the even more rapid changes that have occurred since 2006–2007, with the emerging role of the Internet as a means of delivering media content (see, for example, BARB 2011a; EBU 2008; Ofcom 2007: 19–21, 56–57; Ofcom 2010: 103–106, 177–178; but also Evans 2011: 1).

The intention of this article is to return to the point where Kulik stopped and indicate a way forward for engaging the public with archaeology through audiovisual communication on online platforms, in the changed and changing media landscape. To achieve this aim, the problem is tackled in three stages. Firstly, starting again from the year 2003 we examine how the scenario of television has varied since then, how the offer of archaeological programmes has been reshaped by digital technologies and what operational margins are left, today, for communicating archaeology through televisual broadcasting and narrowcasting. Secondly, based on such an examination, we explore the potential of online thematic channels, run by partnerships which include archaeologists, archaeological companies or institutions that place archaeology at the centre of their mission. This is done through the presentation of two case studies, Archeologia Viva TV[5] (2011) and The Archaeology Channel[6] (2011a), which have proved successful according to audience analyses. Thirdly, the importance of maintaining a television brand when communicating via online audiovisuals is revealed by the less convincing results (primarily in terms of reach and ability to retain viewers) attained by those videos that are uploaded on, or linked to, the webpages of key institutions in the cultural sector as part of a much wider user experience without the intention to create a dedicated, online TV output.

Finally, clarification is needed on the ways in which key concepts, which recur throughout the paper, are understood and addressed. Television is loosely defined as any activity that identifies itself

---

[1] This statement can be also justified in the light of some of the results of Bonacchi's doctoral research *Communicating Archaeology: From Trends to Policy. Public Perceptions and Experience in the Changing Media Environment*, due for completion in 2012.

[2] See footnote no. 11, for the source of the viewing figures for the programme *Pompeii. The Last Day*.

[3] *AVM* was watched, on average, by 10% of the population of the time, whereas *Pompeii* was viewed by over 16% of the population (very close figures). In this picture, however, *Pompeii*'s reach is perhaps more significant, given the tremendously higher number of UK households owning at least one TV set in 2003 compared to the 1950s.

[4] 'Share' can be defined as 'the percentage of television households tuned to a specific station in relation to all households using television ... that is all households with their sets turned on' (Zettl 2006: 391). More specifically, programme share is 'the size of an audience expressed as a percentage of the households or people actually watching television at that time' (McDowell 2006: 86).

[5] Also referred to as AV TV, from now on.

[6] Also referred to as TAC, from now on.

as such and whose mission is to commission and deliver audiovisual content.[7] A television channel is an institution or partnership which provides televisual output, but also the means, the portal via which television is made available to the audience on different platforms (terrestrial, digital, cable, satellite and online). Internet (or online) television is any kind of television distributed through the Internet, whereas Web TV is a form of online television which requires a browser in order to be accessed.

As indicated, online television is examined as a means of promoting public engagement with archaeology, that is of broadening the impact of scientific research (Dolan 2008: 1) by connecting and sharing results with the public (NCCPE 2011). This should not be interpreted as the pursuit of a one-way, transmission form of communication, but, instead, as the provision of spaces where archaeological interpretations are presented and can be discussed, allowing multi-faceted experiences which comprise elements spanning from sociability to the acquisition of information.[8] This is a first component of engagement, the 'sociocultural' one. The second component, 'promotional' and ultimately 'economic', may either be just a consequence of the previous component, or a goal in its own right and consists of marketing the activity carried out by the partners involved in public engagement. Both these elements will be explored as far as possible, with the data that were available regarding the use of online TV channels and Web-based videos.

Television and archaeological TV programmes since 2003

At the present time, in Britain, the overall picture of traditional television dealing with archaeological topics is one of decline,[9] when compared to the situation at the beginning of the century.

In 2003, the main terrestrial channels broadcast around 185 hours of archaeology and ancient history, and a further 90 hours on other heritage-related subjects (Henson 2006).[10] Channel 4 offered popular series, such as *Time Team* (2.7 million viewers, on average), *The Great Pyramid* (2.3 million, on 28 April 2003) and *Secrets of the Dead* (2.3 million, on average).[11] The same year, Channel 5 offered a range of one-off programmes with slightly lower, but still solid, viewing figures. Among them was *Who killed Tutankhamun?* (1.9 million viewers, on 21 February 2003) and *Britain's Finest Ancient Monuments* (1.6 million viewers, on 2 July 2003).[12] However, it was BBC1 and BBC2 that attracted the largest audiences, particularly *Pompeii: The last Day*, which was watched by ten

---

[7] Throughout its history, television has undergone a series of 'definitional crises' (Uricchio 2009: 31, quoted in Evans 2011: 3). It has also always been variously defined depending on the theoretical standing of media and communication researchers and their lines of enquiry, so that different metaphors and paradigms have been and are still used to describe it (for example, see Buonanno and Radice 2008: 27–30; Evans 2011: 4). However, until the penetration of digital technologies, in the late 1990s, there was a 'common' understanding of television as a 'technically highly standardised medium, with fairly similar organizational structure, content types and business models' (Noam 2008: 7). Today this is no longer the case, thus it becomes challenging but critical to explain how television is understood in this article and how online television is distinguished from non televisual, Web-based audiovisual content.

[8] Since the 1990s, the importance of experiences in marketing, economics (Pine and Gilmore 1999; Jensen 1999) and the cultural sectors (with the primacy of museums – for example, Kotler 1999; Lockstone 2007: 62; Pekarik *et al.* 1999) has come to the forefront, although solidly based on literature that dates back, as regards the museum and education sector, at least to the beginning of the 20th century. According to the model of public engagement developed for a research commissioned by Arts Council England *et al.* (2010), instead, 'experience' is defined as one of the five categories in which the 'interaction with arts and cultural content in digital environments can be classified'. It requires more 'sophisticated online skills and behaviour' than 'access' and 'learning', and less sophisticated ones than 'sharing' and 'creating'. The distinction between learning and experiencing that is suggested by this model, however, does not seem to be convincingly applicable to the archaeological sector as it is to the artistic one.

[9] For this article, archaeological TV is defined as a TV offering displaying either one or more of the following: 1) archaeological evidence; 2) archaeological processes of analysis; 3) the results of archaeological research.

[10] Although a definition of heritage is not provided in the paper (Henson 2006), the author (Henson 2011) has later on specified that, by heritage programmes, he meant 'programmes that looked at physical evidence of the past but not in an archaeological way'.

[11] These figures could be retrieved thanks to a Channel 4 audience research commissioned by Furneaux and conducted in November 2003, based on BARB Overnight Figures. Please note that, when available, average views have been included; sometimes, however, only peak views were available.

[12] See footnote no. 11, for the source of the figures that are here presented.

million people (on 20 October 2003), a result that would be hard to imagine today.[13]

In 2010, the archaeological series with the highest number of viewers for a single viewing was *Digging for Britain* (from 1.2 to 2.6 million viewers).[14] Programmes broadcast by Channel 4 had smaller audiences, when compared to the BBC and to Channel 4 figures from 2003; the viewers of *Time Team* and *Time Team Specials*, for example, were between 1.7 and 1.9 million, so roughly one million less than seven years before.[15]

For the foreseeable future, it is likely that archaeology and similar niche factual programming areas will continue to be marginalised on the terrestrial channels, as the survival of broadcasting (and, on a different scale, of digital narrowcasting as well) is based on the provision of 'hits' (Anderson 2004, 2006: 27–40). The latter are essential for commercial channels, but are an important drive also for non-commercial broadcasters in a 'crowded marketplace', although, in this case, their weight is counterbalanced by a PSB[16] requirement.

Being currently tied to the scheduling requirements of terrestrial broadcasters, the number of archaeological programmes on offer via the Internet is also rather limited. It was 45 hours in 2010[17] (up from roughly 25 in 2009,[18] but the figure is still low) and divides into two camps. On the one hand, there is the BBC output, which consists of presenter-led documentary series such as *Ancient Worlds* and is available for a short period of only seven days on BBC's iPlayer, a platform that can be accessed on free-view receivers and over the Internet.[19] On the other hand, there is *Time Team*, offered through Channel 4's 4oD (4 on Demand) service.

A strong argument can be made, however, for online television as a way forward for audiovisual engagement, once untied from scheduling requirements. Over the last decade, the audience has rapidly fragmented with the powerful homogeneity of the previous fifty years now challenged, due to the rise of multi-channel television (satellite, cable and digital terrestrial), which has caused a shift from broadcasting to narrowcasting, from mass production, distribution and consumption, to more niche, personalised ones (Anderson 2004; Buonanno and Radice 2008: 20–26). Multi-channel television's market share increased rapidly from January 2001 (being present in nine million homes) to January 2011 (24.5 million homes) (BARB 2011b). The uptake of this platform has eroded the dominance of the terrestrial broadcasters amongst TV viewers. So, in the ten years from 2001 to 2010, the share of non-terrestrial channels has more than doubled to a figure that today approaches ITV's audience in 1983, the year when Channel 4 was set up (**Table 1**). An increasingly selective and content-focused viewership formed, which, although no longer depending on four or five broadcasters, was still tied to the demands of the schedules on offer to them from any one of the 137 broadcast platforms available in Britain.

The delivery of television over the Internet has liberated viewers from the broadcasters' imposed schedules. In the United Kingdom, a panoply of platforms are available: BBC iPlayer, ITV Player, 4 on Demand, Demand 5, Sky Player, SeeSaw, Blinkbox and Eurosport Player. These platforms provide an online televisual offer accessible to a large part of the population. In the fourth quarter of 2011, 74% of households in Britain had broadband (fixed and mobile), and 27% of adults were smartphone users (Ofcom 2011: 47, 303). Only a few months earlier, in November 2010, 14% of adults in the UK claimed to have watched televi-

---

[13] See footnote no. 11, for the source of the figures that are here presented.
[14] The source of the figures that are presented is BARB 2010.
[15] The source of the figures that are presented is BARB 2010.
[16] PSB is the acronym for Public Service Broadcasting.
[17] The calculation is based on catch-up sites for BBC, Channel 4, Channel 5 and ITV.
[18] The calculation is based on catch-up sites for BBC, Channel 4, Channel 5 and ITV.
[19] Some content has restricted availability outside the UK.

Table 1 Share of terrestrial channels compared with that of other channels (non-terrestrial), from 2001 to 2010.

	BBC1	BBC2	ITV1	C4	Five	Others
1983	37.0	11.0	48.0	4.0	–	–
2001	26.9	11.1	26.7	10.0	5.8	19.6
2010	20.6	6.9	17.0	7.0	4.5	43.7

sion via a PC or a laptop in the previous week, and a further 1.95% via their mobile phone (BARB 2011a). When asked if they had ever watched TV by means of PC or laptop the figure was 34%, up from 27% in 2009, and 5% for mobile phones, up from 3.1% in 2009 (BARB 2011a). It should also be noted that those engaging with television through these devices tend to watch around two hours a week, so, considering the average number of hours watched daily in the UK in 2010 (BARB 2011a), they can be defined as 'light viewers'. Even more striking are the figures for 15 to 34 year olds, where 46% have watched television via PC or laptop, with higher socially stratified sectors (ABC1s) following close behind at 43% (BARB 2011a).

Interestingly, the accessibility of television as a result of its availability on the Internet has been to the advantage of traditional television viewing, not at its expense. This is demonstrated, for example, by the fact that, in 2010, the average number of hours viewed per day reached over four hours (Ofcom 2011: 134; Sweney 2010), for the very first time in the history of television. Clearly, Internet television allows viewers to find what they want to watch when they want to watch it (see also Gibs 2008: 16) and, as a result, this contributes to a higher overall number of hours watched. This trend is matched by a decline in those who say that they would most miss their televisions, with people from 16 to 24 years old placing TV second to mobile phones for the first time ever (Conlan 2011). Even amongst all adults, interest in television has declined over the last year from 50% to 44%, although, for this group, it still ranks ahead of mobile phones (Conlan 2011).

From the analysis that has been conducted, four observations can be made as regards the impact on the communication of archaeology of the way in which digital technologies have changed the offer and consumption of traditional television.

1. The take-up of online TV within the UK is very rapid, mainly due to technological advances driven by the lead-on delivery programme BBC iPlayer, which, in the week ending 9th July 2011, was the sixteenth most visited website in the UK across all categories and the third among entertainment websites (Experian Hitwise 2011).[20]

2. Wider televisual output is changing peoples' TV viewing habits and accelerating the fragmenting of the audience into increasingly smaller and highly discriminatory groups who are now able to be more decisive about the programmes that they like to watch and the modality for doing so.

3. The loss of dominance by terrestrial broadcasters in both the commissioning and transmission of programming creates an opportunity for online 'narrowcasting', especially when it appeals to ABC1s, who may be willing to pay for high quality, niche programming once a business model has been established.

4. Finally, it is suggested that at least a part of these new types of archaeological programming should be free from scheduling requirements and provided by partnerships

---

[20] The calculation was conducted by number of visits.

of archaeology-centred institutions and TV professionals.

Archaeological TV channels online: a possible way forward

The thematic Web channel Archeologia Viva TV (2011) will now be examined, as a successful case of online archaeological narrowcasting, managed by a partnership of the kind that has been suggested in the previous paragraph. The design, audience profile and use, and the economic model of the channel will be analysed and compared to those of its American parallel, The Archaeology Channel (2011a). By doing so, it will be possible to provide specific strategies for an effective communication of archaeology via online television. It should be noticed that the discussion is based on on-site metrics made available by the managers of the two channels. In the case of AV TV, data was derived from the 'visitor reporting tool' Google Analytics (Clifton 2010: 8). Unfortunately, only certain information could be viewed and direct access to metrics, which would have allowed a more detailed and segmented analysis, was not possible.

Archeologia Viva TV (2009) was the first thematic Web channel on archaeology to be produced in Italy. Established in 2009, it was the result of a twenty year-long collaboration between the International Festival of Archaeological Cinema of Rovereto, the first festival of such kind to be organized in Europe, and *Archeologia Viva*, the most popular specialized magazine about archaeology, in Italy, with a circulation of 40,000 copies per month (Pruneti 2011). The mission of the channel is that of promoting public engagement, intended as the facilitation of direct 'encounters' between archaeologists and an interested audience (Archeologia Viva TV 2009).

The structure of the channel is essentially very simple and user-friendly. It is composed of two main sections: 'on air' and 'on demand'. The former has a news format, with short videos streaming according to a schedule that is updated on a bi-weekly timetable, whereas the 'on demand' section is an archive with three different types of videos: news, documentaries and 'conversations' (interviews of specialists). At the time of writing, there are about 177 videos of variable length available on the channel. News videos are generally either 7–8 minutes or 15 minutes in length, while most documentaries are around 30 minutes long and 'conversations' are generally even longer (40 to 60 minutes, or more).

The content has a very broad spectrum and includes archaeological research carried out by Italian teams, both in Italy and abroad, on the most diverse themes and periods, but always maintaining either a journalistic or a narrative-documentary slant, and a tight relationship with the events organised by the magazine *Archaeologia Viva* and the Film Festival of Rovereto.

The audience of AV TV is not as large as that of The Archaeology Channel, for example, but this is both because AV TV is in Italian and because it has just started. Unique visitors (a measure of reach) have been increasing between January 2010 and January 2011 (+36%), and have doubled those of Sperimentarea.tv (2011), the generalist Web TV that is edited and managed by the Museum of Rovereto (23,469 against 14,472). This might well be read as a further sign of the importance of forming an alliance with a strong media brand like the magazine *Archeologia Viva*. The audience of AV TV is a motivated one. Between January 2010 and January 2011, those who casually ended up on the website, or came and soon left disliking it have been few. This is shown by the small number of single-page visits, which is expressed by a very low bounce rate of just 0.5%. A very good figure, if we think that, in general, it is really hard to get a bounce rate under 20% (Kaushik 2007). The bounce rate, also defined as a 'one-page, zero-action visit' (Clifton 2010: 330), is a valuable metric because 'it indicates the immediate reaction of a visitor' (Tonkin *et al.* 2010: 270).[21] Having the opportunity, it would be fruitful to conduct an online survey to ascertain the specific drivers of visitors' motiva-

---

[21] Google Analytics calculates bounce rate as follows: 'percentage bounce rate for a page = number of single page visits to that page with zero actions / number of times that page was an entry page' (Clifton 2010: 330).

tion. It is a loyal audience as well, as shown by the fact that most users (43% of them) arrive at the Web channel directly, by typing the URL into their browser, while only 29% come from referring sites and 28% from search engines (typing 'Archeologia Viva TV' instead of just 'Archeologia Viva', or even less specific key words). As observed by Piero Pruneti, director of *Archeologia Viva*, viewers initially learn about the Web channel reading the magazine *Archeologia Viva*, then they become loyal to the Web channel, and this loyalty helps to reinforce the loyalty towards the magazine.[22] Finally, in spite of the language, the geographic distribution of the audience has been relatively wide in the past year. Most visits have been from Italy (55,397), but along the Tail (with reference to Chris Anderson's Long Tail model) there have been visits from 82 more countries, prevalently Western European, Northern American and Asian. According to Anderson's model (2004, 2006),[23] the entertainment market of the 20th century was based on the logic of selling much of a few, that is selling a very restricted range of products to a mass market. In his view, the media economy of the 21st century is, instead, profoundly different. It has been changed by digital technologies, which have introduced the possibility for overcoming two limitations of the hits-based market: the limitation of space (virtually anything can be made available online) and the limitation of local output: audiences have enlarged and become global. In this context, niche products may also more easily be offered (Anderson 2004, 2006).

On average, visitors stay on the site for about eight minutes and view a little over two pages per visit, suggesting that they find the content they are looking for, view and leave. The most viewed pages are the one showing the most recent videos in the archive (38,026 page views)[24] and the homepage with 'on air' archaeological news (25,617 page views),[25] demonstrating the appeal of the news format and the effectiveness of short, streaming videos, which do not require users to select what they want to watch every time. It is the advantage of having information reaching the audience, as opposed to the audience having to go to the information continuously.

Although the Web channel achieves its mission of public engagement, with a growing, motivated audience, it seems not to be making the most of the potential of online platforms. The channel provides a typically mass mediated communication 'from one to many' (Menduni 2006: 11; McQuail 2005: 4), without offering the audience much space for contributing, if not by sharing on major networking portals (Facebook, Twitter and Myspace). A great advantage of Internet television is that it also allows interaction through user-generated content, which has transformed narrowcasting into 'individual casting' (Noam 2008: 8), and which could be integrated into the format of online thematic channels. In such way, a community who discusses the subject may form, and data on users' preferences and interests can be gathered and analysed in order to improve the overall output.

The effectiveness of the channel depends on the media expertise of the partners, their scientific networks and the brands they hold, which grant visibility and authority to contents. The magazine *Archeologia Viva* provides a strong brand name and the necessary funding to cover the

---

[22] A similar phenomenon has been registered, for example, for the radio series *A History of the World in 100 Objects*, produced by The British Museum, in collaboration with BBC Radio 4 (see also Pett, this volume). The series and the activities organised around it, allowed The British Museum to reach unrecorded levels of popularity, in 2010 (The British Museum 2011b: 12).

[23] It is important to note that Anderson's contribution is a classic one about the new opportunities opened up by digital technologies to make also less 'mainstream' products available. Anderson is a journalist, not an economist, but his analysis on *The Long Tail: Why the Future of Business is selling less of more* (Anderson 2006) has been acknowledged as being an inspiring one also by some cultural economics specialists (e.g. Hjorth-Andersen 2007). Nevertheless, Anderson's work should be referred to more as a thought-provoking reading than as one providing definite answers about business models to implement (Hjorth-Andersen 2007).

[24] Page views refer to the period between March 2010 and April 2011.

[25] Page views refer to the period between March 2010 and April 2011.

costs (paying the company that has developed the structure of the Web channel, for example; Pruneti 2011). Editorial expertise is provided by the staff of the film festival, who collect videos and decide what to show (Di Blasi 2011). Videos reach editors 'naturally', as a result of the activities that are organized by the Film Festival and the magazine *Archeologia Viva* (Di Blasi 2011). This is the case for documentaries, most of which are produced by archaeological research teams and sent to the editorial board to participate in the Film Festival. 'Conversations' are filmed, for the most part, at events held during the Film Festival, where archaeologists and historians are invited and interviewed in the presence of an audience.

The profile and preferences of AV TV's users are similar to those of The Archaeology Channel in three main ways. Firstly, AV TV, like TAC, had a slow beginning. It was established in 2000 but really blossomed only three years later, and in 2008 it achieved eight million page views. In spite of technical problems that caused the website not to work properly on certain days and affected Web traffic, between March 2010 and April 2011 the channel still had 896,563 page views, 322,222 visits and 261,462 unique visitors. Secondly, visitors to TAC are also very motivated, as suggested by the low bounce rate (it has oscillated between 5% and 10% in the past twelve months), by the fact that most visitors access the Web channel directly and by other survey data, published on TAC's website (The Archaeology Channel 2011b). According to the latter, 66 out of 99 respondents hold, at least, a university degree, 22 are working archaeologists and/or teachers and professors, 26 are students and 47 are archaeology enthusiasts. The survey also tells us that, contrary to what might have been expected, age does not constitute a barrier to access, since the age distribution is quite broad, with a mode of 46 to 55 (The Archaeology Channel 2011b). People come from nearly every country on the planet, with a bias towards North America and Western Europe, but with increasing numbers from China, the Middle East, and the developing world. The third and last important similarity with AV TV is the primacy of archaeological news in terms of popularity: the Audio News is currently TAC's most popular programme (Pettigrew 2011).

The business models on which AV TV and TAC are based differ substantially. AV TV lives off the resources and activities of the Film Festival and AV magazine. On the other hand, TAC is sustained by underwriting, which is a scheme by which companies provide funding in exchange for a mention on the site itself (The Archaeology Channel 2011b). Private persons may also contribute, by becoming members. The Archaeology Channel is, in fact, a visitor-supported non-profit public service and membership provides its primary source of revenue to cover expenses (costs of webcasting, website development, new programming, special projects, etc.) (The Archaeology Channel 2011c). Both AV TV and TAC, however, are recognisable as distinct brands of archaeological television, and do not depend on public funding.

Web-based audiovisual content about archaeology: a more casual output

It is important to comprehend how instances of online television discussed in the previous paragraph are manifestly different from single/multiple video(s) that are made available to an online audience in a more casual manner, for example a video on YouTube, or a page of videos. The latter examples generally do not have an editorial board or strategic aim which provides the continuity of vision to create a distinct product or brand of archaeological online television.

First of all, one must try to ascertain why individuals and organisations want to pursue an engagement strategy based on online audiovisuals; is it because it is trendy, is easy, is cheap, or is the Internet now the place to be? In the current financial climate, many archaeological organisations have seen the need to establish a dialogue with their funders (primarily the taxpaying public), and the provision of audiovisual content is a very simple means to achieve this aim. Sometimes, online videos will be the only way of engaging with an archaeological discovery, or the work of a unit. Notable examples of the use of audiovisual communication in the commercial archaeology sector can be found on the Prescott Street (2011), Wessex Archaeology (2011) and Thames Discovery Programme (2011) websites.

A wide array of methods is available to the casual broadcaster (or narrowcaster) to implement their vision, depending on the core reasons that lead the institution to broadcast. For example, one can now make use of a variety of platforms, which include iTunesU (for university based content), Vimeo (19 million users worldwide, and 930,000 in the UK; Google 2011a), YouTube (720 million users worldwide, and 31 million in the UK; Google 2011b), dedicated software like Videola (2011) or Miro Community (2011), and Amazon CloudFront coupled with an embedded open source video player. Some of these are built on open standards, are devoid of advertising and can be freely adapted by the end user; others pay a premium to use the service and present advert-free content. It is now possible to host audiovisuals on an organisation's own hardware, install the correct software and stream the content without the need for third party intervention.

Several factors can influence the methodological path that one chooses for showing Web-based videos; for example the ability to present high definition content, the promise of 99% availability of resources not being blocked by institutional Information Services policy, or a broad interoperability that allows viewing on a panoply of mobile multi-platform devices (e.g. laptops, tablets, hand-held gaming consoles, or smartphones). A great proportion of the United Kingdom's population now carries a device with them daily, which can access on-demand video through the microwave spectrum. The rise of the extremely sophisticated smartphone and its integration into society is evident, as Bell (2011) claims 'phones allow us to expand our influence to other things, people, and places'. This succinct statement sums up what is being achieved by broadcasters who provide their content to mobile platforms.

All of the factors that have been mentioned are extremely desirable. In economic terms, it could be posited that the fiscal burden is primarily placed within the acquisition of audiovisuals rather than the broadcasting. High costs are for producing high quality (or even professional) content and could be seen as being squarely caused by the acquisition of the equipment and the skills to create, rather than by the provision of platforms for engaging with viewers. Those skills include training in the arts of photography, videography, and Web-design.

Organisations and institutions that produce more 'casual' Web-based audiovisual content about archaeology include:

- The Victoria and Albert Museum (V&A): embedded video channel and YouTube presence (The Victoria and Albert Museum 2008);
- The British Museum (BM): YouTube and embedded video (The British Museum 2011a);
- The Thames Discovery Project (TDP): Vimeo and YouTube (UCLTV 2011);
- Wessex Archaeology (WA): YouTube and Vimeo (Wessex Archaeology 2011).

At first glance, it is apparent that the quality of output produced by these Web broadcasters varies greatly in terms of:

- length;
- degree of dynamism;
- production values;
- usage and interaction;
- type of content.

As regards the fourth point, a metric to evaluate the successful use of these 'casual' videos via quantitative analysis is the 'number of views'. Interaction can be measured by noting the number of times they have been shared via social media.[26] When considering the latter argument, however, one should take into account how many people actually use the sharing services provided on a particular website. These include Delicious, Digg, Facebook, Google Buzz, MySpace, Stumbleupon, Yahoo and Twitter. Each of these services has experienced a peak of popularity, and many are now on the

---

[26] The two indicators were chosen also because data for other types of measurements could not be accessed.

wane. MySpace, for example, is shedding users daily (Garrahan 2009; Arrington 2011), whereas Facebook is rapidly gaining speed worldwide and in the UK it is now used by 30 million people, nearly half of the British population (Barnett 2011). Therefore, the volume of sharing on each network will be biased; additionally, many people now have and actively practice poly-social identities on the Web (for example, work and personal Twitter accounts) and might actually share many of these videos multiple times. In spite of the bias, sharing on social media remains a revealing indicator, since, as stated by Arts Council England *et al.* (2010: 44), these have 'become a major tool for discovering as well as sharing information about arts and culture, second only to search through Google'.

Within the five criteria mentioned above, high volumes appear to be mainly achieved for videos which are shorter, punchy and of high production quality. This is because the videos are presented as by-products (usually for marketing reasons), as opposed to stand-alones, with a strongly developed TV brand presence. *Ergo*, these users could be categorised as 'casual'; their main motivation for accessing Web content is not usually that of watching videos, but of visiting a website via search or from an interest developed by chance. Users within this category are often extremely impatient and fickle; their attention is not likely to extend to long broadcasts and time spent on site is not particularly high. They are not dedicated subscribers to the content that these websites produce.

Two examples demonstrate this paradox between short and full length audiovisuals. Wessex Archaeology's video of a Roman coffin being opened has been viewed over 60,000 times (see **Table 2**, for YouTube comparative statistics). As opposed to *Time Team*'s YouTube full length episode entitled *Castle of the Saxon Kings*, which has reached only 1,400 views. In comparing the two, it should be considered that there is at least one mitigating factor for the disparity. Wessex Archaeology is only able to deliver their content over the Web, whilst *Time Team* has the might of their terrestrial and digital TV distributor network, the facility to download full episodes legally via 4 on Demand, or illegally via illegal file sharing, and a much larger market thanks to the strong Channel 4 brand. Hence, the *Time Team*'s YouTube capitalisation is very low compared to a solely Web distributed video offer. Moreover, it can be the case that the WA website has been optimised in such a way (see Goskar, this volume) that it features highly in search results?

Overall, however, the volume of users of this more casual Web-based audiovisual content is not impressive. Contrasting the viewing figures presented above with more light-hearted broadcast entertainment videos – for instance *Simon's Cat* YouTube channel (Simonscat 2011), which has about ten million views per animated video – provides a stark reminder that the market for archaeology is a niche one.

Within the Museum sector, in spite of the high quality of production, audiovisual content from institutions such as the British Museum also attracts few users. Looking at figures[27] produced using the British Museum's analytical software (the sector wide Google Analytics; Finnis *et al.* 2011: section 4) shows a similar pattern for embedded videos within the website (**Table 3**). For example, the exhibition-driven *Afghanistan* teaser video was 1.45 minutes long, showed at 480p resolution (most videos from the cultural sector appear to be standard at 360p), and had audio transcription for accessibility. It was viewed 12,885 times, with average time spent on the page 1.54 minutes and with a high bounce rate of 52.30% (between 1 January 2011 and 31 July 2011), which suggests that people did watch the entire audiovisual, but were likely to leave as soon as they had finished viewing.

The trend of low uptake of Web videos by the casual broad or narrowcaster is confirmed when considering the larger museums that have established a presence on the YouTube platform (**Table 2**). Many of these institutions have archaeological content, are involved in the administration of archaeology or are primarily archaeological by

---

[27] These figures cannot be shared in their entirety.

remit. The subscriber column rarely reaches four digits and there are no videos that approach the million view mark, even though some institutions are prolific producers of audiovisual material (e.g. the Metropolitan Museum of Art and Brooklyn Museum). Figures for the videos produced for the Department of Culture Media and Sport (DCMS) give even worse results, and especially when one considers their status as the administrative national body for culture in the UK. For an early adopter of the technology (joining in June 2006), their output is un-engaging as demonstrated by the fact that the mean on their channel is less than 600 views. This could be attributed to several factors, such as a low appeal to the public, or poor search engine visibility. In this particular case, it is probably a combination of both reasons.

Conclusions: strategies of engagement through online televisual communication

This article has underlined how the loss of dominance by traditional broadcasters has created an opportunity for 'narrowcast' programming and how the UK is a leading online television viewing nation. There is space, therefore, for the development of niche markets of Internet-delivered archaeological television, detached from the offerings and demands of the terrestrial channels operating in Britain.

If engagement is intended as the maximisation of research impact through the achievement of two objectives (marketing and the provision of composite experiences in which learning plays a key role), then the strategy to pursue is not that of relying on a more casual operation of intermittent provision of Web-based audiovisuals. These 'get lost' online; they are difficult to find on YouTube and, arguably, constitute just an element of a much wider user experience when uploaded on the websites of cultural institutions, even national ones such as the British Museum. It seems that, in order for the output to become visible online, strong branding is needed. This is possible if strong archaeological and media brands create a distinct product which is in turn branded as online archaeological television.[28] After all, research carried out on the population of Belgium, the Netherlands and the UK has proved that television is the source of information which is considered to be the most reliable in those countries, after the Internet (InSites Consulting 2009);[29] and Internet, more than the Web. While the former is expanding and gaining speed, the latter is not as much. This is because accessing 'semi-closed platforms that use the Internet for transport, but not the browser for display' is simpler and applications which have become popular after the take up of iOS technology are increasingly preferred to search engines, since they are more structured and 'fit better' into people's lives (Anderson and Wolff 2010).

It is via those platforms as well as websites, which do allow greater interconnectivity, that online archaeological TV could be made available. There, it should be possible to find an 'on air' section with shorter news videos up to 4–5 minutes long, which 'automatically' provide information that users may easily access also through their smartphones, for example. An 'on-demand' section could also be present, with a wide range of longer documentaries and interviews to choose from. Moreover, archaeological TV should not be rigidly institutional, like the Web channel Archeologia Viva TV, but allow interaction (content-sharing and discussion).

---

[28] The importance of brands has been highlighted by several cultural institutions with digital public engagement programmes. In the research commissioned by Arts Council England *et al.* (2010: 6), for example, it is possible to read: 'brands are really important for audiences in discovering and filtering content online'. A second example is that of ArtBabble, the website dedicated to art and art history, run by the Indianapolis Museum of Art. In 2009, the ArtBabble site had 22 institutional partners (Stein *et al.* 2009), and was set up under the premise that 'niche content portals offer better findability and cross-pollination for art content'. This premise is one that the authors also subscribe to when it comes to promoting archaeological audiovisual content and has been applied in the museums sector too, for the aggregation of cultural merchandise through the website CultureLabel.

[29] 'This research data is the result of market research conducted by InSites Consulting in September 2008. In addition to other brands and communication topics, sources and use of word of mouth were also mapped. In all, 900 consumers and 250 marketers took part in this online survey in Belgium, the Netherlands and the UK. The figures are representative for the Internet population of every country in terms of sex and age' (InSites Consulting 2009). The Internet was mentioned by 50% of respondents, television by 23% and newspapers by 13%.

PUBLIC ENGAGEMENT THROUGH ONLINE TV CHANNELS

Table 2 Figures for the consumption of YouTube content as at 2 August 2011.

Institution	Username	Highest views	Channel views	Upload views	Number of videos	Subscribers	Joined YouTube
The British Museum	Britishmuseum	7,284	19,282	62,334	67	422	21/08/2006
Wessex Archaeology	Wessexarchaeology	68,638	11,114	165,166	10	370	10/07/2006
Department for Media Culture and Sport	Dcms	2,122	66,045	22,263	39	169	08/06/2006
Victoria and Albert Museum	Vamuseum	305,863	37,548	855,288	131	1,057	03/03/2008
Metropolitan Museum of Art	Metmuseum	94,344	121,243	1,210,194	390	3,848	5/01/2007
Brooklyn Museum	Brooklynmuseum	29,039	53,892	453,181	162	191	07/07/2006
Penn Museum	pennmuseum	30,961	22,439	211,404	213	616	20/05/2008
Guggenheim	guggenheim	42,026	102,218	n/a	70	n/a	10/12/2005
National Gallery	nationalgalleryuk	32,974	26,021	130,669	54	731	04/02/2008
The Time Team	Channel4[30]	14,326	3,396,224	65,912[31]	9	70,445	22/03/2006
Thames Discovery Project	UCLTV[32]	667	112,428	3,082	9	n/a	15/05/2009

Table 3 Statistics regarding the consumption of a selection of British Museum Web-videos, from 1 January 2011 to 31 July 2011 (URLs are not provided as they are subject to change).

Shortened Video title	Page views	Bounce rate (%)	Length of visit (seconds)	Video length
Afghanistan	12,885	52.30	114	105
Book of the Dead	8,458	61.42	111	98
Karzai's visit	7,968	54.97	127	202
Hidden treasures	8,007	53.33	150	202
Afghanistan crown	7,112	49.83	77	65
A Brief History of Time	5,632	68.08	202	359

---

[30] *Time Team*'s figures are hard to ascertain, as their channel on YouTube covers all Channel 4 output, hence figures for subscriber and channel views are inflated.

[31] This figure is produced from just the *Time Team* videos available on the Channel 4 YouTube account.

[32] The Thames Discovery project also suffers from the same problem as that shown in footnote no. 30.

'People have most trust in each other' even before media, and friends, acquaintances and colleagues are the most trusted, according to the research that was mentioned before (InSites Consulting 2009). Therefore, sharing is not only important for providing a social experience and for facilitating interpretation, but also for reasons related to the marketing of the application itself.

An Internet-supported application of archaeological television is then the strategy that is suggested as a way forward for engaging interested audiences in the results of archaeological research, in a direct manner, easy to produce, distribute and use. Although this path has not been trodden yet, there are signs, especially in the museum sector, which suggest that the proposed approach, or a similar one, may soon be adopted by private or public organizations having archaeology at the core of their mission. During a debate in 2009 at the London School of Economics (LSE), entitled *The Museum of the 21st Century*, the Director of The British Museum, Neil MacGregor, stated:

> The future has to be, without question, the museum as a publisher and broadcaster
> (Higgins 2009; MacGregor and Serota 2009).

Being publishers and broadcasters (possibly in partnership with creative and ICT industries) will help archaeological institutions to diversify their sources of funding and increase their financial sustainability. The importance of establishing networks between or within the creative and cultural sectors, in order to deliver original digital content, has been underlined by recent EU and UK policy as a way in which both sectors may face the current period of austerity, and generate economic growth (e.g. Commission of the European Communities 2007; European Commission 2010; DCMS and BERR 2009; Arts Council England 2010).

Acknowledgements

The authors would like to thank Enrico Crema, Leif Isaksen, Gabriel Moshenska, Jim Mower and Tim Schadla-Hall, for their helpful reviews, comments and for the inspiring insights offered on this paper. Thank you also to Dario Di Blasi, Rick Pettigrew and Piero Pruneti, for the information they provided on Archeologia Viva TV and The Archaeology Channel.

References

Anderson C., 2004. The Long Tail. *Wired* 12.02 [online] October. Available at: http://www.wired.com/wired/archive/12.10/tail.html?pg=1&topic=tail&topic_set (accessed 15 June 2010).

Anderson C., 2006. *The Long Tail. Why the Future of Business is Selling Less of More*. London: Random House Business Books.

Anderson C. and Wolff M., 2010. The Web is Dead. Long Live the Internet. *Wired* 18.08 [online] 17 August 2010. Available at: http://www.wired.com/magazine/2010/08/ff_webrip/all/1 (accessed 15 February 2011).

The Archaeology Channel (TAC), 2011a. Homepage [online]. Available at: http://www.archaeologychannel.org/ (accessed 10 April 2011).

The Archaeology Channel (TAC), 2011b. Underwriting Program [online]. Available at: http://www.archaeologychannel.org/sponsor.shtml (accessed 15 April 2011).

The Archaeology Channel (TAC), 2011c. Invitation to membership [online]. Available at: http://www.archaeologychannel.org/member.html (accessed 15 April 2011).

Archeologia Viva TV (AV TV), 2009. Archeologia Viva TV [online]. Available at: http://www.archeologiaviva.tv/ondemand/archeologia-viva-tv (accessed 10 April 2011).

Archeologia Viva TV (AV TV), 2011. Homepage [online]. Available at: http://www.archeologiaviva.tv/ (accessed 10 April 2011).

Arrington M., 2011. Amazingly, MySpace's Decline Is Accelerating [online] 23 March 2011. Available at: http://techcrunch.com/2011/03/23/amazingly-myspaces-decline-is-accelerating/ (accessed 26 July 2011).

Arts Council England, 2010. *Achieving Great Art for Everyone. A Strategic Framework for the Arts* [online]. Available at: http://www.artscouncil.org.uk/media/uploads/achieving_great_art_for_everyone.pdf (accessed 16 June 2011).

Arts Council England, Museums Libraries and Archives Council, and Arts and Business, 2010. *Digital Audiences: Engagement with Arts and Culture Online* [online] November. Available at: http://www.artscouncil.org.uk/media/uploads/doc/Digital_

audiences_final.pdf (accessed 08 June 2011).

BARB (Broadcasters' Audience Research Board), 2010. *Overnight figures*. London: BARB.

BARB (Broadcasters' Audience Research Board), 2011a. *BARB Bulletin* 26, February 2011. London: BARB [online]. Available at: www.barb.co.uk/news/itemsubscriber/id/214/?source=primary (accessed 01 April 2011).

BARB (Broadcasters' Audience Research Board), 2011b. Multi-Channel Development 1992–2011 (Homes 000's) [online]. Available at: http://www.barb.co.uk/facts/multiChannelDevelopment (accessed 29 July 2011).

Barnett E., 2011. Facebook used by half the UK population. *The Telegraph* [online] 02 March 2011. Available at: http://www.telegraph.co.uk/technology/facebook/8356755/Facebook-used-by-half-the-UK-population.html (accessed 25 July 2011).

Bell T., 2011. Smartphones and spheres of influence. *O'Reilly Radar* [online] 20 July 2011. Available at: http://radar.oreilly.com/2011/07/smartphones-spheres-of-influence.html (accessed 27 July 2011).

The British Museum, 2011a. The British Museum [video online]. Available at: http://www.youtube.com/user/britishmuseum (accessed 25 July 2011).

The British Museum, 2011b. *The British Museum. Reports and Accounts for the Year Ended 31 March 2011* [online] 13 July 2011. Available at: http://www.official-documents.gov.uk/document/hc1012/hc13/1325/1325.pdf (accessed 12 September 2011).

Buonanno M. and Radice J., 2008. *The age of television. Experiences and theories*. Bristol: Intellect Books.

Channel 4, 2011. Time Team [online]. Available at: http://www.channel4.com/programmes/time-team/episode-guide (accessed 15 July 2011).

Clifton B., 2010. *Advanced Web Metrics with Google Analytics*. Indianapolis: Wiley Publishing.

Conlan T., 2011. Young people 'would rather live without TV than mobiles or net'. *Guardian.co.uk* [online] 19 April 2011. Available at: http://www.guardian.co.uk/media/2011/apr/19/young-people-tv-mobiles-net (accessed 02 May 2011).

Commission of the European Communities, 2007. *Communication from the Commission to the European Parliament, the Council, the European Economic and Social Committee and the Committee of the Regions* [online]. Available at: http://eur-lex.europa.eu/LexUriServ/LexUriServ.do?uri=COM:2007:0242:FIN:EN:PDF (accessed 15 September 2011).

Daniel G., 1978. Introduction. In R. Sutcliffe ed., 1978. *Chronicle: Essays from Ten Years of Television Archaeology*. London: BBC.

DCMS and BERR (Department for Culture Media and Sport and Department for Business Innovation and Skills), 2009. *Digital Britain. Final Report* [online] June 2009. Available at: http://webarchive.nationalarchives.gov.uk/20100511084737/http://www.culture.gov.uk/images/publications/digitalbritain-finalreport-jun09.pdf (accessed 02 September 2011).

Di Blasi D., 2011. *Information on Archeologia Viva TV* [telephone interview]. (Personal Communication, 23 April 2011).

Dolan E., 2008. *Mentoring in Academia and Industry*. New York: Springer.

EBU (European Broadcasting Union), 2008. *Broadcasters and the Internet. Executive summary* [online]. Available at: http://www.ebu.ch/CMSimages/en/Internet%20report_Exec%20sum_tcm6-64175.pdf (accessed 20 December 2008).

European Commission, 2010. *Communication from the Commission to the European Parliament, the Council, the European Economic and Social Committee and the Committee for Regions. A Digital Agenda for Europe* [online]. Available at: http://eur-lex.europa.eu/LexUriServ/LexUriServ.do?uri=COM:2010:0245:FIN:EN:PDF (accessed 15 September 2011).

Evans E., 2011. *Transmedia Television*. New York: Routledge.

Experian Hitwise, 2011. Data Center - Top Sites & Engines [online]. Available at: http://www.hitwise.com/uk/datacentre/main/dashboard-7323.html (accessed 29 July 2011).

Finnis J., Chan S., and Clements R., 2011. How to Evaluate Online Success? A New Piece of Action Research. In Trant J. and Bearman D. eds, 2011. *Museums and the Web 2011: Proceedings*. Toronto: Archives and Museum Informatics [online] 31 March 2011. Available at: http://conference.archimuse.com/mw2011/papers/how_to_evaluate_online_success (accessed 26 July 2011).

Garrahan M., 2009. The rise and fall of MySpace [online] 04 December 2009. Available at: http://www.ft.com/cms/s/2/fd9ffd9c-dee5-11de-adff-00144feab49a.html#axzz1TK1iZYYR (accessed July 26 2011)

Gibs J., 2008. The New Screen for Video. In Gerbarg D., 2008. *Television Goes Digital*. New York: Springer, pp. 11–28.

Google, 2011a. Site Profile: vimeo.com. *Doubleclick ad planner* [online]. Available at: https://www.google.com/adplanner/planning/site_profile?hl=en#siteDetails?uid=domain%253A%2520vimeo.com&geo=GB&lp=true (accessed 01 August 2011).

Google, 2011b. Site Profile: youtube.com. *Doubleclick ad planner* [online]. Available at: https://www.

google.com/adplanner/planning/site_profile?hl=en#siteDetails?uid=domain%253A%2520youtube.com&geo=GB&lp=true (accessed 01 August 2011).

Hatley R., 1997. Picks, Shovels ... and a Ton of Hi-Tech Tricks. *London Times*, 22 October, pp. 14–15.

Henson D., 2006. Television archaeology: education or entertainment? *Institute of Historical Research conference publications* [online]. Available at: http://www.history.ac.uk/resources/history-in-british-education/first-conference/henson-paper (accessed on 15 July 2011).

Henson D., 2011. *Heritage Programmes* [email]. (Personal Communication, 01 August 2011).

Higgins C., 2009. Museums' future lies on the Internet, say Serota and MacGregor. *The Guardian* [online] 08 July 2009. Available at: http://www.guardian.co.uk/artanddesign/2009/jul/08/museums-future-lies-online (accessed 25 July 2011).

Hjorth-Andersen C., 2007. Book Review: Chris Anderson, The Long Tail: How Endless Choice is Creating Unlimited Demand. The New Economics of Culture and Commerce. *Journal of Cultural Economics* (2007) 31, pp. 235–237.

InSites Consulting, 2009. InSites Consulting | press release [online] 13 January 2009. Available at: http://www.insites.be/02/MyDocuments/PressreleaseInSitesWOMUK_13_01.pdf (accessed 25 July 2011).

Jensen R., 1999. *The Dream Society. How The Coming Shift From Information To Imagination Will Transform Your Business*. New York: McGraw-Hill.

Jordan P., 1981. Archaeology and Television. In Evans J., Cuncliffe B. and Renfrew C. eds, 1981. *Antiquity and man: essays in honour of Glyn Daniel*. London: Thames and Hudson, pp. 207–213.

Kaushik A., 2007. Standard Metrics Revisited: #3: Bounce Rate. *Occam's Razor* [blog] 06 August 2007. Available at: http://www.kaushik.net/avinash/standard-metrics-revisited-3-bounce-rate/ (accessed 01 April 2011).

Kotler N., 1999. Delivering experience: Marketing the museum's full range of assets. *American Association of Museums* [online]. Available at: http://www.aam-us.org/pubs/mn/MN_MJ99_DeliveringExperience.cfm (accessed 22 October 2011).

Kotler G. and Kotler P., 1998. *Museum strategy and marketing: designing missions, building audiences, generating revenue and resources*. San Francisco: Jossey-Bass.

Kulik K., 2007. A Short History of Archaeological Communication. In Clack T. and Brittain M. eds, 2007. *Archaeology and the Media*. Walnut Creek, California: Left Coast Press, pp. 111–124.

Lockstone L., 2007. Major case study: shape shifters – the role and function of modern museums. In Rentschler R. and Hede A-M. eds, 2007. *Museum Marketing. Competing in the Global Marketplace*. Oxford: Elsevier, pp. 61–68.

McDowell W., 2006. *Broadcast television: a complete guide to the industry*. New York: Peter Lang Publishing.

MacGregor N. and Serota N., 2009. The Museum of the 21st Century [online] 07 July 2009. Available at: http://www2.lse.ac.uk/PublicEvents/events/2009/20090311t1917z001.aspx (accessed 25 July 2011).

McQuail D., 2005. *McQuail's Mass Communication Theory*. London: SAGE.

Menduni E., 2006. *I linguaggi della radio e della televisione. Teorie, tecniche, formati*. Roma: Laterza.

Miro Community, 2011. Introduction [online]. Available at: http://www.mirocommunity.org/ (accessed 25 July 2011).

Mower J., 2000. Trench Warfare: Time Team and the Presentation of Archaeology. *Papers from the Institute of Archaeology* 11 (2000), pp. 1–6.

NCCPE (National Co-ordinating Centre for Public Engagement), 2011. What is Public Engagement? Definition [online]. Available at: http://www.publicengagement.ac.uk/what (accessed 29 July 2011).

Noam E., 2008. TV or not TV: Where Video is Going. In Gerbarg D., 2008. *Television Goes Digital*. New York: Springer, pp. 7–10.

Ofcom (Office of Communication), 2007. *Communications Market Report* [online] 23 August 2007. Available at: http://stakeholders.ofcom.org.uk/binaries/research/cmr/cm07_1.pdf (accessed 20 December 2008).

Ofcom (Office of Communication), 2010. *Communications Market Report* [online] 19 August 2010. Available at: http://stakeholders.ofcom.org.uk/binaries/research/cmr/753567/CMR_2010_FINAL.pdf (accessed 20 July 2010).

Ofcom (Office of Communication), 2011. *Communications Market report: UK* [online] 04 August 2011. Available at: http://stakeholders.ofcom.org.uk/binaries/research/cmr/cmr11/UK_CMR_2011_FINAL.pdf (accessed 17 October 2011).

Pekarik A., Doering Z. D., and Karns D. A., 1999. Exploring satisfying experiences in museums. *Curator* 42/2, pp. 152–173.

Pettrigrew R., 2011. *Information on The Archaeology Channel* [email]. (Personal Communication, 21 April 2011).

Piccini A., 2007. *A survey of heritage television viewing figures* [online]. Available at: http://www.britarch.ac.uk/publications/bulletin/piccini_full.html (accessed 14

April 2011).

Pine J. and Gilmore J., 1999. *The Experience Economy. Work is Theatre and Every Business a Stage.* Boston: Harvard Business School Press.

Prescott Street, 2011. Home [online]. Available at: http://www.lparchaeology.com/prescot/ (accessed 25 July 2011).

360 Production, 2011. Clip: 360 history [online]. Available at: http://www.360production.com/index.php/category/360-history/ (accessed 25 July 2011).

Pruneti P., 2011. *Information on Archeologia Viva TV* [email]. (Personal Communication, 21 April 2011).

Schadla-Hall T. and Morris G., 2003. Ancient Egypt on the Small Screen – from Fact to Fiction in the UK. In MacDonald S. and Rice M. eds, 2003. *Consuming Ancient Egypt.* London: UCL Press, pp. 195–214.

Simonscat, 2011. Simon's Cat [video online]. Available at: http://www.youtube.com/user/simonscat (accessed 25 July 2011).

Sperimentarea.tv, 2011. Homepage [online]. Available at: http://www.sperimentarea.tv/ (accessed 10 April 2011).

Stein R., Incandela D., Munar J., Miller W., Burnette A., Hart D., and Proctor N., 2010. ArtBabble: A Year's Worth of Lessons Learned and Thoughts about Collaborative Content Platforms. In Trant J. and Bearman D. eds, 2010. *Museums and the Web 2010: Proceedings.* Toronto: Archives and Museum Informatics [online] 31 March 2010. Available at: http://www.archimuse.com/mw2010/papers/stein-incandela/stein-incandela.html (accessed 26 July 2011).

Sweney M., 2010. Britons 'watch four hours of TV a day'. *The Guardian* [online] 04 May 2010. Available at: http://www.guardian.co.uk/media/2010/may/04/thinkbox-television-viewing (accessed 25 July 2011).

Taylor T., 1998. *Behind the Scenes at Time Team.* London: Macmillan Publishers Ltd.

Thames Discovery Programme, 2011. Home [online]. Available at: http://www.thamesdiscovery.org/ (accessed 25 July 2011).

Tonkin S., Whitmore C. and Cutroni J., 2010. *Performance Marketing with Google Analytics: Strategies and Techniques for Maximizing Online ROI.* Indianapolis: Wiley Publishing.

UCLTV, 2011. Available at: http://www.youtube.com/user/UCLTV (accessed 11 October 2011).

The Victoria and Albert Museum, 2008. V&A – The Victoria and Albert Museum [video online]. Available at: http://www.youtube.com/user/vamuseum (accessed 25 July 2011).

Videola. Open Source IPTV, 2011. Home [online]. Available at: http://www.videola.tv/ (accessed 25 July 2011).

Wessex Archaeology, 2011. Home [online]. Available at: http://www.wessexarch.co.uk/ (accessed 25 July 2011).

West A., 2004. Archaeology and Television. In Henson D., Stone P., and Corbishley M., 2004. *Education and the Historic Environment.* London: Routledge, pp. 113–119.

Zettl H., 2006. *Television Production Handbook.* Belmont: Thomson Wadsworth.

Smartphones and Site Interpretation: the Museum of London's *Streetmuseum* Applications

Meriel Jeater

Abstract

Developments in mobile phone technology are opening up new ways for the public to access archaeological information and engage with archaeological sites or artefacts. In May 2010, the Museum of London launched its first smartphone software application (app), the augmented reality app *Streetmuseum*. This successful app has paved the way for further developments which extend the use of this technology into archaeology.

This article sets the *Streetmuseum* app in context by looking at the tradition of using handheld and mobile devices in museums and historic sites, discusses the growth in museum smartphone apps and developments in the use of augmented reality in museums, and provides an overview of the other archaeology-themed smartphone apps currently available. The concept and development of *Streetmuseum* is then explained. This article looks at how the technology was advanced and adapted to produce a new app called *Streetmuseum Londinium*, which covers the Roman archaeology of London. It also explores the public response to the apps and details the lessons learnt for similar future projects.

Introduction

Streetmuseum and *Streetmuseum Londinium* (launched by the Museum of London in May 2010 and July 2011 respectively) are location-based augmented reality (AR) smartphone apps. AR inserts digital content into users' views of the real world, creating an immersive experience (Morrison and Gu 2010: 193). The *Streetmuseum* apps use AR technology to overlay historic images and video on the modern street scene as viewed through the camera of a user's smartphone. They are principally designed for use in the streets of London, though the non-AR content can be accessed wherever the user is. This article discusses the development of these apps in the context of the handheld devices, apps and AR projects produced by museums and other historic places.

The context

Museums and historic sites: handheld devices and mobile interpretation

It is very natural that museums should want to enter the market for smartphone apps as these are just the latest in a long line of handheld devices that museums have been experimenting with for many years. The first museum handheld device was introduced by the Stedelijk Museum in Amsterdam in 1952. There, visitors could listen to lectures on artworks via a portable radio and headphones (Tallon 2008: xiii). From these rudimentary beginnings, increasingly sophisticated audio-guides and other multimedia devices have evolved.

Developments in mobile technology have led other cultural sites to experiment with providing visitor content via handheld devices in outdoor venues such as cemeteries, archaeological sites and historic cities. Over the last ten or more years, many trials have taken place using mobile context-aware technology and Global Positioning Systems (GPS), since the earliest work on a location-aware tourist guide called *Cyberguide* in 1996 (Cheverst *et al.* 2000)[1]. Mobile tours are particularly suitable for places where it is impossible to add signs or any other kinds of permanent interpretation (Dow *et al.* 2005). A recent prototype mobile guide was developed for the Shrine of Remembrance in Melbourne, Australia, which showed images, objects, film, video, audio and text relating to parts of the shrine. User testing revealed results that are particularly relevant to *Streetmuseum* and *Streetmuseum Londinium*: lining up historic film with the present day space is an effective way of transporting visitors back in time; visitors responded positively to the presentation of absent objects; visitor attention spans are very short when watching films or listening to audio (Smith *et al.* 2010: 354).

There has also been a drive to create flexible, personalised mobile tours of cultural spaces, which provide information adapted to the personal needs of the user but most ideas have not gone beyond prototype stage (Bonfigli *et al.* 2001; Cheverst *et al.* 2000; Vlahakis *et al.* 2001). The *GUIDE* system, created by Lancaster University, was an early development using a handheld device to help visitors explore historic Lancaster. However, it was limited by the complexity of the system and the battery life of the handheld computer, which was only two hours. Technology has moved on a lot since then, making more powerful, smaller machines available. The developers of *GUIDE* rightly anticipated that mobile phones would become the future method of delivering such content (Cheverst *et al.* 2000).

For a long time handheld devices of all kinds have had their detractors. They are thought to distract visitors from museum objects and isolate visitors from their companions (Gammon and Burch 2008: 38; Filippini-Fantoni and Bowen 2008: 82). One prototype project, *Sotto Voce*, aimed to release visitors from the traditional audio tour bubble by allowing them to eavesdrop on their companions as well as providing visual information on a handheld device, which produced positive results (Aoki *et al.* 2002). It may be that allowing visitors to use their mobile phones in museums is not the solution to this perennial problem (see smartphone apps section below). During experiments at the Shrine of Remembrance, it was demonstrated that visitors using visual mobile guides were reluctant to interact with each other (Smith *et al.* 2010: 354).

Other prototype systems have been developed to enable visitors to share their mobile tours of cultural venues on the basis that a shared experience is more enjoyable. The *George Square* project (a joint project between the University of Glasgow, UK, and the University of Queensland, Australia) allowed a remote visitor to share a visit to *George Square* in Glasgow with a physical visitor. The remote visitor used a laptop and the physical visitor used a handheld tablet computer. Both participants wore headphones and a microphone so they could talk to each other. The physical visitor took photos of what they could see and shared them with the remote visitor by uploading them to the *George Square* system. The premise behind this function was that people enjoy sharing their holiday photos with friends after their visit so why should they not be able to do it during their visit (Brown *et al.* 2005). However, the ability of people to instantly share photos with their entire social circle by uploading them from their mobile phones to websites like Facebook has made this system rather redundant today. The concept of visitors

---

[1] Examples of other trials of mobile context-aware guides can be found in the following publications: Crofts 2011; Arvanitis 2010; Smith *et al.* 2010; Dow *et al.* 2005; Epstein and Vergani 2006; Brown *et al.* 2005.

sharing their responses, experiences and discoveries is something that is predicted to become an increasing part of museum mobile interpretation and is already part of many museums' mobile content (Smith 2009; Proctor 2010).

In recent years it is not just audio content that is available on museums' handheld devices but also elements like video, games and text, making them truly multimedia. The last ten years of developments in mobile multimedia in museums have been discussed at length by Filippini-Fantoni and Bowen (2008: 79–96).

Multimedia handheld devices have been shown to benefit and attract young visitors who have been brought up to expect a high level of audiovisual information and interactivity (Filippini-Fantoni and Bowen 2008: 82). Research has shown that audio tours delivered through users' own mobile phones were most popular with younger audiences (Proctor 2007). A study by the Liberty Science Centre in America found that young people's lives are dominated by their mobile phones. Teenagers constantly share photographs and information about their lives with friends via their phones and the Internet, and therefore mobile phones may provide the key to engaging young people with museums (Bressler 2006).

Providing visitors with information via their own mobile phones is a very logical step for museums. With constant updates to technology and the high cost for museums of loaning visitors handheld devices (costs such as buying the handsets, charging their batteries and maintaining them), it makes sense for visitors to use the handheld device that most carry with them all the time – their mobile phone (Tallon 2008: xviii; Proctor 2007).

Mobile phone technology could bring about huge changes in the way that visitors engage with museums and their collections (Stephens 2010). Koven J. Smith (2009) has argued that mobile multimedia devices could be used to totally change the way that people visit museums and enable them to generate their own tours, find out information about any object in the collection and to post their responses to the displays as they move around the museum while reading the comments that other visitors are also posting.

Museums are increasingly aiming to provide greater access to their collections and their knowledge via digital means (Proctor 2010). The Internet and mobile phones are the ideal medium for achieving this and are 'an alternative means to reproduce, distribute and popularise the museum content' (Arvanitis 2010: 170). Museums thus have the opportunity to enter people's everyday lives and make their content available to people in their own time, not just during a physical visit.

The growth of smartphone apps for heritage and culture

Since 2000 the use and development of smartphones has been widespread and their adoption is growing each year. Over 400 million mobile phones were sold worldwide in the second quarter of 2011 and 25% of these sales were for smartphones (Gartner 2011). Apple launched its iconic iPhone in 2007 (BBC News 2007) and then its iTunes app store in 2008 (Stephens 2010), which provides all kinds of software applications that enable users to access information, games and other content on their iPhones. Android smartphone apps followed soon after. Now apps have entered the museum sector and look set to stay for the near future.

A large number of museums and galleries across the world have developed apps to engage visitors either within their walls or outside. The National Gallery in London was the first museum to develop an iPhone app, *LoveArt*, which was launched in 2009 (Lagoudi and Sexton 2010). Since then many cultural organisations have followed suit[2]. There are currently over 500,000 apps available on iTunes alone and the number is growing daily (Apple 2011).

With the development of the Internet and mobile phone technology, the public now expects to be able to get information on anything, anywhere and anytime. Tallon (2008: xvii) argues that 'To remain relevant to today's public, museums must follow

---

[2] See Bickerseth 2011, Grobart 2011 and Stephens 2010, for details of some of the main museum and gallery apps available.

these trends and meet these evolving visitor expectations'. Therefore, although smartphone apps are relatively new, expensive and could potentially be risky, museums should experiment with them in order to provide what an increasing portion of the public wants.

As smartphone apps are becoming a more common part of a museum or gallery's visitor offer, the Museums Association released an online guide to the subject in 2010 to help institutions who were thinking of investing in an app (Stephens 2010). Apps are seen as a good way of reaching new audiences, increasing the amount of digital collections information available and improving mobile interpretation (Stephens 2010; Proctor 2010). As Proctor (2010) states, 'Web apps and iPhones are the latest great hope, and offer exciting new ways of reaching audiences on-site and beyond'.

The UK government is also encouraging museums to develop new ways of using emerging technologies to engage with wider audiences (Culture24 2010) and the Department for Culture, Media and Sport has issued a best practice document on the subject called *Encouraging Digital Access to Culture* where Margaret Hodge, Minister for Culture and Tourism (DCMS 2010: 2), said 'Our goal must be to use digital media to encourage new audiences to delight in the richness of our arts and culture – and to enrich and deepen the experiences of those who are hungry for more'.

DCMS (2010: 5) advises that while 'no-one can underestimate the huge value of being in a live audience, seeing the real artefact…Digital services can complement and enhance such experiences'. The document (DCMS 2010: 35) recommends that digital services should be 'integrated into real-world experiences'. This is certainly what the *Streetmuseum* apps intend to do: enhance a user's experience of London, revealing the hidden histories behind the modern cityscape.

Apps are evolving that are becoming so much more than the traditional museum audio tour. The American Museum of Natural History has an app (AMNH Explorer) that provides collections information but also, using Wi-Fi triangulation, knows exactly where you are in the museum and can give you precise directions. The AMNH building is huge so having its own version of satellite navigation for visitors is incredibly useful (Grobart 2011).

There is some concern over the use of smartphone apps within the museum setting. There is a fear that visitors will spend their whole time staring at their phone rather than the exhibits or that fiddling with an app will detract from their visit. Bodle (2010) states (regarding art exhibitions): 'The nuances of how a show is hung could easily be lost with most of the audience's heads bent, looking at the corresponding image on their phones'. Other critics have tried various smartphone apps in museums and were left frustrated and distracted. Rothstein (2010) found using an app in The American Museum of Natural History isolated objects rather than connecting them and was more effort than just walking around and looking. For him the Museum of Modern Art's app was 'fussy and interfering' and Brooklyn Museum's app, which allows visitors to 'like' exhibits and 'tag' them, was 'time-consuming' and 'unilluminating'. Ultimately Rothstein viewed the apps he tried as 'flawed works in progress'.

Perhaps the more successful apps may prove to be the type that are not just designed to enhance a physical visit to a museum or gallery but those that take a museum's content and make it relevant to the world outside. According to Grobart (2011), the best museum apps are those that provide information during a visit but can also be used at home to access the collections.

There is also a concern that apps are just a much-hyped, short-lived fad, and an expensive one at that (Connolly 2011; Stephens 2010). Museums are warned to ensure that producing an app is part of their wider mission: this will hopefully prevent the app becoming an expensive mistake that achieves little in terms of public engagement (Connolly 2011).

However, some institutions are fully embracing the new mobile phone technology and making it an integral part of their in-gallery interpretation. MONA, the Museum of Old and New Art in Australia, has no exhibit labels. Instead all their content is delivered via iPod touches which visitors can borrow for free (Bickerseth 2011).

Archaeology apps: what else is out there?

Currently there are few archaeology apps on the marketplace but more are being devised all the time[3]. Most charge a fee for downloading them. The Greek journal *Archaeology and the Arts* has its own app which contains summaries of the last thirty years of content from the journal. There is an *Archaeology iGuide* app available on iTunes for $4.99, which contains information and images of famous archaeological discoveries or objects such as the Vindolanda Tablets and the Staffordshire Hoard. It is also available for Android phones but does not appear to be particularly popular; at time of writing (October 2011) the Android version of the app had less than 100 downloads and only one user comment. *ArchaeoBox* is an iPhone app designed to provide users with up-to-date archaeological news but has been criticised for frequently crashing (Stevebirchard n.d.).

Some companies are producing app tours of historical or archaeological sites *(RAMA)*, such as Pompeii, which costs $2.99. *The Archaeology App* is an Android app to help users find Irish archaeological sites for a fee of €4.99. It uses GPS to find sites closest to you. Again, this seems to have limited appeal so far and has had less than 50 downloads at time of writing. For £6.99 users can download *Discovering Provence – Archaeology Virtual App*, which provides six hour-long programmes containing videos. Interactive Places is a company that specialises in creating location-specific smartphone apps. They have made app-based interactive tours, treasure hunts and trails around towns such as Bristol and London, and as a test project, made an app tour of Chedworth Roman Villa where visitors are guided round by Roman characters.

Other related apps, though not directly archaeological, are the National Trust's app that tells you where your nearest National Trust property is and information about it, and the similar *Heritage App*, which tells you where your nearest heritage property is, including English Heritage sites.

With the exception of the Interactive Places apps, most of the current archaeology-themed apps provide information in a quite simple way and none of them (apart from *Streetmuseum Londinium*) yet feature augmented reality.

Augmented reality

This section looks at previous iterations of AR systems in museums and heritage sites to set *Streetmuseum* in its context[4].

Museums and science centres have been trialling AR systems for several years, such as the National Science Museum in Tokyo, Japan, where AR technology was used to add flesh to dinosaur skeletons in the gallery (Kondo *et al.* 2007). Most systems have been available via a handheld personal digital assistant (PDA) within the museum building. One of the major problems with some of the systems was that they required users to wear or carry bulky equipment such as a backpack and a special head-mounted display. This isolates users from each other and can be a lonely experience (Snyder and Elinich 2010: 88). Not all AR systems were like this; Graz University of Technology developed a 3D interactive AR museum tour and multi-user games which were available on a small PDA with an inbuilt camera. Visualisations and animations were superimposed onto real exhibits to add context (Schmalstieg and Wagner 2005).

The closest previous experience to *Streetmuseum Londinium* was a prototype AR guide developed for the archaeological site of ancient Olympia in Greece, with the first user-testing results published in 2001 (Vlahakis *et al.* 2001). The *ARCHEOGUIDE* (Augmented Reality-based Cultural Heritage On-site Guide) provided AR reconstructions of the ancient ruins and audio information. Developers tested various ways of delivering the guide, including asking users to wear a helmet on which a compass and camera were mounted, AR glasses and a backpack containing the laptop which communicated with the system and had a GPS signal. The other less immersive versions were available via hand-held devices which had more limited

---

[3] See Appendix B for a complete list of the apps mentioned in this section, including URLs.
[4] For further research into AR, see Valeonti 2010 and http://valeonti.com/ (accessed 31 October 2011).

capabilities. The *ARCHEOGUIDE* test group preferred the quality of the AR available with the fully immersive system but did not like the bulky equipment required. Younger audiences with more computer knowledge were the most enthusiastic about the experience. As well as 3D computer reconstructions of Olympic buildings, users could also see computer animated athletes competing in the ancient stadium. These athletes were entirely computer generated, unlike the films of actors used in *Streetmuseum Londinium* (see below). A similar, though non-archaeological, prototype AR system was developed in Atlanta, USA: the *Ghosts of Sweet Auburn* project. Like the *ARCHEOGUIDE* system, users wore head-mounted displays but instead of viewing computer generated figures, they encountered films of actors. The developers felt that users would feel much more emotional involvement when viewing a real person (MacIntyre *et al.* 2001). One of the problems with these prototypes was the expense of the equipment (Vlahakis *et al.* 2001). However, nowadays these problems can be overcome by providing similar experiences via users' own smartphones, as *Streetmuseum* and other apps do.

Though the Museum of London was the first UK museum to produce AR smartphone apps, they were not alone in using this technology. Appropriately, for the first museum to introduce audio tours in the 1950s (Fidel 2010), the Stedelijk Museum in Amsterdam was also one of the first to introduce an AR smartphone app, not for archaeology but for art. Using an application called Layar[5], smartphone users can see virtual artworks 'hung' in real spaces. The app was first launched as part of their *ARtours* programme in May 2010; through the project *Me in Museum Square* student artists were able to virtually hang their works for the public to see on their smartphones in Museum Square in Amsterdam (MobiThinking 2010). At other events that summer and autumn, users could hang images of works from the Stedelijk collection at whatever coordinates they liked and also see where other people had hung them (Fidel 2010). By October 2010, artists had used Layar to add virtual artworks in the Museum of Modern Art in New York without the museum's permission (Porter 2010). Next, the Stedelijk plans to move the *ARtours* project within the museum building and enable visitors to create their own *ARtours* (Stedelijk Museum n.d.).

Streetmuseum is not the only AR system to superimpose historic images onto real street scenes or buildings. The effect of doing this has been investigated for the purposes of archaeological and architectural research. Morrison and Gu (2010: 194) have suggested that 'overlaying the virtual reconstruction onto a real life site can assist in confirming the accuracy and the feasibility of the reconstruction'. In 2009, the Fraunhofer Institute for Computer Graphics Research developed AR software that overlaid historic images onto modern photographs taken on an iPhone. Users could take photographs of the Brandenburg Gate or the Reichstag in Berlin and the software would automatically overlay the historic view, whatever side of the building was photographed (Morrison and Gu 2010: 194). The SARA (Stedelijke Augmented Reality Applicatie) project at the Netherlands Architecture Institute has also used AR to bring historic architecture to life. This smartphone app was launched in December 2009 and like *ARtours*, it uses the AR browser Layar. Users can find out textual information about buildings in Rotterdam and other cities in the Netherlands as well as photos, audio and video. Through their smartphone, users can see past pictures of buildings at specific locations, as well as designs that were never implemented and future plans (Lemmens 2010).

Streetmuseum

What is 'Streetmuseum'?

Streetmuseum is an AR smartphone app, one of the first of its kind to be released. Users can look through their phone's camera in one of over 200 street locations in London and see the past emerge, locked as an overlay across the present

---

[5] Layar (augmented reality browser): http://www.layar.com/ (accessed 31 October 2011).

scene. Historic photographs or paintings from the Museum's collection can be viewed as ghostly alignments, or the archive images can be brought up and explored in detail. Often the results of the overlay can look very dramatic (**Figure 13**). The app also provides information about the image and its historical significance.

One of the advantages of this type of app is that it relates the museum's collections to the world outside, negating the normal criticism that apps divorce visitors from the museum experience (see above). *Streetmuseum* has been designed for use in the street or at home and uses the Museum of London's collection to enhance people's experiences of London (though one of its aims is to encourage subsequent museum visits).

Figure 13. Bomb damage at 21 Queen Victoria Street, 1941, © Museum of London/By Kind Permission of The Commissioner of the City of London Police (see Plate 10).

Where did 'Streetmuseum' come from?

In January 2010, the Museum of London sent out a brief for the creation of a viral marketing campaign to promote its new Galleries of Modern London, which were due to open in May that year. The viral had to link to the main advertising campaign which used the strapline 'You are here' accompanied by historic photographs and paintings of London. These were displayed in relevant locations (for instance a World War II photograph of the bombed Underground station at Bank was used on a poster in the very same station) to encourage the public to make the connection between past and present London, and to prompt people to explore that link in the Galleries of Modern London.

The brief was sent to a creative agency called Brothers and Sisters who were asked to come up with a series of possible concepts. The most exciting and relevant proposal was the creation of an iPhone app which would allow people to stand in certain locations in London and see images of what the streets looked like in the past, using the Museum's extensive collections.

The concept was particularly appealing because it used what was, at the time, very new technology. As the first UK museum to produce an app like this, the Museum of London could show that it was cutting-edge, helping to reposition the organisation as a modern and connected museum. The marketing team felt confident that the app would generate lots of press interest for this reason. An iPhone app was especially appropriate for London as the capital has more iPhone users than anywhere else in the country. In 2010, over 250,000 Londoners owned an iPhone (Brothers and Sisters 2010). Even people without iPhones were likely to be able to see the app in use as users shared their newly downloaded app with friends.

Marketing was not the only driving force behind the app. The Museum of London wanted to try new, dynamic ways of engaging people with London's history and highlighting the fantastic collections that it holds. As Vicky Lee, the Museum's Marketing Manager stated (Attewill 2011), 'The success of *Streetmuseum* has shown that museums can bring history to life in new and exciting ways, taking their collections to the streets rather than relying on visitors coming to them'. Museums across the country are increasingly focusing on outreach and engaging with new users beyond their walls; the Museum of London's iPhone app became the perfect tool to do this.

How was 'Streetmuseum' developed?

The timescale for developing the app was very tight. After the Museum of London briefed Brothers and Sisters in January 2010, the agency came up with the concept in February. Work started on the app at the beginning of March and it was launched on 10 May, quite an achievement considering that the production had taken just over two months. The agency designed and programmed the app but the Museum of London provided all the content, including the images with associated captions written by museum curators.

Each image is geo-tagged with a latitude and longitude to be as accurate as possible to its original location. The agency staff actually cycled around London to physically check all the locations were correct. The Museum's Marketing Manager then double-checked the photo locations by using Google Maps and Google Street View. It is interesting to note that due to the limited time available, the production of *Streetmuseum* was reliant on Internet services such as Google Street View.

In an ideal world, more development time would have been available for user-testing to iron out any quirks. Limited time meant that the app needed to be kept simple so ideas like user-generated content could not be explored.

The cost of producing the iPhone app (**Figure 14**) was approximately £20,000. Normally a project like this would cost double that amount, however Brothers and Sisters worked at a reduced rate providing that the project would be mutually beneficial, resulting in new business leads and media coverage for the agency. They also kept the intellectual property of the technology used in the app. Due to popular demand an Android version of *Streetmuseum* was produced in December 2010, costing £28,000. The Museum of London has trademarked the title '*Streetmuseum*' to protect it from being used by others, at a cost of £200.

The public response to 'Streetmuseum'

There has been a very positive response to *Streetmuseum*, which has demonstrated that museum apps of this kind can promote the public awareness of a museum's brand to a wide audience. On its release *Streetmuseum* generated a huge reaction in the press, a response that continues today. Users still tweet and blog about the app on social networking sites, with new bursts of activity after each new press article. The interest was international as well as national, with people from countries all over the world using the app. The scale of the public reaction was very much to do with timing as we were the first UK museum to produce an AR app. The first museum app, National Gallery's *LoveArt* app, had a similar response after its launch (Lagoudi and Sexton 2010).

In the first year, over 200,000 people downloaded the app, which was 40 times more than the Museum's initial target. At the time of writing, this had increased to over 300,000 downloads. These include users as far away as Argentina and New Zealand.

Streetmuseum has been successful in raising the Museum's profile, particularly amongst young adults who are not part of the traditional museum audience. Users have posted comments on social networking sites like Twitter saying how much they like the app. Hopefully this positive reaction will translate into new visitors who want to see 'the real thing' now that they have had a taste of the Museum's virtual collections.

The Museum of London has also received official recognition for the app. In 2011 *Streetmuseum* won a Webby People's Voice award for 'Best use of device camera'; this award was especially meaningful for the Museum as it was voted for by members of the public. Between May 2010 and July 2011, *Streetmuseum* won other awards too (see Appendix A), including the Jim Blackaby Ingenuity Award at the MUSE Awards in the United States (American Association of Museums 2011a). The MUSE awards are organised by the Media & Technology Committee of

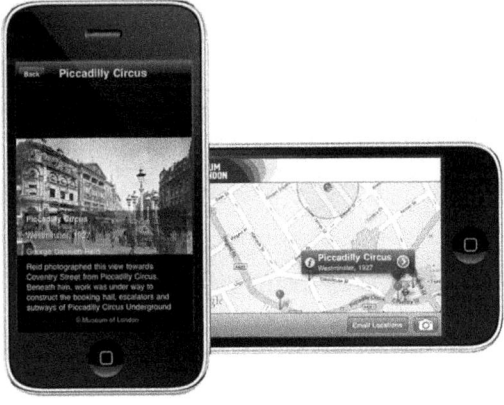

Figure 14. The finished *Streetmuseum* app © Museum of London (see Plate 11).

the American Association of Museums and recognise 'outstanding achievement in museum media'. The awards' judges said (American Association of Museums 2011b), 'The *Streetmuseum* mobile app project was a forerunner in showcasing how augmented reality and geo-location can be combined to export a museum's collections to the street on a large scale, bringing history to life in the context of the real world', which is exactly what the Museum of London was hoping to achieve with the app.

Since *Streetmuseum* launched there has also been a subsequent collaboration with Nokia to produce another app called *Soundtrack to London*, highlighting London's musical heritage.

Further developments: *Streetmuseum Londinium*

Following on from the success of *Streetmuseum*, the Museum of London's Department of Archaeological Collections and Archive wanted to develop a new version of the app specifically for Roman London in order to raise awareness of the Roman landscape in the City and Southwark, as well as outer boroughs. It was also aimed at increasing interest in the development of a new Roman gallery at the Museum.

The new app was developed in partnership with TV channel HISTORY. It used *Streetmuseum* as a model but needed to include innovative new features, which would make it more advanced so that the Museum continued to be seen as a leader in this field. The new features included video and sound, which was produced and supplied by HISTORY as part of their in-kind support for the project, and a virtual dig tool to excavate artefacts.

Like the original app, *Streetmuseum Londinium* guides users around different locations in London using the GPS on their iPhone or iPad. At certain locations they can digitally excavate Roman objects, see reconstruction images of Roman sites, watch scenes of Roman life in situ, or listen to sounds from the Roman city.

Features of the app

The introductory screen of the app includes a scrollable timeline of major Roman events related to London, and associated images, to give users a brief background to the period; this is especially useful for people unfamiliar with Roman London.

The app uses Museum of London Archaeology's Roman London map, which was published in July 2011. The map is the most up-to-date plan of the known buildings and other structures of Roman London. Users can use a slider at the bottom of the screen to gradually reveal or hide the Roman map, which is superimposed over the modern Google map (**Figure 15**). If users are physically on the streets of London, their phone's GPS signal locates where they are on the map. This feature deals with a common problem for many traditional audio tours of museums and other sites, whether delivered via a handheld device or a mobile phone: finding the actual stops (Proctor 2007).

Users can actually 'excavate' Roman objects on their iPhone or iPad screen: by swiping their finger across the screen, they reveal a buried Roman object that was originally found at their location, which can be buried again at the touch of a button (**Figure 16**). iPhone users are even

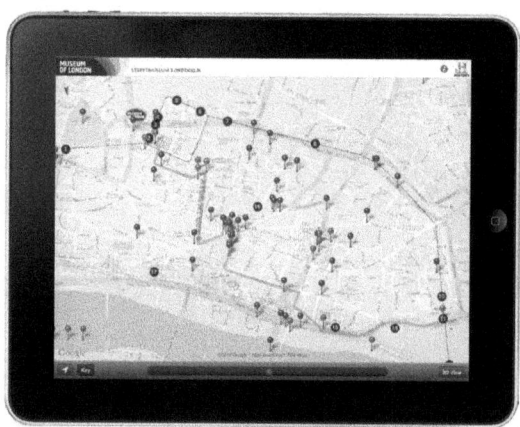

Figure 15. The map of Roman London overlaid on the modern Google map, viewed on an iPad screen © Museum of London (see Plate 12).

able to blow on their screen to remove dirt from the object; they can then 'collect' the object to add it to the total that they have already found and information about the object's history automatically appears once the artefact has been uncovered. Finally, users are able to share their find with their friends by uploading it to the social networking sites Facebook or Twitter. This allows people to show off their new discoveries and also promotes the app to potential new users amongst their online followers. The concept of visitors sharing their discoveries has been discussed above and should hopefully engage young audiences.

Research comparing the way that visitors interact with real and virtual objects in museums found that visitors do not like digital simulations that they cannot interact with (Lindgren-Streicher and Reich 2006). The digging function of *Streetmuseum Londinium* provides that vital interaction and the sense of discovery that should inspire users.

Instead of using only still images, the new app features short videos, which were created by HISTORY. The videos work in the same way as the photographs did on the original *Streetmuseum* app: users can look at the videos through their phone's camera and see them overlaid across the live street scene (the videos were filmed using green screen technology to enable this). Even if users are not actually in situ, they can watch the videos overlaid on a still image of the modern site.

The videos show typical Roman scenes performed by actors in period costume: for example, at the site of the Roman amphitheatre at the Guildhall in the City of London, users can watch a video of gladiators fighting (**Figure 17**). The short length of the videos and audio extracts (only around 15 seconds long) was determined by studies that have shown that visitors have short attention spans when listening to audio[6].

Still images are used to provide extra information about a location. Images are a mixture of excavation site photos and specially commissioned 3D reconstruction models from Museum of London Archaeology. These 3D models show users what key sites would have looked like in Roman times. Reconstructions of ancient buildings have long been shown to be successful in providing visitors with a link to the past (Ogleby and Kenderdine 2001; Coltrain 2009).

Figure 16. An 'excavated' object, viewed on an iPad screen © Museum of London (see Plate 13).

Figure 17. Video of gladiators fighting over a view of Guildhall Yard, viewed on an iPad screen © HISTORY (see Plate 14).

---

[6] For examples of such studies, see Smith *et al.* 2010 and Dow *et al.* 2005.

Finally, *Streetmuseum Londinium* also includes soundscapes at various locations to create a more immersive experience of the past. On the site of the Temple of Mithras users can hear sounds of music and religious incantations; in the area of the Roman fort there is the noise of soldiers marching; at the Diana, Princess of Wales Memorial Fountain in Hyde Park, users can hear typical sounds from a Roman farm to evoke the farmstead that once stood there. The sounds were sourced from HISTORY's audio library as well as from the Museum of London's Roman gallery soundtrack.

The public response to 'Streetmuseum Londinium'

Streetmuseum Londinium has generated very positive feedback from reviewers and users since its launch in July 2011, showing that an archaeology app that links modern topography to the past can be a successful model for archaeological interpretation. The reviews, both formal (from the press) and informal (from users' comments and tweets) have been very useful in revealing which features of the app work best and which may require further development. This in turn will aid the creation of future archaeological and museum apps. The lessons learnt are outlined below.

> Lesson 1: Get press attention. The positive reaction from the press and other websites has been invaluable in promoting the app to the public. In the first three-and-a-half weeks after launch the app was downloaded 40,000 times, helped by iTunes promoting it as their 'App of the Week' in the week beginning 8 August[7]. As there are over 500,000 apps on iTunes, apps can easily get lost without this kind of promotion. The app was featured as the top choice for *The Guardian* newspaper's technology blog 'Apps rush' on the day of launch and was tweeted to their 1.65 million followers (Dredge 2011). *The Times* made the app the focus of a double-page article on 'the 40 best arts apps' (Wagner 2011). *The Sunday Times* also reviewed the app, recommending it on their 'Planet of the Apps' page looking at history apps (Bingham 2011). *Streetmuseum Londinium* was chosen as 'Follow That App of the Week' on the review website Follow That App (2011).

> Lesson 2: Use the iPhone's functionality as an integral part of the app. Follow that App (2011) described the app as an 'excellent follow up' to *Streetmuseum* which 'makes good use of the iPhone's possibilities', referring to the digging capabilities of the app. Reviews of other apps such as *LoveArt* have shown that users loved playing with functions that are part of their iPhone: for *LoveArt* it was the zoom function that scored most highly in user reviews (Lagoudi and Sexton 2010).

> Lesson 3: Quirky game elements should be optional. The digging function of *Streetmuseum Londinium* has had mixed reviews. The Follow That App reviewer (2011) felt that 'the novelty soon wears off'. This feeling is echoed by a comment posted on iTunes (Apple, iTunes 2011) from a user who was very positive overall but said 'it would be nice to turn off the 'dig' function'. However, *The Times*' journalist (Wagner 2011) was excited by it, saying 'The digging really does produce gasps of delight from me and my son'. It seems that children

---

[7] For a list of previous apps of the week, including *Streetmuseum Londinium*, see Apple's iTunes app page, 'Previous apps of the week' (iTunes application required to access): http://itunes.apple.com/WebObjects/MZStore.woa/wa/viewRoom?cc=gb&fcId=395808350&id=25206&mt=8.

may enjoy the digging activity best whereas adults would prefer to turn it off after a few tries.

Lesson 4: Maps are a good way of relating archaeology to the modern city. The overlay of the Roman map across the modern map was particularly liked by reviewers on iTunes (Apple iTunes 2011) and in other website reviews (Nicholas 2011). *Apps Magazine* (Anon. 2011) described *Streetmuseum Londinium* as 'a must-have app for all history buffs', saying 'we particularly like the two-layer map that allows you to fully appreciate the evolution of the city'. Follow That App (2011) said the map was 'well executed' but suggested an improvement: 'to save on tired fingers and to make the content easier to read, it would be useful to have a text view to explore'.

Lesson 5: Use new technology to interpret the past. One archaeologist blogger (Meyers 2011) was particularly pleased with the app and how it highlights the importance of archaeology. She also commented: 'For now, augmented reality may just be the equivalent of having a Kindle with every travel book programmed in, but in the future this could be a powerful tool for extending the museum beyond the walls of its building and creating a deeper connection between history and space'. It is important to keep pushing the technology further however. The technology of *Streetmuseum Londinium* did not impress one user whose comment featured in the Follow That App review (2011): 'Well, I'll admit that the map is helpful and well organised and one gets an interesting tour, but the main problem is that the tech is very basic. It used compass and GPS, but there is nothing clever as far as AR is concerned'.

The future of 'Streetmuseum Londinium'
Streetmuseum Londinium launched on 25 July 2011 and at the time of writing this article, was available free of charge from iTunes for iPhones and iPads. Depending on public demand and the sourcing of extra funding it is possible that this latest app may be released for Android smartphones at a later date.

The trademarking of the *Streetmuseum* name ensures that we can bring out a series of themed apps in the future, linked to other exhibitions, galleries or time periods, which will create a strong sub-brand for the Museum of London. Where possible, we aim to offer the apps for free to attract the widest audience possible. The download rate for the *LoveArt* app dropped dramatically after the National Gallery introduced a charge of £1.99, ten weeks after launch (Lagoudi and Sexton 2010) so it may be that providing free apps is the way to ensure wide usage. Indeed, charging may set up high expectations about the content amongst users that could be disappointed. *The Archaeology App* has been criticised for its price by one user (Seandalaiocht 2011): 'Nice design and good idea but very little content for the price'.

Pros and cons of smartphone apps
Stephens (2010) and Proctor (2010) both provide a good overview of the pros and cons of smartphone apps. Here are some of the main issues:

Pros
- Apps can reach out to new audiences;
- Mobile phone technology has been shown to be popular with younger visitors;
- Apps can provide a fun, interactive and immersive experience;
- Apps can provide new ways of making a museum's collection relevant to the daily lives of people outside the museum;
- With the right 'hook', apps can be a very effective way of marketing your museum and spreading the knowledge of your brand;

- Software is being developed that will make app production easier, quicker and cheaper;
- The number of smartphone users is growing all the time – sales of smartphones increased by 74% from last year (Gartner 2011) and in a year's time it is predicted that half of all UK mobile phones will be smartphones (Arthur 2011).

Cons

- Mobile phone technology can be tricky to use within museum buildings as the structure can interfere with GPS signals, network connections and the phones' inbuilt compass;
- Users may be put off using apps if they are worried about how much their phone company may charge them;
- Apps can take up quite a lot of space in a phone's memory so there is a limit to how many people will download;
- Apps can be expensive to produce;
- At the moment apps require bespoke development for each mobile platform (e.g. iPhones and Android), which adds to the expense;
- Apps are currently very popular and the technology is growing and increasing in sophistication but will something new come along to supplant them soon?

Like most museums, the Museum of London has very limited funds to invest in new technology. None of the Museum's apps would have been possible without working in partnership with outside companies such as Brothers and Sisters or HISTORY, who sponsored the *Streetmuseum Londinium* app as a way of both reaching new audiences and of making history more accessible. As technology changes at lightning speed, museums risk being left behind or creating products that quickly become obsolete or too expensive to update. Partnership and collaboration are key to avoiding these pitfalls. By working with external organisations with similar goals, museums and other archaeological organisations can develop exciting new ways of interpreting the past which would normally be beyond their means.

Limitations of the *Streetmuseum* project

While many other multimedia devices developed for museums and other heritage sites have been subject to much formative evaluation and summative user testing, *Streetmuseum* has not. That is beyond the scope of the project, which was primarily to increase awareness of the Museum of London brand, generate media coverage and to reach out to new audiences, which it certainly has achieved. We have not conducted studies to track how visitors are using it, how it influences their behaviour, whether it enhances their interactions with their companions or encourages them to visit the Museum of London (it is not currently possible to find out from Apple who is downloading the app, apart from their country of origin). However, it would be very interesting to research more deeply the impact of this type of archaeological interpretation on users. It would be useful to know whether people are using *Streetmuseum* or *Streetmuseum Londinium* to conduct their own tours of London, how long they spend using the app, which features they use the most and how often they use the app. This knowledge would feed into the development of future apps.

Conclusion

Streetmuseum Londinium offers users an interactive and fascinating way to discover Roman London, its finds and its archaeological sites. It provides the Museum of London with the opportunity to expand its audience and raise awareness of its brand and collections. The possibilities for the future are endless and as new technology develops, the idea can be taken in a wide range of directions. A location-based app is perfect for the interpretation of archaeology, a discipline that is so tied to 'place'. It is also a highly effective way of ensuring that archaeology is seen as fun and connected to the modern world. An app designed to be used outside the museum also avoids some of the problems of in-museum use, such as visitors being distracted from displays, and instead makes museum collections relevant to the outside world. More research is needed in this area to discover the impact of apps on users.

Appendix A: *Streetmuseum* awards gained between May 2010 and July 2011

1. Visit London – Gold award for Best Marketing & PR campaign.
2. Guild of PR Practitioners – Heralds Award for best PR campaign.
3. Webby Award (People's Voice): *Streetmuseum* – Best Use of Device Camera.
4. Bronze Pencil Award – *Streetmuseum*.
5. Creative Review Annual: Best in Book – *Streetmuseum*.
6. MUSE Awards – Jim Blackaby Ingenuity Award for *Streetmuseum*.
7. Digital Revolution Awards – *Streetmuseum* Best Innovation Award.
8. Digital Revolution Awards – *Streetmuseum* Best Use of Mobile Award.
9. Campaign Big Award – *Streetmuseum* (digital category for Sport, Travel and Leisure).
10. Kinsale Shark Award – *Streetmuseum* (Utilities/Tools/Widgets/Applications category).

Appendix B: Selected heritage/archaeology apps

- Archaeology and the Arts app: http://www.topappreviews101.com/archaeology-ipad-app-5539.html.
- Archaeology app, iPhone version (iGuide): http://itunes.apple.com/us/app/archaeology-iguide/id383903123?mt=8.
- Archaeology app, Android version (Smart Guide): http://www.androidzoom.com/android_applications/books_and_reference/archaeology-smart-guide_rlay.html.
- ArchaeoBox app: http://itunes.apple.com/ca/app/archaeobox/id406223742?mt=8.
- The Archaeology App: http://www.androidzoom.com/android_applications/travel_and_local/the-archaeology-app_bhkhb.html.
- Discovering Provence – Archaeology Virtual App: http://appshopper.com/travel/discovering-provence-archaeology-virtual-app.
- Heritage app: http://heritage-app.com/.
- Interactive Places apps: http://www.interactiveplaces.co.uk/; Chedworth Roman Villa Tour: http://www.interactiveplaces.co.uklocation-specific-appschedworth-roman-villa.
- National Trust: http://itunes.apple.com/gb/app/national-trust/id360792792?mt=8.
- RAMA: http://itunes.apple.com/us/app/rama/id391888636?mt=8.

Acknowledgements

I would like to sincerely thank Vicky Lee, Marketing Manager at the Museum of London, for providing me with so much information on the *Streetmuseum* apps and many valuable comments on previous drafts of this paper. I would also like to thank Chiara Bonacchi, Rhiannon Looseley, John Joyce and Claire Ross for their extremely helpful advice and suggestions.

References

American Association of Museums, 2011a. Jim Blackaby Ingenuity Award [online]. Available at: http://www.mediaandtechnology.org/muse-awards/2011-muse-awards/jim-blackaby-ingenuity-award/ (accessed 29 July 2011).

American Association of Museums, 2011b. Muse Awards [online]. Available at: http://www.mediaandtechnology.org/muse-awards/ (accessed 14 July 2011).

Anon., 2011. Time Travel on iPad. Visit Ancient London with *Streetmuseum*. *Apps Magazine*, 01 September 2011, pp. 9–10.

Aoki P. M., Grinter R. E., Hurst A., Szymanski M. H., Thornton J. D. and Woodruff A., 2002. Sotto Voce: Exploring the interplay of conversation and mobile audio spaces. *ACM Conference on Human Factors in Computing Systems (CHI 2002)*. Minneapolis, MN, USA, 20–25 April 2002. NY: ACM, pp. 431–438.

Apple, 2011. App Store information [online]. Available at: http://www.apple.com/iphone/from-the-app-store/ (accessed 05 October 2011).

Apple iTunes, 2011. iTunes Streetmuseum Londinium page [online]. Available at: http://itunes.apple.com/gb/app/streetmuseum-londinium/id449426452?mt=8 (accessed 21 September 2011).

Arthur C., 2011. Smartphones head to 'tipping point'. *The Guardian* [online] 11 July 2011. Available at: http://www.guardian.co.uk/technology/2011/jul/11/ios-android-blackberry-smartphone-data (accessed 07 October 2011).

Arvanitis K., 2010. Museums Outside Walls: mobile phones and the museum in the everyday. In Parry R. ed., 2010. *Museums in a Digital Age*. Leicester Reader in Museum Studies. London: Routledge, pp. 170–176.

Attewill F., 2011. An i on London's past. Museum app reveals the sights and sounds of city's Roman heritage. *Metro* (London) 18 July 2011, p. 29.

BBC News, 2007. Apple iPhone debuts in UK stores [online] updated 10 November 2007. Available at: http://news.bbc.co.uk/1/hi/technology/7085643.stm (accessed 05 October 2011).

Bickerseth J., 2011. Museums, Smartphones and mobile applications [online] 31 January 2011. Available at: http://bickersteth.blogspot.com/2011/01/museums-smartphones-and-mobile.html (accessed 21 September 2011).

Bingham M., 2011. Planet of the Apps. *The Sunday Times*, 25 September 2011, p. 23.

Bodle K., 2010. Pros and Cons of Smartphones in the Museum [online] updated 26 October 2010. Available at: http://www.bocamuseum.org/index.php?src=blog&srctype=detail&blogid=44 (accessed 21 September 2011).

Bonfigli M. E., Cabri G., Leonardi L. and Zambonelli F., 2001. Mobile Devices to Assist Cultural Visits. In Bearman D. and Garzotto F. eds, 2001. *International Cultural Heritage Informatics Meeting: Proceedings from ichim01, Cultural Heritage and Technologies in the Third Millennium*. Milan, Italy, September 3–7 2001, pp. 333–340 [online]. Available at: http://www.archimuse.com/publishing/ichim01_vol2/bonfigli.pdf (accessed 21 September 2011).

Bressler D., 2006. Mobile Phones: A New Way To Engage Teenagers In Informal Science Learning. In Trant J. and Bearman D. eds, 2006. *Museums and the Web 2006: Proceedings*. Toronto: Archives & Museum Informatics [online]. Available at: http://www.archimuse.com/mw2006/papers/bressler/bressler.html (accessed 21 September 2011).

Brothers and Sisters, 2010. *Discussion on development of Streetmuseum* [conversation]. (Personal communication, February 2010).

Brown B., Chalmers M., Bell M., Hall M., MacColl I. and Rudman P., 2005. Sharing the square: collaborative leisure in the city streets. In Gellersen H., Schmidt K., Beaudouin-Lafon M. and Mackay W. eds, 2005. *Proceedings of the Ninth European Conference on Computer-Supported Cooperative Work*. Paris, France, 18–22 September 2005. Dordrecht: Springer, pp. 427–447.

Cheverst K., Davies N., Mitchell K., Friday A. and Elfstatiou C., 2000. Developing a Context-aware Electronic tourist Guide: Some Issues and Experiences. *Proceedings of ACM SIGCHI Conference of Human Factors in Computing Systems (CHI'00)*. The Hague, Netherlands, 1–6 April 2000. NY: ACM, pp. 17–24.

Coltrain J., 2009. A picture is worth 1000 pasts: how 3D virtual reconstructions can bridge the gap between visitor interest and scholarly debate. In Seal A. with Keene S. and Bowen J. eds, 2009. *EVA London 2009: Electronic Visualisation & the Arts. Proceedings of a conference held in London 6–8 July 2009*. BCS, pp. 84–91 [online]. Available at: http://www.bcs.org/upload/pdf/ewic_ev09_s4paper1.pdf (accessed 21 September 2011).

Connolly R., 2011. Museums, Archaeology and Mobile Apps. *Archaeology, Museums & Outreach* [online] 22 August 2011. Available at: http://rcnnolly.wordpress.com/2011/08/22/mobile-apps/ (accessed 03 October 2011).

Crofts C., 2011. Technologies of seeing the past: the Curzon Memories app. In Dunn S. with Bowen J. and Ng K. eds, 2011. *EVA London 2011: Electronic Visualisation & the Arts. Proceedings of a conference held in London 6–8 July*. BCS, pp. 163–170 [online]. Available at: http://ewic.bcs.org/upload/pdf/ewic_ev11_s9paper1.pdf (accessed 21 September 2011).

Culture24, 2010. Culture24 to develop new smartphone app to unlock museum and gallery collections [online] 01 April 2010. Available at: http://www.culture24.org.uk/sector+info/art77524 (accessed 03 October 2011).

DCMS (Department for Culture, Media and Sport), 2010. *Encouraging Digital Access to Culture* [online] Available at: http://fm.typepad.com/files/dcms_encouraging_digital_access_to_culture.pdf (accessed 03 October 2011).

Dow S., Lee J., Oezbek C., MacIntyre B. J. and Gandy M., 2005. Exploring spatial narratives and mixed reality experiences in Oakland Cemetery. *ACE '05, Proceedings of the 2005 ACM SIGCHI International Conference on Advances in computer entertainment technology*. Valencia, Spain, June 15–17, 2005. NY: ACM, pp. 51–60.

Dredge S., 2011. Apps Rush: Streetmuseum Londinium, Tekken Bowl, Buildings and more. *The Guardian* [online] 25 July 2011. Available at: http://www.guardian.co.uk/technology/appsblog/2011/jul/25/apps-rush-Streetmuseum-londinium-tekken-bowl-buildings?utm_source=twitterfeed&utm_medium=twitter (accessed 27 July 2011).

Epstein M. and Vergani S., 2006. History Unwired: mobile

narrative in historic cities. *Proceedings of the working conference on Advanced Visual Interfaces, AVI 2006.* Venezia, Italy, May 23–26, 2006. NY: ACM, pp. 302–305 [online]. Available at: http://web.mit.edu/frontiers/History_Unwired_Preliminary_Findings.pdf (accessed 21 September 2011).

Fidel A., 2010. Art Gets Unmasked in the Palm of Your Hand. *The New York Times* [online] 01 December 2010. Available at: http://www.nytimes.com/2010/12/02/arts/02iht-rartsmart.html (accessed 21 September 2011).

Filippini-Fantoni S. and Bowen J. P., 2008. Mobile Multimedia: Reflections from Ten Years of Practice. In Tallon L. and Walker K. eds, 2008. *Digital Technologies and the Museum Experience. Handheld Guides and Other Media.* AltaMira Press, pp. 79–96.

Follow That App, 2011. Streetmuseum Londinium review: Follow That App of the Week [online] 05 August 2011. Available at: http://followthatapp.co.uk/2011/08/05/Streetmuseum-londinium-review/ (accessed 16 August 2011).

Gammon B. and Burch A., 2008. Designing Mobile Digital Experiences. In Tallon L. and Walker K. eds, 2008. *Digital Technologies and the Museum Experience. Handheld Guides and Other Media.* AltaMira Press, pp. 35–62.

Gartner, 2011. Gartner Says Sales of Mobile Devices in Second Quarter of 2011 Grew 16.5 Percent Year-on-Year; Smartphone Sales Grew 74 Percent [online] 11 August 2011. Available at: http://www.gartner.com/it/page.jsp?id=1764714 (accessed 05 October 2011).

Grobart S., 2011. Multimedia Tour Guides on Your Smartphone. *The New York Times* [online] 16 March 2011. Available at: http://www.nytimes.com/2011/03/17/arts/design/apps-give-museum-visitors-multimedia-access.html?_r=2 (accessed 21 September 2011).

Kondo T., Shibasaki J., Arita-Kikutani H., Manabe M., Inaba R. and Mizuki A., 2007. Mixed Reality Technology at a Natural History Museum. In Trant J. and Bearman D. eds, 2007. *Museums and the Web 2007: Proceedings.* Toronto: Archives & Museum Informatics [online]. Available at: http://www.archimuse.com/mw2007/papers/kondo/kondo.html (accessed 21 September 2011).

Lagoudi E. and Sexton C., 2010. Old Masters at Your Fingertips: the Journey of Creating a Museum App for the iPhone and iTouch. In Trant J. and Bearman D. eds, 2010. *Museums and the Web 2010: Proceedings.* Toronto: Archives & Museum Informatics [online]. Available at: http://www.archimuse.com/mw2010/papers/lagoudi/lagoudi.html (accessed 03 October 2011).

Lemmens P., 2010. Connecting the Collection: From Physical Archives to Augmented Reality in the Netherlands Architecture Institute. In Trant J. and Bearman D. eds, 2010. *Museums and the Web 2010: Proceedings.* Toronto: Archives & Museum Informatics [online]. Available at: http://www.archimuse.com/mw2010/papers/lemmens/lemmens.html (accessed 21 September 2011).

Lindgren-Streicher A. and Reich C., 2006. Visitor Interactions with Digitized Artifacts. In Trant J. and Bearman D. eds, 2006. *Museums and the Web 2006: Proceedings.* Toronto: Archives & Museum Informatics [online]. Available at: http://www.archimuse.com/mw2006/papers/lindgren/lindgren.html (accessed 21 September 2011).

MacIntyre B., Bolter J. D., Moreno E. and Hannigan B., 2001. Augmented Reality as a New Media Experience. *International Symposium on Augmented Reality (ISAR 2001).* New York, NY, October 29–30, 2001 [online]. Available at: http://www.augmentedenvironments.org/lab/wp-content/uploads/2009/11/isar01-narrative.pdf (accessed 21 September 2011).

Meyers K., 2011. Revealing Londinium Under London: New AR App [online] 21 July 2011. Available at: http://chi.matrix.msu.edu/2011/07/21/revealing-londinium-under-london-new-ar-app/ (accessed 16 August 2011).

MobiThinking, 2010. How museums can bring their collections to life: an interview with Stedelijk Museum Amsterdam ARtours' Hein Wils [online]. Available at: http://mobithinking.com/how-museums-use-augmented-reality (accessed 05 October 2011).

Morrison T. and Gu N., 2010. What architectural historians can learn from augmented reality technologies. In Seal A. with Bowen J. and Ng K. eds, 2010. *EVA London 2010: Electronic Visualisation & the Arts. Proceedings of a conference held in London 6–8 July.* BCS, pp. 191–196 [online]. Available at: http://ewic.bcs.org/upload/pdf/ewic_ev11_s10paper2.pdf (accessed 21 September 2011).

Nicholas D., 2011. Explore Roman London with new mobile app. *History Today* [online] 27 July 2011. Available at: http://www.historytoday.com/blog/2011/07/explore-roman-london-new-mobile-app (accessed 16 August 2011).

Ogleby C. and Kenderdine S., 2001. Ancient Olympia as a Three Dimensional Museum Experience. In Bearman D. and Garzotto F. eds, 2001. *International Cultural Heritage Informatics Meeting: Proceedings from ichim01, Cultural Heritage and Technologies in the Third Millennium.* Milan, Italy, 3–7 September

2001, pp. 333–340 [online]. Available at: http://www.archimuse.com/publishing/ichim01_vol2/ogleby.pdf (accessed 21 September 2011).

Porter E., 2010. Is That a Dagger I See? *The New York Times* [online] 21 October 2010. Available at: http://www.nytimes.com/2010/10/22/opinion/22fri4.html (accessed 21 September 2011).

Proctor N., 2007. When In Roam: Visitor Response To Phone Tour Pilots In The US And Europe. In Trant J. and Bearman D. eds, 2007. *Museums and the Web 2007: Proceedings.* Toronto: Archives & Museum Informatics [online]. Available at: http://www.archimuse.com/mw2007/papers/proctor/proctor.html (accessed 21 September 2011).

Proctor N., 2010. The Museum Is Mobile: Cross-platform Content Design for Audiences on the Go. In Trant J. and Bearman D. eds, 2010. *Museums and the Web 2010: Proceedings.* Toronto: Archives & Museum Informatics [online]. Available at: http://www.archimuse.com/mw2010/papers/proctor/proctor.html (accessed 21 September 2011).

Rothstein E., 2010. From Picassos to Sarcophagi, Guided by Phone Apps. *The New York Times* [online] 01 October. Available at: http://www.nytimes.com/2010/10/02/arts/design/02apps.html?_r=1 (accessed 21 September 2011).

Schmalstieg D. and Wagner D., 2005. A Handheld Augmented Reality Museum Guide. *Proceedings of IADIS International Conference on Mobile Learning 2005.* Qawra, Malta 28–30 June 2005.

Seandalaiocht, 2011. Comment. *Comments and Ratings for The Archaeology App* [online] 24 August 2011. Available at: http://www.androidzoom.com/android_applications/travel_and_local/the-archaeology-app_bhkhb_comments.html (accessed 30 October 2011).

Smith K., 2009. The Future of Mobile Interpretation. In Trant J. and Bearman D. eds, 2009. *Museums and the Web 2009: Proceedings.* Toronto: Archives & Museum Informatics [online]. Available at: http://www.archimuse.com/mw2009/papers/smith/smith.html (accessed 29 September 2011).

Smith W., Lewi H., Darian-Smith K. and Pearce J., 2010. Re-connecting visual content to place in a mobile guide for the Shrine of Remembrance. In Seal A. with Bowen J. and Ng K. eds, 2010. *EVA London 2010: Electronic Visualisation & the Arts. Proceedings of a conference held in London 6–8 July.* BCS, pp. 347–354 [online]. Available at: http://www.bcs.org/upload/pdf/ewic_ev10_s15paper1.pdf (accessed 21 September 2011).

Snyder S. L. and Elinich K. J., 2010. Augmented reality for interpretive and experiential learning. In Seal A. with Bowen J. and Ng K. eds, 2010. *EVA London 2010: Electronic Visualisation & the Arts. Proceedings of a conference held in London 6–8 July.* BCS, pp. 87–92 [online]. Available at: http://www.bcs.org/upload/pdf/ewic_ev10_s4paper4.pdf (accessed 21 September 2011).

Stedelijk Museum, n.d. ARtours: The Augmented Reality project of the Stedelijk Museum Amsterdam [online]. Available at: http://www.stedelijk.nl/en/now-at-the-stedelijk/spotlight/artours (accessed 05 October 2011).

Stephens S., 2010. Mobile phone apps. *Museum Practice* [online] (15 June 2010) Available at: http://www.museumsassociation.org/museum-practice/apps (accessed 08 September 2011).

Stevebirchard, n.d. Comment. *Archaeobox. Customer Reviews* [online]. Available at: http://itunes.apple.com/ca/app/archaeobox/id406223742?mt=8 (accessed 30 October 2010).

Tallon L., 2008. Introduction: Mobile, Digital and Personal. In Tallon L. and Walker K. eds, 2008. *Digital Technologies and the Museum Experience. Handheld Guides and Other Media.* AltaMira Press, pp. xiii–xxv.

Valeonti F., 2010. Research: Augmented Reality for Museums [online] 12 May 2010. Available at: http://valeonti.com/?p=366 (accessed 05 October 2011).

Vlahakis V., Karigiannis J., Tsotros M., Gounaris M., Almeida L., Stricker D., Gleue T., Christou I. T., Carlucci R. and Ioannidis N., 2001. ARCHEOGUIDE: First results of an Augmented Reality, Mobile Computing System in Cultural Heritage Sites. *Proceedings of the Conference on Virtual Reality, Archaeology, and Cultural Heritage (VAST'01).* Glyfada, Greece, 28–30 November 2001, pp. 131–140 [online]. Available at: http://archeoguide.intranet.gr/papers/publications/ARCHEOGUIDE-VAST01-1.pdf (accessed 21 September 2011).

Wagner E., 2011. A world of culture in your hands: the 40 best arts apps. *The Times, Saturday Review*, 16 July 2011, pp. 4–5.

Uses of Social Media within the British Museum and Museum Sector

Daniel Pett

> Use social media to help deliver specific marketing, learning and participation goals – don't do it for the sake of it (Imagemakers 2011: 8).

Abstract

Social media can be defined in many ways, but this paper focuses primarily upon platforms that allow community members to engage with each other by creating profiles and online content (see the often cited Kaplan and Haenlein 2010, and Atkinson 2011), or *'social capital'* (Ellison *et al.* 2007).

This paper demonstrates how social media can be used and implemented within the museum sector, for marketing (with specific reference to the author's institution), for a participatory multivocal dialogue and for creating a strong online brand and a research presence. It will also consider the relative merits of pertinent case studies and suggest how others could emulate and innovate within the archaeological and museum sectors.

Social media: what is it?

The use of social media in the digital arena now permeates our life, with many of us participating via a range of methods and devices (the mobile device now becoming especially ubiquitous and presenting its own particular challenges). Social media can range from high profile platforms (e.g. Facebook and Twitter) to meet-up groups, forums and knowledge banks and online games, which will be discussed below. They provide a way to interact and engage in dialogue with a new audience. For example, a younger or worldwide public could now be courted by a local museum, where previously this may have been beyond their means. It is a mechanism for broadcasting cultural propaganda, to influence target audiences and create new relationships. However, these channels of communication are two-way and not just unidirectional (as many marketing tools are traditionally): social media are ultimately about the creation of social capital. They are extensions of the news generated in the traditional hard copy, allowing anyone to break stories, become a valued influence and develop a wider network of interested people. Marketing via social media has thus expanded into a new realm: that of community-building and direct interaction and all of this can be achieved relatively cheaply and with low numbers of dedicated personnel.

The recent publication of national reports on digital markets in various sectors of UK life demonstrates the importance of taking this market seriously. For example, the Arts Council England, Museums, Libraries and Archives Council and Arts & Business (ACE *et al.* from here on) research document, *Digital audiences: engagement with arts and culture online* (2010: 4, 18), suggests that 53%

of the online population[1] have used the Internet to engage with arts and culture in the past 12 months (with an increase to 62% for those in the 16–34 year old age bracket).

The report identifies five main online interaction categories: access, learn, experience, share, and create. These five factors indicate the importance of museums and cultural institutions being active on social media platforms and making them a key marketing channel; furthermore, such factors nicely align with the '4 pillars of enterprise' that Rangaswami[2] discusses (**Table 1**).

Table 1 Synergy between Rangaswami's '4 pillars of enterprise' and the ACE *et al.* criteria.

ACE *et al.* report criteria	Rangaswami's pillars of enterprise
Access	Search
Share	Syndication
Experience | Learn | Share	Fulfilment
Create | Share	Conversation

The report demonstrates that Internet users are creative and want to engage with the online resource that they are interacting with; however, it should be noted that, if the 90-9-1 (also known as 'participation inequality') rule is applied, then the potential creative audience is relatively small (circa 10%, the tip of the pyramid; see Nielsen 2006 and Wallis 2010: 27).

Another finding from the ACE *et al.* (2010: 17) report is that 'those engaged in arts and culture online are also engaged in arts and culture offline. There is great potential for cross-promoting and cross-fertilising audiences'. This produces an opportunity for the conversion of online relationships into offline and on-site ones with the knock-on potential for income generation. Such opportunity will be returned to below, but it is worth saying now that limitations within the cultural sector (physical resources, knowledge, personnel and time) can prevent full exploitation of the potential of online platforms, and of social media ones particularly, and lead to out-sourcing for implementation. Institutions need to choose carefully the aspects of digital media to which to devote their efforts, if they are to achieve a positive return on their investment. Simplistically, institutions will migrate towards platforms with the largest audience share. However, is an institution's engagement with social media simply pandering to a niche market? The Office for National Statistics (2011) states that there are 62.26 million people in the UK[3], but are only 100,000 people interested in the British Museum's social media output? Is the marketing output really not reaching the correct audience? Is the investment worthwhile? Are people interested in culture? Should you focus on the marketing practices, or more on executing social media tools effectively?

Platforms for engagement: choice abounds

In the last few years, an explosion of social media platforms has led to a huge array of options for anyone wishing to create an online persona, whether the latter is an 'avatar'[4] or an accurate representation of the user, and to generate their own content. Social media is about creating references to self, or 'Me media', as Cassidy (2006) styles it. This projected persona can heavily influence the interactions and engagements that users have with one another and with various services (for example, see Morgan 2009: 479–481, on the Second Life recreation of Çatalhöyük, or Dimicco and Millen's work [2007] on identity projection and interaction via Facebook). Each social media platform attempts to produce a unique selling point (USP), whether this involves an emphasis

---

[1] 18 million fixed broadband lines exist at the end of 2010 (Ofcom 2011).
[2] http://confusedofcalcutta.com/category/four-pillars-of-enterprise-application-architecture/ (accessed 20 October 2011).
[3] Population figures were obtained from http://www.ons.gov.uk/ons/rel/pop-estimate/population-estimates-for-uk--england-and-wales--scotland-and-northern-ireland/mid-2010-population-estimates/rft---mid-2010-population-estimates.zip (accessed 06 September 2011).
[4] An avatar is the incarnation of a person as they perceive themselves or wish to be perceived by others, for example someone's Wii Mii avatar; for more details on the concept of Nintendo Wii Mii avatars see http://en.wikipedia.org/wiki/Mii (accessed 27 September 2011).

on geographic (Location Based Service – LBS), audio-visual (e.g. photo and video sharing), prose-based (blogs), or micro update services. A limited selection of the wide range of platforms available for social media participation is displayed in **Table 2**.

Social media use has been prevalent for a long time within the archaeological and museum sectors, for example in the form of mailing lists and chat forums (e.g. in the UK, BRITARCH[5] and MCG[6], hosted on JISCMAIL servers). Social media and the Internet allow everyone to have a voice (Kolbitsch 2007) and an opinion on any subject that they choose; Breen (2010: 36) states the following for archaeology, but the comments are also relevant for museums:

> The Web has opened up publishing to everyone, and that may yet save Irish archaeology from a dispiriting trend. The recent boom in archaeology and the development of many national monuments with ... admission charges have made the public more aware, but also seem to give many people the impression that actually going out and studying their local antiquities is ... best left to the experts ... It is a relief therefore

Table 2 A list of social media tools by type defined by the author (not comprehensive and sustainability of many of these is questionable).

Service type	Examples
Micro updates	Twitter
Location based	Foursquare, GoWalla, Google Latitude, Facebook places, Geocaching, History Pin
Photo sharing	Flickr, Picasa
Multipurpose or community sites	Facebook, Google+, Ning, Buddypress, Orkut, Friends Reunited, MySpace[7], Lanyrd, Yammer, Naseeb, Muxlim, Muslimbook
Video sharing	YouTube, Vimeo
Link shortening	bitly, tinyurl, Goo.gl
Mobile phone based applications	Tweet and Grow, Streetmuseum, History Pin
Social gaming	X-box, Second Life, Civilization, World of Warcraft
Video conferencing and communications	Skype
Discussion lists and fora	JISCMAIL, phpBB, Vanilla
Interactive glyphs or barcodes	Quick Response (QR), Augmented Reality
Messaging services	Yahoo!, Google, BlackBerry messenger
Link sharing	Delicious, StumbleUpon, Digg, reddit
Professional services	Linkedin, Academia
Knowledge bases	Yahoo! Answers, Google Groups, Wikipedia
Archiving tools	Storify[8], Twapperkeeper, Thinkupapp
Match making	Match, Mysinglefriend
Review	TripAdvisor, Yelp
Monitoring tools	Klout, TweetLevel, Peerindex
Code repository software	GitHub
Music	Spotify, Last FM
Sports	Adidas miCoach, Nike Running

[5] https://www.jiscmail.ac.uk/cgi-bin/webadmin?A0=britarch - British Archaeology mailing list (accessed 20 October 2011).
[6] https://www.jiscmail.ac.uk/cgi-bin/webadmin?A0=mcg - Museums Computer Group mailing list (accessed 20 October 2011).
[7] Friends Reunited and MySpace's troubles are well documented as they have declined (Garrahan 2009; Arrington 2011).
[8] The CASPAR workshop back channel was documented via Storify see: http://storify.com/jessogden/acrncaspar (accessed 20 October 2011).

to see that a number of enthusiasts have started websites where they post photographs and descriptions of monuments they have visited.

Breen, in essence, has captured a more general trend of the Web as it has moved from one-way didacticism towards engaged learning and a culture of dialogue, and sociability.

Bevan (this volume) refers to Fiske's (1991) models of social agency and suggests that many social media platforms deliberately espouse a logic of 'community sharing', and it is true that, for example, Twitter and Facebook invite their users to share 'status updates' (see also Richardson, this volume). More generally, of the platforms available to marketing professionals, it is indeed those focussed on engagement through content or in community sharing of content that are perhaps the most important for museums to consider, such as YouTube and Flickr, location-based interaction services like Foursquare, Gowalla and Facebook check-ins, and the most widely used platforms of Facebook and Twitter. The nascent Google+ platform has the potential to become Facebook's main competitor, but, given that other Google offerings such as Wave, TV and Buzz (see Bisson and Branscombe 2011) have seen little enthusiasm from the social media aware online demographic and were soon withdrawn from service, it is probably too early to predict how Google+ will fare. What is clear is that Darwinian principles (O'Brien 1996) apply to social media networks, with end users choosing the platform(s) that are fit for their purposes and augment their experiences elsewhere (Rangaswami 2008). The best platforms adapt and integrate well with the rest of the Web ecosystem: for example, the combination of Flickr's interface with Twitter to allow users to share recent photo uploads, or Facebook's growth to enable photographic content to be posted (Cassidy 2006).

Klebe Treviño *et al.* (2000: 166) note that 'individuals are more likely to choose rich media (e.g. face-to-face meetings) and they are less likely to choose lean media (e.g. letters, fax) when message equivocality is high'. This statement could apply equally well to the Facebook age: the richer experience offered by online platforms that allow for text, images, sound and even video chat has now started to impact on social interactions offline. People now have a wide circle of online friends and this may in many cases eventually enable them to meet in the offline world. Likewise, social media allows long distance friendships to be maintained, or in the case of institutions, they can sustain a relationship with people who may have been only briefly interested in a particular collection or have visited one time in their life, but now have an opportunity to keep up with events.

Social media currently percolates to all societal levels; it allows for conference participation via back-channels (see Ross *et al.* 2011, for discussion about relative merits of this concept); it enables companies to 'search for their brand on Facebook' or use Google voice search (see **Figure 18** for an example); it lets unverified information enter into journalistic output, with articles based entirely around Twitter[9] comment. Mainstream television programmes can now display a hash tag without any explanation due to the ubiquitous nature of social media. For example, the recent 'Arab Spring' revolt was reported worldwide and co-ordinated with a heavy reliance on social media (Howard 2011), as were the August riots (Halliday 2011) in the United Kingdom; so much so, Government agencies mooted that social media usage should be restricted (Rainey 2011).

The Facebook phenomenon

Facebook has undoubtedly transformed social media, with museums now sometimes even using it as a replacement for a separate online presence of their own. Reams of analysis can be found on the social media powerhouse that is Facebook, but simple quantitative results demonstrate how game changing this platform has been. For example, Facebook's registered user base would equal the population of the world's third largest country (640

---

[9] Twitter launched publicly in August 2006 and is still searching for viable monetisation strategies to survive; it is limited in its scope for advertising when compared to Google or Facebook.

Figure 18. One of Google's social Web adverts at Piccadilly Circus underground station[10] (see Plate 15).

million users), the site receives 310 million visits daily and, in an average 20 minute period in 2010, 5.9 million wall posts, 10.2 million comments were made and 2.7 million photos were posted (Ward 2011). In contrast, if we consider other platforms, 49% of registered Twitter users never check their timeline (although Twitter claims to have 100 million active users[11]), Wikipedia article volume has grown by 21% from 2010 to 2011, and Flickr now hosts over six billion images, with 3,500 new ones added each second (Ward 2011). Facebook, however, still has potential to grow further, especially if developing nations expand their Internet capacity, relax online censorship and the platform proves useful to these communities.

Earlier in this paper, reference was made to the research document issued by the Arts Council England *et al.* Here, specific emphasis is placed upon the value of Facebook to the arts and culture community (2010: 6): 'social media – and in particular **Facebook**[12] – has become a major tool for discovering as well as sharing information about arts and culture, second only to organic search through Google and other search engines'.

Why and how does the British Museum use social media?

The British Museum (BM) aims to be 'a museum of the world for the world' (British Museum 2008: 3), and by utilising social media tools and platforms it can attempt to meet this mission statement. The BM is currently the United Kingdom's most visited paid for heritage attraction (Kennedy 2011), with 5.8 million visitors and a comparable online attendance (5.866 million unique visitors to just the main website in the calendar year, for 2010[13]). This similarity in scale of online visits and physical footfall perhaps points to the intimate connection of these two activities, as discussed in a different context by Ellison *et al.* (2007).

The centrepiece of the BM's website is the Museum's collection[14], with an emphasis on making it more accessible to the public, documenting its physical conservation and presenting the ongoing research conducted with it. A project to enable the dissemination of the collection online has now seen nearly two million objects being made available for public consumption worldwide; fulfilling the institutional remit outlined in an Act of Parliament in 1753 that states that the BM collection should be available to 'all curious and studious persons'. Secondly, the BM wishes to use the online presence to increase revenue via the BM Company, through increased membership of the 'Friends' programme and by enhanced ticket sales to exhibitions. The BM's focus on digital engagement is outlined as follows: 'by 2012, the Museum's physical presence in London will be complemented by a globally accessible media resource, including multimedia products, digitised archives and broad-

---

[10] Image by Annie Mole, Creative Commons licensed, available at: http://www.flickr.com/photos/anniemole/5573997732/sizes/z/in/photostream/ (accessed 7 September 2011).

[11] http://blog.twitter.com/2011/09/one-hundred-million-voices.html (accessed 20 October 2011).

[12] Author's emphasis in bold.

[13] The British Museum has a Web presence, with around ten constituent parts that get returned overall annually. Online visit figures are obtained from Google Analytics (11 September 2011).

[14] 20% of the BM website visits are for use of the collection online section (Ghey 2011: 68)

cast programmes which will make the Museum's world-class collections available to a global audience' (British Museum 2008: 12, 23).

Over the past forty years, the increasing ease of international travel has meant not only that more visitors from abroad can come to London to use the collection, but that the latter can more easily travel to them, and be put to public use in new local contexts (e.g. touring exhibitions and loans). As a complement to this, however, it has also become increasingly important to engage with an online audience that may not be able to physically engage with the Museum. Social media are just one of the tools used by the BM's Marketing and Web teams to offer access to digital content, communicate ideas, encourage and facilitate discussion, and market to a world-wide online audience. It is an adjunct to the methods of public engagement already employed (e.g. family learning and educational activities, lectures, the Partnership UK programme, exhibitions) and is easy to integrate into existing public programming activities. Recent examples of the Marketing department's use of social media include the *Grayson Perry* and *Hajj* exhibitions. For the *Hajj* exhibition, Web and Marketing have developed a campaign that reaches out to Muslim audiences and provides engaging and informative content for non-Muslims who want to know more about the pilgrimage to Mecca. The Web presence for this exhibition allows those who have been on the *Hajj* to submit their experiences online[15] in the form of text, pictures and video; once moderated, these are then displayed on the BM website and a selection may feature in the exhibition multimedia guide and possibly within the exhibition itself.

Social media experimentation

a) *A History of the World*

Before analysing the BM's social media activities, it is worth considering some of the departmental work that feeds into the institution's persona and enlists a variety of crossover audiences. A multi-department (and indeed multi-institutional) project that led to substantial user generated content (UGC) and was deemed to be highly successful[16], is *A History of the World (AHOW)*. This was a radio series, fronted by the BM Director, Neil MacGregor, and backed by a team of curators who researched and synthesised the data. When short listing *AHOW* for their 2011 award, the Art Fund described it as a 'groundbreaking and enormously successful project exploring world history through the British Museum's unparalleled collection' (British Museum 2011: 51).

The online component of this project allowed people to download podcasts of the radio programme, of which over 19 million were realised (British Museum 2011: 35), and also to upload their own objects to the BBC developed series website. The final object to be presented in this project sparked online suggestions for objects that represented life in 2010 (Cock 2011), prompting lively and sometimes heated debate. Five objects were nominated by the BM, with the Didier Drogba Chelsea Football Club shirt generating the most interest. The online collection of objects nominated by the project's 551 institutional participants was enhanced and complemented by over 4,000 objects uploaded by the public (0.1% of the overall visits; Cock 2011), and these all had the facility for social interaction via commentary or sharing mechanisms.

During the judging for the Art Fund 2011 award, Michael Portillo commented:

> Above all, we felt that this project, which showed a truly pioneering use of digital media, has led the way for museums to interact with their audiences in new and different ways. Without changing the core of the British Museum's purpose, people have and are continuing to engage with objects in an innovative way as a consequence of this project (Brown 2011).

The series also inspired third party developers to build related content, with the History

---

[15] http://www.britishmuseum.org/whats_on/exhibitions/hajj/hajj_stories.aspx (accessed 3 October 2011).

[16] Winner of the 2011 Art Fund Prize for Museums (Brown 2011; Prudames 2011).

Hack Day 2011[17] winner producing a mobile phone based application[18] that allowed the user to interact with the entire series in the space of around only 12 hours.

b) Wikipedia

The BM has also innovated through a project called *Wikipedian-in-residence*[19] that was initiated in 2010 and hosted by the department of Learning, Volunteers and Audiences (LV&A) (Wyatt 2010; Cohen 2010; see also Thornton in this volume for further discussion of this platform and its potential for archaeological research). This partnership project invited Wikipedia and its immense user base to interact with the BM collection and staff, and produce a series of collaborative works including:

- An object challenge, to enhance one individual object page: the Hoxne Hoard[20];
- A series of five prizes for the first featured articles to be written;
- Collaborative working between curators and Wikipedians (this is ongoing, with the department of Prehistory and Europe and a series of Prehistoric pages being produced or enriched);
- A 'backstage pass' day, where the Wikipedia community could see the internal workings of the BM;
- Departmental presentations.

Since the conclusion of the project, collaboration has been continued by many of the participants, with the department of Portable Antiquities and Treasure (PA&T) providing Creative Commons licensed images for the Wikimedia Commons and information for a variety of cases, for example the Frome[21] and Staffordshire[22] hoards. This project was described by one blogger as: 'a model for institutions on how to deal with the Internet revolution. It's clever, it costs them nothing, it gains the institution respect and traction on the Internet… there is, in truth, no downside' (Pearse 2010). Such a statement captures nicely the kind of social traction that the BM can gain from interacting with the Wikipedia community; as the cited articles show (e.g. Wyatt 2010, Cohen 2010) the project was well received around the world.

Internal social media use for an external audience

Another example of the heavy use of social media can be seen in the author's own department, that of PA&T, which has been engaging with such approaches since 2005 (see also Goskar in this volume for Wessex Archaeology's similar emphasis). The PA&T website[23] is fully integrated with social media tools via the use of APIs[24]; it retrieves content from a variety of sources – Flickr, Yahoo!, Google Maps, etc. (Pett 2011b: 76). The highest profile example, so far, of the role of social media in this department has been the launching of the Staffordshire Hoard website[25] (in September 2009), which used Flickr to solicit for interaction and host a set of images that gained over 1.5 million views, several thousand comments and 250,000 visitors in a period of three days (Pett 2010) solely via that platform.

A specialised, digitally native department within the BM that is fully immersed with social media technology is the Samsung Digital Discovery Centre

---

[17] http://historyhackday.org/ (accessed 20 October 2011).
[18] http://historyhackday.org/ (accessed 20 October 2011).
[19] http://en.wikipedia.org/wiki/Wikipedia:GLAM/BM (accessed 27 September 2011).
[20] http://en.wikipedia.org/wiki/Hoxne_hoard (accessed 20 October 2011); view the edit history, with particular reference to June's edits.
[21] http://en.wikipedia.org/wiki/Frome_Hoard (accessed 20 October 2011).
[22] http://en.wikipedia.org/wiki/Staffordshire_hoard (accessed 20 October 2011).
[23] http://finds.org.uk (accessed 20 October 2011).
[24] API: Application Programming Interface, a method for interacting with software.
[25] Originally published at http://www.staffordshirehoard.org.uk and now at http://finds.org.uk/staffshoard (accessed 20 October 2011), as the Staffordshire Hoard partnership replaced the old site with a magazine style format.

(SDDC). This is a dedicated young person's learning facility in the Clore Educational Centre which uses a variety of tools, platforms and techniques to bring archaeology and the world of museums to life. Examples of their work include the production of video news bulletins around the discovery of such iconic objects as the Sutton Hoo ship burials and then uploading these to Vimeo, to enable comment and dialogue with the creators and their families. Staff within the department are currently working on a video-conferencing experiment based around best practice and public archaeological discovery (Warry 2011), which will use social media tools to enhance children's learning experiences.

Figure 19. A QR code in the BM *Australia Garden* exhibition on the West forecourt 2011. The QR code on the sign is shown on the right and when scanned goes to http://bit.ly/lHPhkB a short URL for a mobile webpage at: http://www.britishmuseum.org/mobile/australia_trail/australia_stop_1.aspx (Photo by author). This follows best practice for using the glyphs and mobile devices (see Plate 16).

QR code and glyph based technology

Whilst not fully engaging in the use of QR and glyphs within the BM for innovative social media based exercises (a concept that has been applied for different campaigns at museums around the world[26]), several examples of their use can be found within the BM's estate. Projects have made use of QR code technology for enabling access to enhanced resources, with this year's outdoor collaboration with Kew Gardens (the Australia Garden on the West lawn of the forecourt) containing labels integrated with QR codes. These allow anyone equipped with the correct handset and software to interact with information online (see **Figure 19** for an example of one such labels). Secondly, an exhibition on the Akan Dum[27], held in 2010[28], had a QR code that linked to a mobile site, which allowed people to access enhanced information and download an MP3 track of the drum being played[29] from Spotify or iTunes. Whilst not promoting a two-way dialogue, these glyphs can be a doorway to social interaction: a Facebook check-in to a place facilitated by a code is one such use.

Eden (2011) has also conducted experimental work on the QRpedia project within the BM galleries (see also the Derby Museums project), where codes could be placed on labels and scanning would take the consumer directly to the Wikipedia page (he specifically discusses the Rosetta Stone), and this could also be relevant for Museum webpages.

Prior to these implementations, QR codes[30] have been utilised elsewhere within the BM; the PA&T website produces a glyph via Google Charts for each individual artefact recorded and the SDDC has also experimented with the use of AR glyphs within exhibition spaces (Mannion 2011a and 2011b).[31]

Many in the marketing (and indeed museum) industry believe that QR codes have had their day and technology has moved on, for example towards Near Field Communication (NFC) or Augmented Reality (AR) (see Rossoff 2011).

---

[26] For information on mobile based projects worldwide see http://wiki.museummobile.info/ (accessed 09 September 2011).

[27] http://www.bbc.co.uk/ahistoryoftheworld/objects/iTEvLsbQRxilYjAO5TZ3mA (accessed 09 September 2011).

[28] http://www.britishmuseum.org/whats_on/archive_exhibitions/akan_drum.aspx (accessed 09 September 2011).

[29] http://www.britishmuseum.org/whats_on/all_current_exhibitions/akan_drum/akan_drum_playlist.aspx (accessed 09 September 2011).

[30] They do produce an intended (narrow) audience, cost and use limitation: those without access to the correct hardware and software are excluded from interacting with them and overseas visitors can incur high costs for roaming bandwidth usage (let alone language specific delivery.) Not everyone knows how these codes can be utilised.

[31] This use has been documented by staff in a comprehensive video, appropriately shared on the social media platform Vimeo; see http://vimeo.com/25782400 (accessed 20 September 2011).

Nevertheless, they are seen in very varied locations, most often print based, but sometimes in innovative places, as in the case of Betfair's use of QR code on the GB volleyball team uniform (Eleftheriou-Smith 2011).

The British Museum on Facebook

The BM's Facebook page (**Figure 20**) has been in operation since April 2009 and is used as a discursive interface for the Museum's activities. At the time of writing (5 September 2011), the profile has attracted 137,776 'likes' and has had 6,178 check-ins. The information page provides clear links to the Museum's other social personas for other audiences (of which it has several, just as many individuals also project multiple distinct identities on the Web; Dimicco and Millen 2007). All of the BM's activities online and via the creative departments are aided by the strong brand awareness and high visibility in the world's press (see Bonacchi *et al.*, in this volume, for further discussion of the importance of brand). This is of course something that many organisations can only aspire to, and the author appreciates his privileged position. All of the above concepts are tied to specific benchmarks which help to determine whether the media chosen are worthwhile; for example, on Facebook, a target of 200,000 '*likes*'[32] has already been reached, and for Twitter, the target of 100,000 '*followers*'[33] should be realised by March 2012.

The BM has many areas of contention that can spark intense online debate (e.g. issues such as repatriation[34] of objects or human remains) and, therefore, the institution's Facebook presence offers a clear statement of expectation and rules of engagement for host and participants:

> This page is an open forum where anyone is welcome to contribute. Discussion is encouraged, but please be aware that any offensive, defamatory, obscene or harassing comments or personal attacks of any kind will be removed. Spamming, repeat submissions of the same (or very similar) contributions or content that is off-topic may also be removed.[35]

The marketing department of the BM is responsible for the social media output, in conjunction with the department of LV&A. Facebook is primarily used to broadcast information about the Museum and partner museums' activities worldwide, about a scientific research, and excavation discoveries; and it elicits commentary and 'likes' by inviting people to interact and give examples of how certain events are celebrated in their part of the world. Quantitative analysis is conducted on the postings via the 'insights' facility; the mean 'likes' for posts is around 147 and the most popular ones, which are usually Egypt-related, receive over 85,000 views. Other posts that rank highly include simple facts about the museum, news pieces, behind-the-scenes videos and links to blogs; asking direct questions to the BM fan base usually elicits substantial feedback.

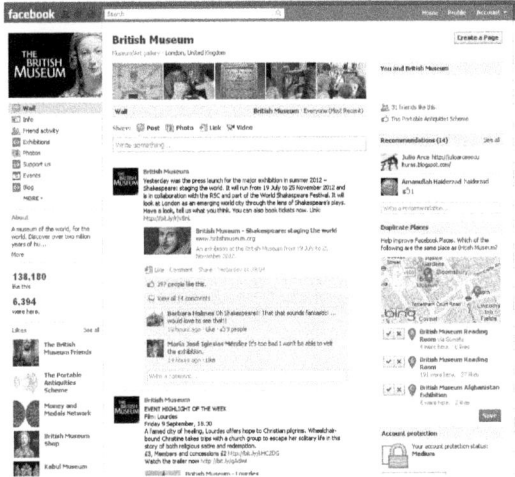

Figure 20. The British Museum's presence on Facebook (see Plate 17).

---

[32] A 'like' is a user interaction, where one shows appreciation for a webpage, an object or event.
[33] A 'follower' on Twitter is basically a subscriber to a list of comments, much like deciding to listen to a radio station. One can turn off at will.
[34] For example, the Parthenon marbles restitution, Cyrus Cylinder to Iran and Benin Bronzes arguments.
[35] https://www.facebook.com/britishmuseum?sk=info (accessed 20 September 2011).

The demographic breakdown of users for the page is relatively straightforward to obtain from the 'Insights' interface (unless people lie about date of birth and gender, which some do because of privacy concerns; Ellison *et al.* 2007) and produces some interesting figures:

- The largest proportion of fans is from the United Kingdom;
- The city with the most fans is Madrid (Spain);
- English is by far the most spoken language of users;
- 35% of the audience on this platform are between 25 and 44 years old (with potential for family interaction within this age bracket).

The British Museum on Twitter

The BM has been active on Twitter since January 2009. It currently has 62,604 followers, but it only follows 439 users; this suggests a low level of interaction or reciprocity, an aspect which is discussed further below. The BM account has gathered new followers at a rate of circa 10% per month and has seen peaks in interest around certain news updates. The frequency of Twitter status updates (see Richardson in this volume for the mechanics of this process, and also for the appropriate use of hash tags) varies between one and two times per day and is carefully managed (unless a specific campaign requires more organised question and answer techniques)[36].

Twitter campaigns are planned to fit in with current events and future exhibitions, notable recent examples include[37]:

- Main hashtag (#britishmuseum): it is used for broadcasting information about the museum (854 tweets since April 2011; however, tweets mentioning the phrase **britishmuseum** number 1,724, in same period).
- Stunt bear (#stuntbear): a competition[38] run around the *Grayson Perry* exhibition, which solicited entries for three teddy bears to stand in for the artist's own teddy bear (Alan Measles) on the back of his motorbike (60 tweets since September 2011). This competition attracted 300 entries and over 2,000 votes for the 12 bears that were shortlisted.
- Craftdebate (#craftdebate): another social media campaign based around the *Grayson Perry* exhibition; this featured a live Twitter debate with the artist responding to people's comments and opinions on how art and craft can be seen within the digital age.
- *Afghanistan* exhibition (#afghanistanBM): it broadcasted information on the *Afghanistan* exhibition and allowed seeing how people interacted or developed an empathy with the objects/content (503 tweets since April 2011).
- *Australia garden* (#australiaBM): used for broadcasting information about the garden and related events (261 tweets since April 2011).

The BM has several accounts that actively broadcast: the main identity, the BM Company for the shop, to promote products, and also one for the book club; the Portable Antiquities Scheme interacts too, under the @findsorguk account, and some of their staff also have regional accounts.

The British Museum and video

The BM has a dedicated and specialised broadcast unit, staffed by an ex BBC producer, a broadcast assistant and a team of experienced freelance professionals. All of this is in line with MacGregor's statement (also referenced in Bonacchi *et al.*, this volume) that: 'The future has to be, without question, the museum as a publisher and broadcaster' (Higgins 2009; MacGregor and Serota 2009). In particular, the BM has begun to focus on broadcasting via narrowcasting on the Web[39]

---

[36] For example, Twitter campaigns for #askacurator or #craftdebate.
[37] Figures obtained from an install of yourTwapperKeeper; software available at: http://your.twapperkeeper.com/ (accessed 20 September 2011).
[38] http://www.britishmuseum.org/whats_on/exhibitions/grayson_perry/competition.aspx (accessed 20 September 2011).
[39] See Bonacchi *et al.* in this volume.

and larger broadcasts on mainstream TV, which have been negotiated via the unit. The BM's presence on YouTube was re-launched in August 2010 (British Museum 2011: 37), with a strategic plan to upload new high quality (sometimes high definition) content two or three times per month. Many of these videos are thematic (e.g. a brief history of time telling[40]), or exhibition based (e.g. an Afghanistan exhibition teaser video).

The BM's Marketing department and the Web team strategically plan when video will be released and cross-publicise it via the various social media platforms that they maintain. Salient examples are discussed in this volume within Bonacchi *et al.*, with analysis of viewing figures of the videos on the video sharing social media platforms.

The British Museum blogs

The BM's Web team have maintained a blog[41] since April 2010 and PA&T has curated a variety of dedicated self hosted blogs[42] since August 2005. Both have used the ubiquitous Wordpress open source blogging platform. The blogs run by British Museum staff discuss and document the diversity of BM activities; posts are carefully selected by the Web team (this platform, unlike the other social media utilised, is not maintained by the marketing team). Recent topics include updates on the Chisledon Cauldrons, discussion of the discoveries at Amara West (Egypt), news and install information for the *Treasures of Heaven* and *The Tomb of the Unknown Craftsman* exhibitions, and information about the Future Curators programme and the participants' experience. In line with blogs around the world (Arthur 2009), commentary is relatively small compared to the 'participatory' nature of the other platforms that the BM runs. Consumers of BM social media can now comment on their own terms, without moderation, on other platforms: for example, by sharing links via Facebook or Twitter with comment attached.

Strategies for engagement

As with all professional activity, the development of a clear strategy is imperative. As the saying goes: fail to plan, plan to fail. When attempting to engage an audience via social media for institutional gain, it pays to follow a set agenda. The kinds of questions that might be addressed are:

- What do we, as an institution, want to achieve by engaging our public/professional or funding audience? What resources will be needed?
- Does the knowledge or skill set exist within the institution or can it be learnt?
- Does a third party need to be engaged or new staff members recruited?
- Are you going to develop bespoke applications or use existing platforms; and if the latter, which platforms?
- Can we link our use of various platforms together to produce a holistic social media offering?
- Does the institution actually allow social media to be used internally? Does it have a social media policy (for example, see Civil Service 2009a, Simon 2008, BBC n. d.)?
- What are the institutional benchmarks?
- What are we going to say and what are we going to participate in? How frequently will the platforms be updated?
- Will each platform be its own individual silo? Or will the approach be holistic, with cross platform pollination?
- Is failure an option and, if not, why not? Social media are experimental by nature and failure is likely; Orgel's second rule (evolution is cleverer than you are), should also be applied. Software developers cannot predict how their platform will develop.
- What are the guidelines for creating a dialogue? What is acceptable?
- Have you staked the claim to your identity – for example using your institution name on social media (e.g. facebook.com/britishmu-

---

[40] http://www.britishmuseum.org/explore/young_explorers/discover/videos/brief_history_of_time_telling.aspx (accessed 20 September 2011).
[41] http://blog.britishmuseum.org (accessed 2 September 2011).
[42] http://finds.org.uk/blogs (accessed 1 September 2011).

seum, twitter.com/britishmuseum) or taking ownership of your venue on Foursquare?
- What copyright stance are you going to assume for your social media output? A Creative Commons licence without a non-commercial clause will allow more take up and reuse, but does not suit all.
- Has your legal adviser or team checked 'Terms and Conditions' or your policies? Are they enforceable? When one puts something online, control is lost.
- Are you able to deal with privacy of your users?
- How does your institution feel about the embedded advertising prevalent on many mainstream platforms? Can you leverage it to your advantage?
- Will an archive of content be maintained?
- When do you decide to 'turn off' or 'retire' a social media channel?

Strategy documents for museums and archaeological institutions and organisations are few and far between, probably due to the youthfulness of the medium and the fact that good strategy has yet to be defined! A few reasonable pieces published specifically for museums do exist (for example, Stewart 2010; Smithsonian Institution 2009) and more generally, social media policy draws inspiration from Sir Gus O'Donnell's exhortations (Civil Service 2009b) to the civil service to:

a) Be credible: Be accurate, fair, thorough and transparent.
b) Be consistent: Encourage constructive criticism and deliberation. Be cordial, honest and professional at all times.
c) Be responsive: When you gain insight, share it where appropriate.
d) Be integrated: Wherever possible, align online participation with other offline communications.
e) Be a civil servant: Remember that you are an ambassador for your organisation. Wherever possible, disclose your position as a representative of your department or agency.

This is sage advice for all professional engagement online, but in reality it is impossible to actually control social media output by institutional employees and general encouragement to behave with common sense is a much better tactic to adopt than outright regulation.

Problems with social media

Institutional use of social media is fraught with potential problems. While there have been many successful social media projects, it is important to also outline some of the remaining issues which include:

- Copyright;
- Terms of service changes (for example, Twitter);
- Privacy concerns;
- Exposure of young participants to audiences;
- Flash-point subjects;
- Bullying and anti-social behaviour, dealing with trolls and vexatious bloggers;
- Lack of expertise in implementing the right social media solution for a particular situation;
- Local authority/ council/ institution blocking of social media (Gibbins 2011). For example PA&T employees are routinely blocked from using Flickr (Basford 2011; Darch 2010; and Adams 2011);
- Maintenance of an archive can be tricky or impossible (see archiving section below);
- Choice of software for interactions can be detrimental to the experience;
- Management of poly/single identity can be time consuming if working on a highly interactive topic;
- How do you mitigate for staff absence, is the duty devolved elsewhere?
- Institutional buy-in;
- Encouraging participation versus lurking (the 90% of Nielsen's 2006 model).

The problems outlined above, are mostly self explanatory and further discussion is outside the scope of this paper.

Measuring impact and effectiveness

As with all activities, the perceived worth of the engagement will decide whether or not it has longevity. Measuring social media output, and indeed input, is now possible via a variety of methods, with 'key performance indicators' (KPI) being a frequently used term (Fishkin 2011).

a) Analysis

Simple things can be measured on most well-known platforms. For example, URLs that you share should be shortened (when using QR codes or disseminating via Twitter or Facebook) and tracked via the shortener's (e.g. Bitly) interface. Raw figures can be assessed and patterns established, benchmarks can be compared with peers, and resources can be better aligned towards projects that work. Techniques such as sentiment analysis or natural language processing can be applied to determine how people interact with the social media platform; if a platform looks like it is not performing, then maybe your audience are not there, the outcomes are not positive and you should scale down interaction! Analysis can be as simple as a graph, or as detailed as nodal analysis using sophisticated techniques in software like Gephi; but without raw data, it is hard to achieve. One example, which is discussed further within Richardson's paper (this volume), is the change in terms and conditions of Twitter's export API (Watters 2011), where you now have to source data from a third party at considerable cost.

Table 3 gives some idea of what you might want to measure for five key social media platforms.

Table 3 What you might want to measure for five key social media platforms.

Platform	Attachment or affiliation	Engagement & Metrics
Facebook	Fans	Click rate to links Volume of comments Shares 'Likes' Traffic to site Post views
Twitter	Followers	Retweets (RT) Mentions (@) Direct replies (starting with @) Institution/ brand/ URL mentions Traffic to site Direct retweets using built in Twitter functions
Flickr	Contacts	Comments Gallery additions Embeds Traffic to site Views
YouTube	Subscribers	Views Embeds Shares Comments Traffic to site
Google+	Circles (like followers)	Number of circles Mentions (+name) Shares Institution/ brand/ URL mentions +1 Traffic to site

Below are a couple of site metrics for the author's Twitter identity. Both measures demonstrate how a fallow period of use has affected the social 'score' that was being maintained; see **Figure 21**, where the graph shows a downwards trend whilst the author was on leave and did not use the platform.

Figure 22 shows how the Twitter user's profile of tweets can be categorised into distinct topics of conversation, while **Figure 23** shows a so-called Tweetlevel index. There are inherent problems with these different influence measuring tools, to do, for example, with the speed at which the data is refreshed, the degree to which people block access to the third party programmes because of privacy concerns, and the lack of openness of the algorithm involved.

Bevan (this volume), discusses the concept of 'value' and 'authority' and how it can be applied to the museum and archaeological sectors. When

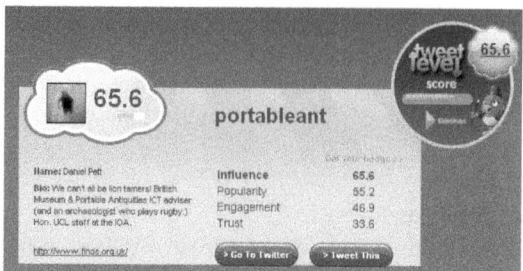

Figure 23. The author's Tweetlevel score.

people interact with the social media personas of the museum world, are they trying to develop ties with the institution, to assert authority over their peers by having comments replied to as definitive? Do people choose their social relationships carefully to maintain a 'cultured' or 'informed' online presence so that people believe that they are influential? Is reciprocity of interaction carefully gauged in order to make the most impact? For example, does a large national museum respond to all tweets on a subject, or just ones that have perceived social standing (e.g. a world famous broadcaster)? Institutions can also take steps to reconfirm their authority, authenticity and voice within the social media arena in a variety of ways; Twitter, for example, provides a verification seal for accounts.

b) Impact?

The measurement of impact and influence has been developed via specialised software, via the creation of social indices that analyse networks and try to determine user's spheres of influence, their audience numbers and their trust levels. These tools are now being used for academics and museum practitioners to establish whether their engagement is worthwhile.

Effective monitoring of social media output is vital; without being able to prove the benefit of the medium as a means of engagement, awkward questions arise such as the following:

- Why should a board of trustees or a senior management team allow time to be wasted on these platforms?
- Has the chosen social media output made an impact on the desired audience? Has it changed

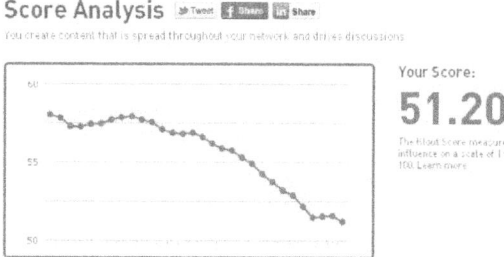

Figure 21. The author's Klout score, showing significant decrease after a week on leave.

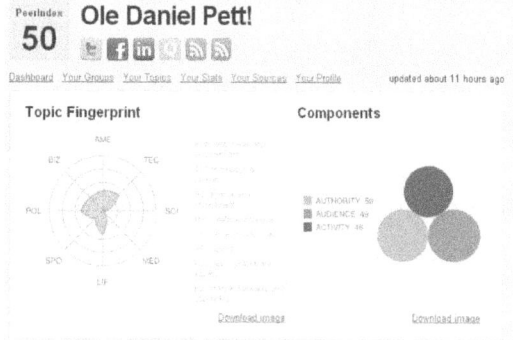

Figure 22. The principle author's peerindex scores (@portableant on Twitter).

their opinion? Taught them something new? Brought them in as new membership?

A recent project led by the Culture24 organisation aimed at determining how best to measure the impact and effectiveness of social media use, across the museum sector, in various countries, and was presented at the 2011 Museums and the Web conference (Finnis *et al.* 2011a). The methodology behind the project was relatively simple, and reasonably effective; researchers used sector wide Google Analytics data from the institutional website, with all 17 partners harvesting the same metrics (including mobile device usage) from their reports and collating these via project management software. One of the key aims of this project was to 'move beyond measuring numbers and begin to measure quality/value of engagement/ meaning: not just usage but interaction' (Finnis *et al.* 2011b).

The Web metrics were backed with quantitative data from social platforms and institutional surveys to determine similarities between investment in time, people and technologies employed. The eventual outcome of this project has provided an authoritative, common sense based methodology for assessing museum sector Web metrics and social engagement (see Finnis *et al.* 2011b).

Further examples of the use of social media in the museums sector

The previous section reflected on social media use within the British Museum; however, the usage of these platforms and tools within the museums sector is richer than simply that tried so far at the BM. There are myriad opportunities for innovative and original applications to be produced, although very few are the really successful projects that have penetrated into the online community, and the numbers of participants are usually relatively small compared to the figures for Internet usage cited previously. This final section offers a brief discussion of a selection of the applications, creative integrations and campaigns out there at present, and it attempts to demonstrate how social media and museums are entwined.

a) Location based: *Streetmuseum*

Museums and archaeological organisations are now realising the potential for location based services; collections contain objects, pictures and artefacts that can be identified with time and place; something that the public can easily assimilate with. The advent of cheaper GPS chips within smartphones is now enabling social media applications to work outside the confines of desktop computers (Kaplan and Haenlein 2010: 57) and allows us 'to expand our influence to other things, people, and places' (Bell 2011).

Earlier in this volume, Jeater discusses the *Streetmuseum*[44] smartphone AR application developed by Brothers and Sisters for the Museum of London (MOL), which now has two distinct themes: Londinium or Roman London and the original release (see also Pett 2011a: 119–120, 2011c; and Museum of London 2011). The former is currently only available on the iOS operating system (iPhone), whilst the latter is available on Android and iOS, therefore capturing a wider audience. The Apple iOS system is more aspirational, the operating system is locked to one piece of expensive hardware and hence limits the social demographic able to acquire the application and feel part of the community. However, this application was expensive to produce and could have perhaps saved a physical job from being lost in the recent job cuts that MOL announced. The HLF commissioned a rather lightweight report by Imagemakers (2011: 48) which states: 'the app has generated an estimated £750,000 worth of PR for the museum and driven an estimated three-fold increase in footfall'. *Ergo*, this is probably deemed to be a successful project and has recouped the costs.

b) Location based: *Historypin*

The Google sponsored partnership project with We Are What We Do, the *Historypin* project has actively sought collaboration from Museums, Libraries and

---

[44] http://www.museumoflondon.org.uk/Resources/app/you-are-here-app/index.html (accessed 20 October 2011).

Archives[45] (MLAs) in much the same way as the Flickr Commons programme. This website collates images via crowd sourcing with meta data for geographical location and time, attaching stories and anecdotes and it builds a photographic archive via place in a very simple model. The platform is now live on the two main mobile operating systems iOS and Android. One museum that has consistently engaged in early adoption of new technology, Brooklyn Museum of Art (see Bernstein 2011), decided to post a series of photographs[46] from their collection from unknown locations and then they invited people to geo-locate them.

c) Location based: Foursquare

The American museum community has been the market leader when it comes to interaction via the LBS platform Foursquare. The Metropolitan Museum of Art (MET) has worked in partnership with the social platform to develop badges for check-in rewards, as has Brooklyn Museum of Art. These rewards, which come in a variety of forms (e.g. if you are Mayor, most frequent visitor, check-in special etc.) are achieved after 'following' the institution on the Foursquare platform, and then checking in and thereby declaring your presence. The platform's API also allows for innovative reuse of data from their check-in log, for example Brooklyn built a Foursquare community page[47]. Examples of museum based rewards that are currently on offer in New York include:

1. Metropolitan Museum of Art (check-in special): Receive a complimentary reusable tote bag with your merchandise purchase of $20 or more at The Met Store, main shop only.

2. Brooklyn Museum of Art (Mayor special): 'If you're our mayor on First Saturday, show the Membership desk and we'll honor you with your very own 1st fans Membership for one year'.

3. The Museum of Sex (check-in special): The Museum of Sex is now serving alcohol! Celebrate our liquor license with $2 off any drink - aphrodisiac cocktails, wine and champagne. Head down to our subterranean OralFix Bar. CODE: FSFIX01

4. Queens Museum of Art (loyalty special): Thanks for being such a loyal fan of the Queens Museum of Art! To show our appreciation, we're giving you a FREE QMA t-shirt! To redeem, present this message to the Gift Shop.

d) Social network: *1st Fans*

Brooklyn Museum has leveraged the social networking of Twitter to produce an exclusive subscription based club (a tax deductable $20 per annum to participate). This initiative is labelled *1st Fans*[48] and provides the opportunity to participate in certain more exclusive museum activities (events, free luggage storage, queue jumping; for further discussion, see Simon 2009). While the efforts of Brooklyn's team have sometimes been discussed online in less than complimentary ways (MacManus 2011), the museum sector as a whole has recognised them as being effective, pioneering and innovative. Brooklyn has a wide array of social media outposts in its engagement portfolio and has found it hard to maintain a full profile on all of them.

e) Social network/ mobile gaming: *Tweet & Grow*

Kew Gardens has developed an application that can be played on the Web or via iOS or Android devices. This application is labelled *Tweet and Grow*[49] and revolves around gaming and decision

---

[45] http://www.historypin.com/community-partners-lams/ (accessed 20 September 2011).
[46] http://www.historypin.com/profile/view/Brooklyn%20Museum (accessed 20 September 2011).
[47] http://www.brooklynmuseum.org/community/foursquare/ (accessed 20 September 2011).
[48] http://www.brooklynmuseum.org/support/1stfans (accessed 20 September 2011).
[49] http://www.kew.org/visit-kew-gardens/summer/tweet-and-grow/index.htm (accessed 8 September 2011).

making, with discount codes built into the process. The application has a multi-faceted role; it is an educational and marketing tool within one silo, whilst also leveraging the power of social networks to get users to return, perhaps purchase items from the shop, interact and play the game. It provides a series of 'virtual' or in-game rewards as your plant is nurtured and grows, as well as a set of 'real' rewards. **Figure 24** below shows some baseline statistics for game play interaction.

Figure 24. The *Tweet & Grow* 'Global Garden' screen (see Plate 18).

Some of the gaming being done around the Museum sector allows for reconstruction of past lives and archaeologists' and museologists' interpretation of how they believe the past might have looked. Joyce and Tringham (2007: 348) comment on reconstruction: 'engage with the process of how I have reached my interpretations and how and why other archaeologists have reached theirs, with the ultimate aim of them creating their own plausible interpretations as narratives or scenarios'.

Hence, when creating a reconstruction of the past with which an audience is meant to engage, detail and the ability to tell a story can colour others' interpretations. When it comes to gaming, perhaps this is key and the authority that the institution can provide is vital.

Conclusion

This paper opened with a quotation that attempted to dictate why and how one should be using social media. The discussion that followed hopefully has gone some way towards explaining more about the exact process by which an institution leverages such tools. The adoption and adaption of social media is now an important agenda throughout the sector. When executed correctly, the results are extremely beneficial to a museum or archaeological institution's engagement with a wider audience. Social media can provide a platform for broadcasting propaganda, but need not cost a fortune, as the platforms that provide the greatest possibilities for audience interaction are typically also those that are free. Some institutions have adopted a pay wall model for accessing digital media (e.g. the Brooklyn Museum of Art) or have developed a digital club based around exclusivity (like the misguided *Time Team Digital* experiment, which broadcasts to Twitter via Facebook and interacts poorly). Experimentation is vital to establish what works and what does not. Failure is an option.

Many institutions are still exploring the correct level of licensing, with very few adopting an open access model. There are several innovators that should be seen as exemplars, and provide inspiration for others to emulate, for example the aforementioned Brooklyn Museum, the Tate and Indianapolis Museum of Art; but not every museum can follow the same approach. Regardless of the exact details, a successful social media strand to museum life demands a clear strategy, commitment, resources and personnel, directorate buy-in, marketing nous, a unique selling point (such as a particular collection) and a fan base to cultivate.

Questions remain about exactly what audience museums are gathering via social media. Are the people who follow or interact with museums online not already the ones who are well aware of these institutions' worth in society? Are such institutions thereby just further excluding part of their audience? There are clearly still issues here to unravel, but social media is about conversation. Make the conversation a good one and engagement will follow.

Acknowledgments

The author would like to thank Ian Richardson, Lena Zimmer, Ruth Levis, Katharine Kelland and

Matthew Cock (The British Museum), Tyler Bell (Factual Inc.), Chiara Bonacchi and Andy Bevan (University College London), for their comments on this article.

References

Adams K., 2011. *Flickr use* [conversation]. (Personal Communication, 03 November 2011).

Arrington M., 2011. Amazingly, MySpace's Decline Is Accelerating [online] 23 March 2011. Available at: http://techcrunch.com/2011/03/23/amazingly-myspaces-decline-is-accelerating/ (accessed 26 July 2011).

Arthur C., 2009. The long tail of blogging is dying. *The Guardian* [online] 24 June 2009. Available at: http://www.guardian.co.uk/technology/2009/jun/24/charles-arthur-blogging-twitter (accessed 06 September 2011).

Arts Council England, Museums Libraries and Archives Council, and Arts and Business, 2010. *Digital Audiences: Engagement with Arts and Culture Online* [online]. Available at: http://www.artscouncil.org.uk/media/uploads/doc/Digital_audiences_final.pdf (accessed 08 June 2011).

Atkinson R., 2011. Developing a social media strategy in Museum practice [online] 15 March 2011. Available at: http://www.museumsassociation.org/museum-practice/social-media (accessed 01 July 2011).

Basford F., 2011. *Flickr use* [email]. (Personal Communication, 2011).

BBC, n. d. Social Networking, Microblogs and Other Third Party Websites: BBC Use [online]. Available at: http://www.bbc.co.uk/editorialguidelines/page/guidance-blogs-bbc-full (accessed 06 September 2011).

Bell T. W., 2011. Smartphones and spheres of influence [online]. Available at: http://radar.oreilly.com/2011/07/smartphones-spheres-of-influence.html (accessed 27 July 2011).

Bernstein S., 2011. Help us pin Brooklyn to the map! [online] 21 June 2011. Available at: http://www.brooklynmuseum.org/community/blogosphere/2011/06/21/help-us-pin-brooklyn-to-the-map/ (accessed 08 September 2011).

Bisson S. and Branscombe M., 2011. Google's real problem: the smartest kids in the room [online] 18 August 2011. Available at: http://www.zdnet.co.uk/blogs/500-words-into-the-future-10014052/googles-real-problem-the-smartest-kids-in-the-room-10024153/ (accessed 06 September 2011).

Breen T. C., 2010. Irish archaeology on the Internet - Fifteen years on. *Archaeology Ireland* 24 (3), pp. 35–36

British Museum, 2008. *Strategy to 2012* [online]. Available at: http://www.britishmuseum.org/pdf/Strategy%20to%202012%20web%20version.pdf (accessed 05 September 2011).

British Museum, 2011. 2010–2011 *Review* [online]. Available at: http://www.britishmuseum.org/pdf/annualreview1011.pdf (accessed 05 September 2011).

Brown M., 2011. British Museum wins Art Fund prize. *The Guardian* [online] 15 June 2011. Available at: http://www.guardian.co.uk/culture/2011/jun/15/british-museum-wins-arts-fund-prize (accessed 05 September 2011).

Cassidy J., 2006. Me media. *The New Yorker* [online] 15 May 2006. Available at: http://www.newyorker.com/archive/2006/05/15/060515fa_fact_cassidy (accessed 06 September 2011).

Civil Service, 2009a. Principles for participation online [online]. Available at: http://www.civilservice.gov.uk/about/resources/participation-online.aspx (accessed 01 September 2011).

Civil Service, 2009b. Sir Gus' vision: The Four P's [online]. Available at: http://www.civilservice.gov.uk/about/values/vision.aspx (accessed 06 September 2011).

Cock M., 2011. On Air, Online and Onsite: The British Museum and BBC's 'A History of the World' [online]. Available at: http://conference.archimuse.com/mw2011/papers/on_air_online_and_onsite_the_british_museum_an (accessed 26 September 2011).

Cohen N., 2010. Venerable British Museum Enlists in the Wikipedia Revolution. *The New York Times* [online] 04 June 2009. Available at: http://www.nytimes.com/2010/06/05/arts/design/05wiki.html (accessed 05 September 2011).

Darch E., 2010. *Flickr use* [email]. (Personal Communication, 2010).

Dimicco J. M. and Millen D. R., 2007. Identity Management: Multiple Presentations of Self in Facebook. *GROUP'07* [online]. NY: ACM, pp. 383-386. DOI: 10.1145/1316624.1316682.

Eden T., 2011. Introducing QRpedia [online] 03 April 2011. Available at: http://shkspr.mobi/blog/index.php/2011/04/introducing-qrpedia/ (accessed 07 September 2011).

El Dahshan M., 2011. Facebook has little to fear from Muslim social networking sites. *The Guardian* [online] 31 May 2011. Available at: http://www.guardian.co.uk/commentisfree/belief/2011/may/31/muslim-social-networking (accessed 07 September 2011).

Eleftheriou-Smith L., 2011. Betfair puts QR codes on beach volleyball bum [online]. Available at: http://www.marketingmagazine.co.uk/news/1084029/

Betfair-puts-QR-codes-beach-volleyball-bums/ (accessed 06 September 2011).

Ellison N. B., Steinfield C. and Lampe C., 2007. The benefits of Facebook 'friends': Social capital and college students' use of online social network sites. *Journal of Computer-Mediated Communication* 12 (4) [online]. Available at: http://jcmc.indiana.edu/vol12/issue4/ellison.html (accessed 02 September 2011).

Finnis J., Chan S. and Clements R., 2011a. How to Evaluate Online Success? A New Piece of Action Research. In Trant J. and Bearman D. eds, 2011. *Museums and the Web 2011: Proceedings*. Toronto: Archives & Museum Informatics [online]. Available at: http://conference.archimuse.com/mw2011/papers/how_to_evaluate_online_success_a_new_piece_of_ (accessed 09 June 2011).

Finnis J., Chan S. and Clements R., 2011b. Let's get real: How to evaluate online success. Brighton: Culture24.

Fishkin R., 2011. *Tracking the KPIs of Social Media* [online]. Available at: http://www.seomoz.org/blog/tracking-the-roi-of-social-media (accessed 08 September 2011).

Fiske A., 1991. *Structures of Social Life: The Four Elementary Forms of Human Relations*. New York: The Free Press.

Garrahan M., 2009. The rise and fall of MySpace. *FT Magazine* [online] 04 December 2009. Available at: http://www.ft.com/cms/s/2/fd9ffd9c-dee5-11de-adff-00144feab49a.html#axzz1TK1iZYYR (accessed 26 July 2011).

Ghey E., 2011. Collections online at the British Museum. In Cook B. ed., 2011. *The British Museum and the future of UK numismatics*. London: British Museum Press, pp. 68–70.

Gibbins W., 2011. Local authorities should realise the potential in social media. *The Guardian* [online] 03 March 2011. Available at: http://www.guardian.co.uk/guardian-professional/2011/mar/03/engagement-hr (accessed 03 November 2011).

Halliday J., 2011. London riots: how Blackberry Messenger played a key role. *The Guardian* [online] 08 August 2011. Available at: http://www.guardian.co.uk/media/2011/aug/08/london-riots-facebook-twitter-blackberry (accessed 05 September 2011).

Higgins C., 2009. Museums' future lies on the Internet, say Serota and MacGregor. *The Guardian* [online] 08 July 2009. Available at: http://www.guardian.co.uk/artanddesign/2009/jul/08/museums-future-lies-online (accessed 25 July 2011).

Howard P. N., 2011. Digital media and the Arab Spring [online] 16 February 2011. Available at: http://blogs.reuters.com/great-debate/2011/02/16/digital-media-and-the-arab-spring/ (accessed 05 September 2011).

Imagemakers, 2011. *Digital Participation and Learning: 22 Case Studies* [online]. Available at: http://www.hlf.org.uk/aboutus/howwework/Documents/Digital_report_Sept2011.pdf (accessed 08 September 2011).

Joyce R. A. and Tringham R. E., 2007. Feminist Adventures in Hypertext. *Journal of Archaeological Method and Theory* 14 (3), pp. 328–358.

Kaplan A. M. and Haenlein M., 2010. Users of the world, unite! The challenges and opportunities of Social Media. *Business Horizons* 53 (1), pp. 59–68.

Kennedy M., 2011. British Museum remains UK's top attraction for fourth year running. *The Guardian* [online] 28 June 2011. Available at: http://www.guardian.co.uk/culture/2011/jun/28/british-museum-top-attraction (accessed 07 September 2011).

Klebe Treviño L., Webster J. and Stein E. W., 2000. Making Connections: Complementary Influences on Communication Media Choices Attitudes and Use. *Organization Science* 11 (2), pp. 163–182.

Kolbitsch J., 2007. Kōrero: An Integrated, Community-Based Platform for Collaboration [online]. Available at: http://www.kolbitsch.org/research/papers/2007-Korero.pdf (accesseed 02 November 2011).

MacGregor N. and Serota N., 2009. *The Museum of the 21st Century* [online] 07 July 2009. Available at: http://www2.lse.ac.uk/PublicEvents/events/2009/20090311t1917z001.aspx (accessed 25 July 2011).

Mannion S., 2011a. AR adventures at the British Museum [online]. Available at: http://www.slideshare.net/s.mannion/ar-adventures-at-the-british-museum (accessed 06 September 2011).

Mannion S., 2011b. Research on tablets for learning [online] 25 May 2011. Available at: http://wiki.museummobile.info/archives/91923 (accessed 07 September 2011).

MacManus R., 2011. Social media case study: Brooklyn Museum [online] 05 September 2011. Available at: http://www.readwriteweb.com/archives/social_media_case_study_brooklyn_museum.php (accessed 06 September 2011).

Morgan C., 2009. (Re)Building Çatalhöyük: Changing Virtual Reality in Archaeology. *Archaeologies: Journal of the World Archaeological Congress* 5 (3), pp. 468–487.

Museum of London, 2011. Museum of London Apps [online]. Available at: http://www.museumoflondon.org.uk/Explore-online/Apps/ (accessed 06 September 2011).

Nielsen J., 2006. Participation Inequality: Encouraging More Users to Contribute [online] 09 October 2006. Available at: http://www.useit.com/alertbox/participation_inequality.html (accessed 06 September 2011).

O'Brien M. J., 1996. *Evolutionary archaeology: Theory and applications*. Salt Lake City: University of Utah Press.

Ofcom (Office of Communication), 2011. Facts & Figures [online]. Available at: http://media.ofcom.org.uk/facts/ (accessed 15 April 2011).

ONS (Office for National Statistics), 2011. Population Estimates for UK, England and Wales, Scotland and Northern Ireland, Mid-2010 Population Estimates [online]. Available at: http://www.ons.gov.uk/ons/publications/re-reference-tables.html?edition=tcm%3A77-231847 (accessed 06 September 2011).

Pearse R., 2010. Wikipedia and the British Museum [online] 08 June 2010. Available at: http://www.roger-pearse.com/weblog/?p=4451 (accessed 05 September 2011).

Pett D. E. J., 2010. Meeting public interest in the hoard. *British Archaeology* 110, p. 51.

Pett D. E. J., 2011a. A review article. *Public Archaeology* 10 (2), pp. 119–127. DOI 10.1179/175355311X1 308661712664.

Pett D., 2011b. Distributing the wealth. In Cook B. ed., 2011. *The British Museum and the future of numismatics*. London: British Museum Press, pp. 71–80.

Pett D., 2011c. #ACRNCASPAR Workshop on Archaeologists & the Digital: Towards Strategies of Engagement. *7 Pillars of Wisdom* [online] 17 May 2011. Available at: http://www.7pillarsofwisdom.co.uk/acrncaspar-workshop-on-archaeologists-the-digital-towards-strategies-of-enga gement/ (accessed 06 September 2011).

Prudames D., 2011. *A History of the World wins Art Fund Prize for the British Museum* [online] 16 June 2011. Available at: http://www.bbc.co.uk/blogs/ahistory-oftheworld/2011/06/winning-the-art-fund-prize.shtml (accessed 05 September 2011).

Rainey J., 2011. Social media crackdown? It'd be more than unsociable. *Los Angeles Times* [online] 17 August 2011. Available at: http://www.latimes.com/entertainment/news/la-et-onthemedia-20110817,0,632518.column (accessed 06 September 2011).

Rangaswami J. P., 2008. Why I still use Facebook, and other musings on social networks [online] 18 January 2008. Available at: http://confusedofcalcutta.com/2008/01/18/why-i-still-use-facebook-and-other-musings-on-social-networks/ (accessed 06 September 2011).

Richardson L., 2011. My research [online]. Available at: http://digipubarch.org/myresearch/ (accessed 08 June 2011).

Ross C., Terras M., Warwick C. and Welsh A., 2011. Enabled backchannel: conference Twitter use by digital humanists. *Journal of Documentation* 67 (2), pp. 214–237. DOI: 10.1108/00220411111109449.

Rossoff M., 2011. Google kills off those little squares you scan with your phone. *Business Insider* [online] 31 March 2011. Available at: http://www.businessinsider.com/those-little-square-codes-you-scan-with-your-phone-are-dead-2011-3 (accessed 06 September 2011).

Simon N., 2008. How (and why) to develop a social media handbook. *Museum 2.0* [online] 27 October 2008. Available at: http://museumtwo.blogspot.com/2008/10/how-and-why-to-develop-social-media.html (accessed 07 September 2011).

Simon N., 2009. 1stfans: An Audience-Specific Membership Program at the Brooklyn Museum. *Museum 2.0* [online] 12 February 2009. Available at: http://museumtwo.blogspot.com/2009/02/1stfans-audience-specific-membership.html (accessed 06 September 2011).

Smithsonian Institution, 2009. Smithsonian Web and New Media Strategy [online]. Available at: http://smithsonian-webstrategy.wikispaces.com/Strategy+-+Table+of+Contents (accessed 08 September 2011).

Stewart E. P., 2010. Developing a Social Media Strategy. In MuseumsEtc, 2010 *Twitter for Museums: Strategies and Tactics for Success*. Milton Keynes: MuseumsEtc.

Wallis C., 2010. Who Uses Twitter. In MuseumsEtc, 2010. *Twitter for Museums: Strategies and Tactics for Success*. Milton Keynes: MuseumsEtc, pp. 22–31.

Ward W. J., 2011. How Quickly Has Social Media Grown And How Large Is The Global Impact? #infographic [online]. Available at: http://www.dr4ward.com/dr4ward/2011/09/how-quickly-has-social-media-grown-infographic.html (accessed 04 September 2011).

Warry E., 2011. *Classroom CSI: developing a video conferencing model for investigating British Archaeology in Schools*. University College London, unpublished Master's thesis.

Watters A., 2011. How recent changes to Twitter's terms of service might hurt academic research [online] 03 March 2011. Available at: http://www.readwriteweb.com/archives/how_recent_changes_to_twitters_terms_of_service_mi.php (accessed 01 June 2011).

Wyatt L., 2010. The British Museum and me [online]. Available at: http://www.wittylama.com/2010/03/the-british-museum-and-me/ (accessed 07 June 2011).

Wikipedia and Blogs: New Fields for Archaeological Research?

Amara Thornton

Abstract

Wikipedia and blogs have become a feature of modern life. Within what archaeologists might call the blink of an eye (the past decade), paper-based information exchange has been replaced by the Internet. Due to the huge popularity of search engines such as Google, Wikipedia has become the portal for quick facts, despite being the product of multiple authors and editors of varied backgrounds and claims to authenticity (see Lim 2009; Magnus 2009; Rosenzweig 2006). This paper discusses the value of Wikipedia and blogs for assessing public engagement in archaeology. It proposes that both can play an active role in introducing archaeological research to an increasingly active virtual community who can simultaneously challenge the 'academic' view of archaeology, its classifications and its terminology while yearning for more information to satisfy an ever growing thirst for accessible knowledge.

Introduction

In today's financially constrained environment, academia has been faced with the increasing importance of impact and accessibility as the 'value' of academic disciplines is assessed. The public facing branches of said disciplines are working to keep up with the rapid pace of the production of knowledge, which has changed immeasurably as the Internet has become a part of daily life. These developments have affected the way that academic research is conducted, opening new doors as previously relatively inaccessible materials and research have 'gone viral'. The field of public archaeology (see Ascherson 2000; Merriman 2004; Moshenska 2009; Schadla-Hall 1999) is now associated with defining the many ways in which archaeology/archaeologists and the public interact. Understanding how 'the public' understands archaeology is an essential part of this process. Examining how Wikipedia articles on archaeology are structured, when they were created and their edit and user history can inform archaeologists' conception of the nature of public understanding of and appreciation for archaeology. This approach also provides the potential for quantitative assessment of how the public interacts with archaeology online. Through conducting such an examination, this paper will assess how archaeology can be 'consumed' (see Moshenska 2009) by the public, while also highlighting the different routes of access to archaeology on Wikipedia. Similarly, moving beyond the numerous blogs created and maintained by practicing archaeologists, this paper uses publicly accessible blogs published in *The Guardian* online to explore the interaction between academic and practicing archaeologists and other scholars, and the public.[1]

Wikipedia: a brief history

Wikipedia was begun in 2001; its creation is largely attributed to American entrepreneur Jimmy Wales, although Wikipedia's history page states that Wikipedia was a group effort (see Edemariam 2011; Wikipedia 2011: History of Wikipedia; Jimmy Wales). Its basic structure enables any 'user' to create new articles or modify pre-existing ones; the quality of the resulting articles has been questioned throughout Wikipedia's history and remains problematic today (Wilkinson and Huberman 2007; Magnus 2009; Wikipedia 2011: Wikipedia: About). In addition, information presented on Wikipedia is edited anonymously; Wilkinson and Huberman state that 'While the wiki interface does facilitate coordination, it cannot resolve cultural or philosophical differences which result in a significant number of "edit wars" and mass deletions' (2007: 158).

Kittur *et al.* present data on how Wikipedia is edited and used, arguing that editing has shifted from a group of 'elite' users – such as Wikipedia administrators or prominent participants – to a wider group of 'common' users (Kittur *et al.* 2007: 1–2). Lim's research on how university students use Wikipedia included research indicating that its high ranking with search engines such as Google contributes to its popularity (Lim 2009: 2190). Lim also notes work indicating that Web-users' priority lies in functionality, usability and ease of access rather than individual author's identity and that these criteria may override information deemed 'credible' (2009: 2191). Magnus, presenting evidence for Wikipedia's difference from 'traditional' encyclopedias, discusses both its accessibility and its breadth in covering 'matters about which traditional encyclopedias are silent' (2009: 78–79). This last observation is particularly relevant for public archaeology as it enables archaeology to be incorporated *publicly* and *anonymously* into areas beyond the boundaries of the archaeological sector through linked layers of knowledge; Wikipedia enables a flexibility of approach to information presentation within a pre-formed framework – the Wikipedia 'Manual of Style' (2011; see also Mihalcea and Csomai 2007: 233). Highly specialised information can be accessible through layers of links, and anyone's interest can be accommodated through linkages.

Currently, Wikipedia has an ongoing project called *WikiProject Archaeology*[2] to improve the coverage of archaeology on Wikipedia and create new articles on archaeology or topics relating to archaeology. A tool linked to the 'view page statistics' button on the 'view history' page of any Wikipedia entry enables searches of Wikipedia statistics in different projects (i.e. the English Wikipedia). This tool publishes periodic lists of the Top 1000 most visited pages on Wikipedia; the latest list, dated December 2010, demonstrates that Wikipedia use is heavily dependent on the time of year – 'Christmas' being number ten on the list. The Top 1000 list also correlates to Spoerri's research on the Top 100 most visited Wikipedia pages between September 2006 and 2007, referenced in Lim (2009: 2190), which indicates that politics, history and entertainment were the top categories for Wikipedia searches (see also Rosenzweig 2006: 128). Archaeologically related articles that appeared on the Top 1000 list in December 2010 included: 'Acropolis of Athens' (No. 122), 'List of Greek mythological figures' (No. 538), 'Greek alphabet' (No. 596) and 'Great

---

[1] This paper is not intended to be a comprehensive survey of blog commentaries in online portals. *The Guardian* was chosen because it has a free and accessible online presence and is easily searchable, as opposed to *The Times* online, which operates a paywall system. However, a future research project could assess online commentary on archaeological news, whether on individual blogs or newspapers online more comprehensively.

[2] The Wikipedia: WikiProject Archaeology page (2011) also lists a number of related projects, which include: WikiProject Near East, WikiProject Ancient Egypt, WikiProject History, WikiProject Mesoamerica, WikiProject Science, WikiProject Bible and WikiProject Historic Sites.

Wall of China' (No. 852) demonstrating archaeology's links to sites, geographic regions/countries and cultures.[3]

Archaeology on Wikipedia

Rosenzweig's 2006 article on the future of Wikipedia's role in history writing offers some interesting insights and approaches well worth considering for archaeology given the mutual interest in 'the past' that the two disciplines espouse, albeit with different approaches. He emphasises Wikipedia's accessibility as one of its most important characteristics, arguing that, being more openly accessible than other more 'scholarly' sources, Wikipedia's policy of easy editing adds to its attractiveness as a highly popularly-utilized source.[4] Exploring Wikipedia's reliability against *Encarta* and *American National Biography Online* by in depth assessments of word counts, readability and references, he finds that, although Wikipedia holds its own in comparison to *Encyclopedia Britannica* and *Encarta*, it cannot match the scholarly, nuanced entries in *American National Biography* (2006: 127–130). However, he discusses Wikipedia's use as a teaching and training tool, examining how the structure of creating Wikipedia articles forces users to engage with the historical process and confront the fact that 'the "facts" of the past and the way those facts are arranged and reported are often highly contested' (Rosenzweig 2006: 138). Archaeologists, take note.

Voss refers to 'Wikipedia articles and the links between them' as 'a network of concepts' (2005: 9). Identifying keywords and linking to other Wikipedia articles is considered one of the key tasks in contributing to Wikipedia (see Mihalcea and Csomai 2007: 234). Although Wikipedia's Manual of Style warns against over-linking which might decrease an article's readability (Wikipedia 2011: Wikipedia: Manual of Style; see also Mihalcea and Csomai 2007: 235), Bryant *et al.* have found that linking often leads Wikipedia 'novices' to dip their proverbial toes into the Wikipedia pool and become involved in the editing and eventual creation of Wikipedia articles themselves (2005: 5). One of Wikipedia's most obvious benefits is in the ability for contributors to insert links where other media (i.e. print) or scholarly conventions might not make linking possible. Taking Magnus's point about the ability of Wikipedia to present information not traditionally covered by other encyclopedias, within Wikipedia articles it is possible and easy to link concepts together – improving the potential for information to become accessible and prominent. Wikipedia is, in essence, a way to choose your own adventure – from science to art, history, film, music and beyond.

The 'Archaeology' entry on Wikipedia is 6,258 words as of 19 July 2011. It was created on 3rd November 2001, has 1,526 users, and has been revised 3,092 times in total, with 1,054 being minor edits (Wikipedia 2011: Archaeology). It has ten sections, 334 linked terms, 77 footnotes, and a bibliography referencing 52 works, including Renfrew and Bahn's popular introductory textbook *Archaeology: Theories, Methods and Practice* (2004). An additional 16 works listed as 'Further Reading' and 20 'External links' make the entry appear fairly thorough, well referenced and authoritative, although heavily reliant on UK and US based publications.[5] As Wikipedia instructs article authors to verify information through citation and referencing (see Wikipedia 2011: Wikipedia: Verifiability), if a member of 'the public' with no introduction to archaeology were to read this Wikipedia page, he or she would, at the very least, be given a plethora of references and internal and external links to continue learning about archaeology and related fields or concepts. Archaeology is defined in Wikipedia as:

---

[3] The Wikipedia Top 1000 page views can be found at: http://stats.grok.se/en/top (accessed 30 October 2011). A general list of statistics for Wikipedia entries can be found at: http://en.wikipedia.org/wiki/Wikipedia:Statistics (accessed 30 October 2011).

[4] See Bryant *et al.* (2005) for an analysis of Wikipedia contributors' initial motivations for creating articles.

[5] Rosenzweig (2006: 128) also notes the tendency for Wikipedia's English project to reference 'Western' source material. See Magnus (2009) for a discussion of authority and Wikipedia 2011: Wikipedia: Verifiability for an outline of Wikipedia policies on article referencing.

the study of **human society**, primarily through the recovery and **analysis** of the **material culture** and environmental data that they have left behind, which includes **artifacts**, **architecture**, **biofacts** and **cultural landscapes** (the **archaeological record**) [words in bold represent internal links to Wikipedia entries on the respective terms] (Wikipedia 2011: Archaeology).

Of the terms linked within this initial definition, **human**, **artifacts**, **biofacts**, and **archaeological record** link back to **archaeology**. **Material culture** links back to **archaeology** through the hyperlinked term **archaeologist** which automatically redirects visitors to **archaeology**. **Society** and **cultural landscapes** refer to general concepts within the archaeological sphere but do not link directly back to **archaeology**. From this definition, a reader can find out an enormous amount about the value of archaeology. By clicking on **human** a reader is instantaneously transported to an article of over 9,000 words, with several sections dealing directly with archaeology in which links include **Middle Palaeolithic**, **out of Africa**, **hunter-gatherers**, **Neolithic Revolution**, **human settlements**, **Acheulean**, **artifacts**, and **stone tools**. And so the Web continues (see Milne and Witten 2008; Wikipedia 2012: Human; Artifact (archaeology); Biofact (archaeology); Archaeological record; Material culture; Society; Cultural landscapes).

The helpful hand of Indiana Jones?

Rosenzweig comments on Wikipedia's role as a repository for information on obscure or fictional persons, places and events. Referencing Wikipedia's article 'Why Wikipedia is not so great', Rosenzweig shows that at the beginning of Wikipedia's history those creating entries were more likely to be 'English-speaking, males, and denizens of the Internet' (2006: 127). The commonalities between 'Wikipedians' (see also Bryant *et al.* 2005) led to a higher number of lengthy mathematical and scientific articles than equivalent articles on culture, history or geography. However, Rosenzweig also states that entries follow current affairs closely, ensuring that articles on news events are as long or longer as important events in history, albeit with a strong 'Western' bias (2006: 127–128). Similarly, he notes that bias towards the subject of the entry is evident in Wikipedia articles, and, given the medium's democratic ethos, subjects which might be considered quite trivial are given what some might consider unmerited excess attention, although this judgment is entirely a matter of perspective (2006: 131, 141–142).

Indiana Jones, the fictional treasurer-hunter/archaeologist, darling of popular culture whom archaeologists love to love and hate in equal measure, provides as helpful a route into accessing archaeological information on Wikipedia as he has done in inspiring a generation (or more) of prospective archaeologists (see Gowlett 1990; Holtorf 2007, Chapter 5; Colley 2005). The 4,625 word entry on **Indiana Jones**, created on 2 July 2001, has 2,333 users and 4,773 revisions (of which 1,065 were minor edits) and merits a page view status of 1231. It has had 161,878 views in the last 30 days to 28 July 2011, compared to the 38,002 visitors to **archaeology**, ranking at 6704 for page view traffic, in the same period (Wikipedia 2011: Indiana Jones).[6] It would seem wise, given these figures, for archaeologists to consider where links can be made to archaeological Wikipedia articles. While the entry on Jones tends to reflect the intricacies of the film, television, video game and theme park bonanza that capitalises on the original storyline, there is room to insert a few more archaeological links. The 'Origins and Inspirations' section already links to **H. Rider Haggard** and **Arthur Conan Doyle**'s **Professor Challenger**, while 'Models' for Indiana Jones include **archaeologists Roy Chapman Andrews**, **Giovanni Battista Belzoni**, **James Henry Breasted**, **T. E. Lawrence**, **Percy Fawcett** and **Otto Rahn**.

A further section in the **Indiana Jones** entry could list some of the archaeological sites and civilisations (e.g. **Petra** and the **Nabataeans**)

---

[6] These figures have been obtained by using the 'Revision history statistics' and 'page view statistics' buttons on the 'Indiana Jones' and 'Archaeology' articles on Wikipedia.

associated with the films (e.g. **Indiana Jones and the Last Crusade**); some of which are covered in other Wikipedia entries (Wikipedia 2011: Petra; Nabataeans; Indiana Jones and the Last Crusade). Alternatively, if one wanted to dissect the films in more detail, in the first 30 minutes of *Indiana Jones and the Last Crusade* (Spielberg 1989), Flinders Petrie's excavation at Naukratis in 1885 is mentioned as the homework for Professor Jones' class. **Flinders Petrie** and **Naukratis** both have pre-existing Wikipedia articles – another link potential. *Raiders of the Lost Ark* (Spielberg 1981) presents even more links: Professor Jones lectures his love-struck students on the **Neolithic** barrow at **Turkdean**, **Gloucestershire**, with its associated **cist**s (chambers), and the danger of local legend-inspired **looting** (the current Wikipedia article on looting includes a section on archaeological removals and a link to **Grave robbery**) (Wikipedia 2011: Flinders Petrie; Neolithic; Turkdean; Gloucestershire; Cist; Looting; Grave robbery; Wikipedia 2012: Naukratis).[7] Even more divisive topics emerge in the following scene, where Jones is called an 'expert on the **occult** and obtainer of rare **antiquities**' (Wikipedia 2011: Archaeology; Occult; Antiquities). Shortly afterwards, Jones is sent to investigate German excavations at **Tanis**, another nice link back to **Flinders Petrie**, who excavated there in 1884.[8] While the Wikipedia page on **Tanis** includes links to articles on **Flinders Petrie** and **Raiders of the Lost Ark**, there is no link from **Flinders Petrie** to **Raiders of the Lost Ark**, and likewise no link from **Raiders of the Lost Ark** to **Flinders Petrie** (Wikipedia 2011: Flinders Petrie; Raiders of the Lost Ark; Tanis). This example helps to justify the need for well placed links between popular culture and archaeological articles – in one click readers can obtain references and links to scholarly articles on archaeological topics merely by following an interest in Indiana Jones.

Through compiling a list of key terms in the **archaeology** and **Indiana Jones** Wikipedia articles, it is evident that given Wikipedia's high Google rankings, an alliance with popular culture and incorporation with broader concepts on Wikipedia would be beneficial, with great potential for archaeology to become more visible and more publicly accessible. Providing adequate links can encourage new users to Wikipedia, and create a route by which to improve the integration of archaeological fact (or interpretation) and popular culture.

Wikipedia and beyond

Wikipedia's scope is not limited to the information contained on www.wikipedia.org. As mentioned above, its popularity can be perhaps greatly attributed to its high Google ranking – the order in which webpages or sites appear if a term is entered into the Google search box. In addition, Rosenzweig notes that Wikipedia's entries reach beyond the high Google ranking through the extrapolation and re-publication of Wikipedia entries onto sites such as Answers.com and Reference.com (2006: 134, 136–137).

For scholars, this breadth can have a tangible bonus. An independent network of historians has been using Wikipedia's references section to link to historical research on topics pertaining to the Wikipedia entries. In a recent letter to *The Guardian* they noted that:

> a few dozen links increased visitors from Wikipedia to H & P [History and Policy] significantly, moving the online encyclopedia from below 10th to the third most popular source of traffic to our site. We intend to continue embedding links to our papers in relevant Wikipedia entries (Berridge *et al.* 2011).

Wikipedia is now actively searching for more input from academics, conducting a survey, now closed, entitled *Expert Barriers to Wikipedia* (see Corbyn 2011). The British Museum has also recently begun to engage with Wikipedia, arranging

---

[7] Currently, the Wikipedia article on Turkdean has a section on Jones' use of the site in his classroom; however, the *Raiders of the Lost Ark* Wikipedia article does not link to the Turkdean page (Wikipedia 2011: Raiders of the Lost Ark; Turkdean).

[8] A list of Petrie's excavations by season can be found at: http://www.digitalegypt.ucl.ac.uk/archaeology/petriedigsindex.html (accessed 30 October 2011).

for a temporary 'Wikipedian in residence' in 2010 to cement the relationship and enhance the Wikipedia entries relating to the Museum and its collections (Wikipedia 2011: Wikipedia: GLAM/BM/Wikipedian in Residence; Cohon 2010). Current projects include events to construct and edit Wikipedia articles on the Bronze Age and Ice Age (Wikipedia 2012: Wikipedia: GLAM/BM), and the *Wikipedia in Residence* project has expanded to other institutions such as the US National Archives (National Archives 2011).

It is also forging connections to popular social media platforms – in April 2010, Facebook launched 'Community pages', which are defined as 'pages based on topics of interest to the community that are not maintained by a single author' (Park 2010). Under a Creative Commons License, content from Wikipedia, as collectively authored content of the community, can now be accessed on Facebook (Park 2010). Facebook's 'like' feature is another way to gauge how people respond to archaeology, through the number of 'likes' archaeologically-related Wikipedia Facebook pages generate. John Garstang, a British archaeologist and first Professor of the Methods and Practice of Archaeology at Liverpool University's Institute of Archaeology, which he helped establish in 1902, has generated three 'likes' as of July 2011 (see Facebook 2011: John Garstang; Gurney and Freeman 2004). Flinders Petrie, much better known, has generated 242 'likes' as of July 2011 (Facebook 2011 a, b: Flinders Petrie). Another facet of archaeology on Facebook is the ability for famous archaeologists to acquire Facebook pages. Some of these pages link them to their 'friends' who also have Facebook pages, and provide details of their personal and professional lives (see Facebook 2011 b: Flinders Petrie). Sir R. E. Mortimer Wheeler, founder of the Institute of Archaeology in London, currently has three separate Facebook profile pages (Facebook 2011 a, b, c: Mortimer Wheeler).

Blogs and archaeology

Although Facebook 'likes' and comments shared on Facebook pages represent some quantitative and qualitative data on the public – although a very skewed proportion – response to archaeology on the Web, further quantitative and qualitative assessment of how the public views archaeology can be found in the public response to archaeological articles, by reading through the comment section in *The Guardian*'s online blogs. There are an increasing number of blogs by archaeologists and archaeological interest groups on the Web. A recent entry on the 'Electric Archaeology' blog notes that Archaeological blogs are becoming more and more popular (*The Archaeological Blogosphere*; see Graham 2011), but it is difficult to tell how accessible they are to those outside the academic blogging community. Tom Goskar has recently published a list of archaeological blogs from a range of archaeologists and heritage professionals (Goskar 2011). There are also networks of archaeological bloggers, such as the Ancient World Bloggers Group (AWBG 2011). However, it remains difficult to assess how effective these blogs are in engaging 'the public' in archaeological research. Quantitative information on visitors to blogs can be gathered using a number of open-access tools, but unless the blog creator chooses to make this information visible on the blog the numbers go undocumented in any public sense.

However, blogs about archaeological topics published in *The Guardian* online, can be much more informative about the public view of archaeology. The paper's online forum enables 'the public' to comment and share or 'like' articles via Twitter and Facebook. These features enable those interested in the public response to archaeological information to have some idea of how many people have read and/or shared that information with others in a way that was not possible for paper-based media.

A recent blog by *The Guardian* art critic Jonathan Jones, entitled 'Who are the Coptic Christians', published on 11 May 2011, by 13 May 2011 had generated 153 comments, 73 tweets and it was shared by 467 people on Facebook. The blog contained a link to the Petrie Museum of Egyptology, and references to material found in archaeological contexts. It also represents the timeliness of such a piece just a few days after violent clashes between Copts and Muslims in Cairo (Jones 2011). Another blog with less political relevance, 'Did aliens establish a primitive postcode system in Ancient Britain', posted on *The Guardian* on 21 April 2011, generated only 31 comments and 88 tweets, but was shared by 728 people on Facebook by 13 May 2011 (Parker 2011). A more nuanced blog by Richard Sugg of Durham University's English Department, explained some of the historical context behind drinking from human skulls, following an article on drinking vessels made from skulls found by archaeologists in Cheddar, Somerset. This blog, written by an academic, generated 111 comments, 21 tweets and was shared by 76 people on Facebook (Sugg 2011). Finally, historian of ancient history Richard Miles' lengthy post on a recently discovered purported Roman era refugee camp near Hadrian's Wall, published in *The Guardian*'s 'Comment is Free' section on 24 June 2011, demonstrates how effective the intermingling of past and present can be for generating interest (whether positive or negative) around a contentious topic – in this case, the treatment of 'refugees' or 'asylum seekers' by the Romans (Miles 2011). Miles' article generated 165 comments and 22 tweets. Clearly there is potential and a comment-friendly audience for more guest bloggers on archaeology. In addition, these platforms can help archaeologists to assess how information about archaeology is processed and shared by the English-speaking public, if even a small portion of it. This is a new feature of our Internet-dominated age – the ability to generate a vast amount of surveyable information which is maintained and stored on websites. Qualitative and quantitative analysis of the comments on these articles could prove informative for future strategies in public engagement for archaeology.

Conclusion

This brief exploration into the potential of Wikipedia and blogs for the public's reception of information about archaeology demonstrates that the digital information age we are currently experiencing can be harnessed and used for the benefit of the subject and its practitioners. Both Wikipedia and blogs are clearly important public forums for informative communication, discussion and debate. The archaeological network, in its widest sense, should embrace these platforms and familiarise itself with the tools they provide to gauge public reception and become more aware of the power of search engine promotion. Both Wikipedia and blogs enable the academic community to promote informed, engaged access to information about the past.

As academia finds itself under pressure to demonstrate assessable public impact and value in this period of economic distress, all the myriad ways in which these calls for assessment can be addressed should be acknowledged and utilized. Archaeological blog networks can be encouraged to monitor visits to their blogs and feed these results into future research, while making sure that their blogs are as openly accessible as possible. In order to do this effectively, we need to continue raising awareness within the sector of the terminology (e.g. sharing, tweeting and retweeting, 'liking') associated with social media and the Internet, and the potential assets both methods represent for assessing impact and value of archaeological publications and features. This awareness will enable us to mine comments for information on how information on archaeology is being interpreted and reinterpreted by members of the public, given the open-access platform that online publications such as *Guardian Online* encapsulate.

The studies referenced in this paper show Wikipedia's pervasiveness in popular culture, especially when considering its articles often occupy the top positions on Google. Archaeological institutions such as the British Museum are now beginning to take advantage of this prime Internet position. As Wikipedia itself urges academics to become more involved in contributing and editing articles, the academy has, in part, responded with questions about how and whether to add collaboration and creation with Wikipedia to their already heavily burdened shoulders when contributions may be challenged or edited and there is no prospect of remuneration or acknowledgement for their efforts (Corbyn 2011). However, as other scholars have noted, Wikipedia remains an increasingly important readily available source of information, encapsulating the invested interest of many thousands (if not more) of anonymous contributors. In engaging with Wikipedia as scholars, we should consider the structure and form of articles – making sure that subdivisions and wider links are exploited as much as possible. Learning how to link effectively, drawing the reader into more and more sophisticated levels of information, can ensure the survival of academia and research today, given Wikipedia's high profile. The recognition potential academic contributers seek will come from drawing public attention through references to external sites – using Wikipedia as the portal it is meant to be. Although the online encyclopedia's entries may not reflect the priorities, accuracy or literary panache of other publications, the only solution to these problems is the investment of time and knowledge for the benefit of society – and perhaps the future of education for all. Wikipedia's very flexibility works in our favour – we can contribute as much or as little as we want, taking advantage of the breadth of coverage to expand our own horizons, making links wherever we see fit.

Acknowledgements

Thanks are due to Dan Pett, Tom Goskar, Dr Andy Bevan, Drs John Thornton and Linda Heywood and my two anonymous reviewers for their comments.

References

Ancient World Bloggers Group, 2011. *Ancient World Bloggers Group (AWBG)* [online]. Available at: http://ancientworldbloggers.blogspot.com/ (accessed 12 May 2011).

Archaeology – article revision statistics, 2011. *General Statistics, Year Counts, Edits over Time* [online]. Available at: http://toolserver.org/~soxred93/articleinfo/index.php?article=Archaeology&lang=en&wiki=wikipedia (accessed 25 July 2011).

Ascherson N., 2000. Editorial. *Public Archaeology* 1 (1), pp. 1–4.

Berridge V., Reid A. and Szreter S., 2011. Footnotes, history and Wikipedia. *The Guardian* [online] 08 April 2011. Available at: http://www.guardian.co.uk/technology/2011/apr/08/footnotes-history-wikipedia?INTCMP=SRCH (accessed 11 May 2011).

Bryant S. L., Forte A. and Bruckman A., 2005. Becoming Wikipedian: Transformation of Participation in a Collaborative Online Encyclopedia. *Proceedings of the 2005 International ACM SIGGROUP Conference on supporting group work* [online]. Available at: http://dl.acm.org/citation.cfm?id=1099205 (accessed 26 July 2011).

Cohen N., 2010. Venerable British Museum Enlists in Wikipedia Revolution. *The New York Times* [online] 04 June 2010. Available at: http://www.nytimes.com/2010/06/05/arts/design/05wiki.html (accessed 29 July 2011).

Colley S., 2005. 'Consumer choice' and public archaeology in and beyond the academy. *Australian Archaeology* 61, pp. 56–63.

Corbyn Z., 2011. Wikipedia wants more contributions from academics. *The Guardian* [online] 29 March 2011. Available at: http://www.guardian.co.uk/education/2011/mar/29/wikipedia-survey-academic-contributions (accessed 13 May 2011).

Edemariam A., 2011. The Saturday interview: Wikipedia's Jimmy Wales. *The Guardian* [online] 19 February 2011. Available at: http://www.guardian.co.uk/theguardian/2011/feb/19/interview-jimmy-wales-wikipedia (accessed 16 July 2011).

Facebook, 2011.

———a. Flinders Petrie [online]. Available at: http://www.facebook.com/pages/Flinders-Petrie/104075192962645 (accessed 09 October 2011).

———b. Flinders Petrie [online]. Available at: http://www.facebook.com/FlindersPetrie (accessed 09 October 2011).

———. John Garstang [online]. Available at: http://www.facebook.com/pages/John-Garstang/104051999631197 (accessed 09 October 2011).

———a. Mortimer Wheeler [online]. Available at: http://www.facebook.com/pages/Mortimer-Wheeler/112943805386294 (accessed 09 October 2011).

———b. Mortimer Wheeler [online]. Available at: http://www.facebook.com/pages/Sir-Mortimer-Wheeler/96164868952 (accessed 09 October 2011).

———c. Mortimer Wheeler [online]. Available at: http://en-gb.facebook.com/people/Mortimer-Wheeler/100002536786185 (accessed 09 October 2011).

Goskar T., 2011. Archaeology Blogs. *Past Thinking: Archaeology, Heritage and Museums – It's Everybody's Past* [online] April 2011. Available at: http://www.pastthinking.com/links/ (accessed 12 May 2011).

Gowlett J. A., 1990. Review: Indiana Jones: crusading for archaeology? *Antiquity* 64, p. 157.

Graham S., 2011. The Archaeological Blogosphere. *Electric Archaeology: Digital Media for Learning and Research* [online] 01 April 2011. Available at: http://electricarchaeologist.wordpress.com/author/

fhg1711/ (accessed 12 May 2011).

Gurney O. R. and Freeman P. W., 2004. Garstang, John Burges Eustace (1876–1956). In *Oxford Dictionary of National Biography* [online ed.] Oxford University Press. Available at: http://www.oxforddnb.com/index/33/101033341/ (accessed 30 November 2011).

Holtorf C., 2007. *Archaeology is a brand! The meaning of archaeology in contemporary popular culture*. Walnut Creek, CA: Left Coast Press.

Jones J., 2011. Who are the Coptic Christians? *The Guardian* [online] 11 May 2011. Available at: http://www.guardian.co.uk/artanddesign/jonathanjones-blog/2011/may/11/coptic-christians-ancient-egypt (accessed 13 May 2011).

Kittur A., Chi E., Pendleton B., Suh B. and Mytkowicz T., 2007. *Power of the Few vs. Wisdom of the Crowd: Wikipedia and the Rise of the Bourgeoisie* [online]. Available at: http://www.viktoria.se/altchi/submissions/submission_edchi_1.pdf (accessed 11 May 2011).

Lim S., 2009. How and why do college students use Wikipedia? *Journal of the American Society for Information Science and Technology* 60 (11), pp. 2189–2202.

Magnus P. D., 2009. On Trusting Wikipedia [online]. Available at: http://www.euppublishing.com/doi/pdfplus/10.3366/E1742360008000555 (accessed 16 June 2011).

Merriman N. ed., 2004. *Public Archaeology*. London: Routledge.

Mihalcea R. and Csomai A., 2007. Wikify! Linking Documents to Encyclopedic Knowledge. *CIKM '07: Proceedings of the sixteenth ACM Conference on information and knowledge management* [online]. Available at: http://www.cse.unt.edu/~rada/papers/mihalcea.cikm07.pdf (accessed 26 July 2011).

Miles R., 2011. Comment is Free: What the Romans can teach us about refugees. *The Guardian* [online] 24 June 2011. Available at: http://www.guardian.co.uk/commentisfree/2011/jun/24/roman-refugees-battle-adrianople (accessed 01 August 2011).

Milne D. and Witten I. H., 2008. Learning to Link with Wikipedia. *CIKM '08: Proceedings of the 17th ACM conference on information and knowledge management* [online]. Available at: http://dl.acm.org/citation.cfm?id=1458150&bnc=1 (accessed 01 August 2011).

Moshenska G., 2009. What is public archaeology? *Present Pasts* 1, pp. 46–48.

National Archives, 2011. National Archives announces First 'Wikipedian in Residence' [online]. Available at: http://www.archives.gov/press/press-releases/2011/nr11-130.html (accessed 14 October 2011).

Park J., 2010. *Wikipedia on new Facebook community pages* [online] 21 April 2010. Available at: https://creativecommons.org/weblog/entry/21721 (accessed 12 May 2011).

Parker M., 2011. Did aliens establish a primitive postcode system in Ancient Britain? *The Guardian* [online] 21 April 2011. Available at: http://www.guardian.co.uk/science/blog/2011/apr/21/aliens-postcode-system-ancient-britain (accessed 01 August 2011).

Renfrew C. and Bahn P. G., 2004. *Archaeology: Theories, Methods and Practice*. London: Thames & Hudson.

Rosenzweig R., 2006. Can History be Open Source? Wikipedia and the Future of the Past. *Journal of American History* 93 (1), pp. 117–146.

Schadla-Hall T., 1999. Public Archaeology. *European Journal of Archaeology* 2 (2), pp. 147–158.

Spielberg S., 1981. *Indiana Jones and the Raiders of the Lost Ark*. Paramount Pictures/Lucasfilm.

Spielberg S., 1989. *Indiana Jones and the Last Crusade*. Paramount Pictures/Lucasfilm.

Sugg R., 2011. Brain Food: The History of Skull Drinking. *The Guardian* [online] 18 February 2011. Available at: http://www.guardian.co.uk/commentisfree/2011/feb/18/1 (accessed 13 May 2011).

Voss J., 2005. Measuring Wikipedia. *International Conference of the International Society for Scientometrics and Infometrics*. Stockholm, Sweden, 24–28 July 2005 [online]. Available at: http://hapticity.net/pdf/nime2006_180-works_cited/MeasuringWikipedia2005.pdf (accessed 26 July 2011).

Wikipedia, 2011.

———. Antiquities [online] 09 October 2011. Available at: http://en.wikipedia.org/wiki/Antiquities (accessed 09 October 2011).

———. Archaeology [online] 19 July 2011. Available at: http://en.wikipedia.org/wiki/Archaeology (accessed 26 July 2011).

———. Archaeology: Revision history statistics [online] July 2011. Available at: http://toolserver.org/~soxred93/articleinfo/index.php?article=Archaeology&lang=en&wiki=wikipedia (accessed 26 July 2011).

———. Arthur Conan Doyle [online] 09 October 2011. Available at: http://en.wikipedia.org/wiki/Arthur_Conan_Doyle (accessed 09 October 2011).

———. Cist [online] 09 October 2011. Available at: http://en.wikipedia.org/wiki/Cist (accessed 09 October 2011).

———. Flinders Petrie [online] 09 October 2011. Available at: http://en.wikipedia.org/wiki/Flinders_petrie (accessed 09 October 2011).

———. Giovanni Battista Belzoni [online] 09 October. Available at: http://en.wikipedia.org/wiki/Giovanni_Battista_Belzoni (accessed 09 October 2011).

———. Gloucestershire [online] 09 October 2011. Available at: http://en.wikipedia.org/wiki/Gloucestershire (accessed 09 October 2011).

———. Grave Robbery [online] 09 October 2011. Available at: http://en.wikipedia.org/wiki/Grave_robbery (accessed 09 October 2011).

———. H. Rider Haggard [online] 09 October 2011. Available at: http://en.wikipedia.org/wiki/H._Rider_Haggard (accessed 09 October 2011).

———. History of Wikipedia [online] 05 May 2011. Available at: http://en.wikipedia.org/wiki/History_of_Wikipedia (accessed 11 May 2011).

———. Indiana Jones [online] 26 July 2011. Available at: http://en.wikipedia.org/wiki/Indiana_Jones (accessed 28 July 2011).

———. Indiana Jones and the Last Crusade [online] 09 October 2011. Available at: http://en.wikipedia.org/wiki/Indiana_Jones_and_the_Last_Crusade (accessed 09 October 2011).

———. James Henry Breasted [online] 09 October 2011. Available at: http://en.wikipedia.org/wiki/James_Henry_Breasted (accessed 09 October 2011).

———. Jimmy Wales [online] 10 May 2011. Available at: http://en.wikipedia.org/wiki/Jimmy_Wales (accessed 11 May 2011).

———. Looting [online] 09 October 2011. Available at: http://en.wikipedia.org/wiki/Looting (accessed 09 October 2011).

———. Nabataeans [online] 09 October 2011. Available at: http://en.wikipedia.org/wiki/Nabataeans (accessed 09 October 2011).

———. Neolithic [online] 09 October 2011. Available at: http://en.wikipedia.org/wiki/Neolithic (accessed 09 October 2011).

———. Occult [online] 09 October 2011. Available at: http://en.wikipedia.org/wiki/Occult (accessed 09 October 2011).

———. Otto Rahn [online] 09 October 2011. Available at: http://en.wikipedia.org/wiki/Otto_Rahn (accessed 09 October 2011).

———. Percy Fawcett [online] 09 October 2011. Available at: http://en.wikipedia.org/wiki/Percy_Fawcett (accessed 09 October 2011).

———. Petra [online] 09 October 2011. Available at: http://en.wikipedia.org/wiki/Petra (accessed 09 October 2011).

———. Professor Challenger [online] 09 October 2011. Available at: http://en.wikipedia.org/wiki/Professor_Challenger (accessed 09 October 2011).

———. Raiders of the Lost Ark [online] 09 October 2011. Available at: http://en.wikipedia.org/wiki/Raiders_of_the_Lost_Ark (accessed 09 October 2011).

———. Roy Chapman Andrews [online] 09 October 2011. Available at: http://en.wikipedia.org/wiki/Roy_Chapman_Andrews (accessed 09 October 2011).

———. T. E. Lawrence [online] 09 October 2011. Available at: http://en.wikipedia.org/wiki/T._E._Lawrence (accessed 09 October 2011).

———. Tanis [online] 09 October 2011. Available at: http://en.wikipedia.org/wiki/Tanis (accessed 09 October 2011).

———. Turkdean [online] 09 October 2011. Available at: http://en.wikipedia.org/wiki/Turkdean (accessed 09 October 2011).

———. Wikipedia: About [online] 22 July 2011. Available at: http://en.wikipedia.org/wiki/Wikipedia:About (accessed 25 July 2011).

———. Wikipedia: GLAM/BM/Wikipedian in Residence [online] 26 July 2011. Available at: http://en.wikipedia.org/wiki/Wikipedia:GLAM/BM/Wikipedian_in_Residence (accessed 29 July 2011).

———. Wikipedia: Manual of Style [online] 26 July 2011. Available at: http://en.wikipedia.org/wiki/Wikipedia:Manual_of_Style#Links (accessed 26 July 2011).

———. Wikipedia: Verifiability [online] 08 October 2011. Available at: http://en.wikipedia.org/wiki/Wikipedia:Verifiability (accessed 08 October 2011).

———. Wikipedia: WikiProject Archaeology [online] 07 May 2011. Available at: http://en.wikipedia.org/wiki/WikiProject_Archaeology (accessed 16 July 2011).

Wikipedia, 2012.

———. Archaeological record [online] 23 January 2012. Available at: http://en.wikipedia.org/wiki/Archaeological_record (accessed 23 January 2012).

———. Artifact (archaeology) [online] 23 January 2012. Available at: http://en.wikipedia.org/wiki/Artifact_(archaeology) (accessed 23 January 2012).

———. Biofact (archaeology) [online] 23 January 2012. Available at: http://en.wikipedia.org/wiki/Biofact_(archaeology) (accessed 23 January 2012).

———. Cultural landscapes [online] 23 January 2012. Available at: http://en.wikipedia.org/wiki/Cultural_landscapes (accessed 23 January 2012).

———. Human [online] 23 January 2012. Available at: http://en.wikipedia.org/wiki/Human (accessed 23 January 2012).

———. Material culture [online] 23 January 2012. Available at: http://en.wikipedia.org/wiki/Material_culture (accessed 23 January 2012).

———. Naukratis [online] 23 January 2012. Available at: http://en.wikipedia.org/wiki/Naukratis (accessed 23 January 2012).

———. Society [online] 23 January 2012. Available at: http://en.wikipedia.org/wiki/Society (accessed 23 January 2012).

———. Wikipedia: GLAM/BM [online] 23 January 2012. Available at: http://en.wikipedia.org/wiki/Wikipedia:GLAM/BM (accessed 23 January 2012).

Wikipedia article traffic statistics, 2011 [online]. Available at: http://stats.grok.se/ (accessed 16 July 2011).

Wikipedia article traffic statistics: most viewed articles in 201012, 2010 [online] December 2010. Available at: http://stats.grok.se/en/top (accessed 16 July 2011).

Wilkinson D. and Huberman B., 2007. Cooperation and Quality in Wikipedia. *WikiSym '07*. Montreal.

A Call for Open Scholarship in Archaeology

Brian Hole

Abstract

Open Scholarship is a term that covers a range of information sharing mechanisms, including e-Publishing, Open Access and Open Data. This chapter argues that these behaviours need to become more widely adopted in archaeology, especially in the context of an environment where funding is difficult to obtain and there is strong competition from other disciplines. It makes nine recommendations on how to achieve this, including the use of data journals to maximise research impact.

Introduction

Along with other disciplines in the humanities, archaeology is in a difficult position when the government funding it depends upon is provided under competitive conditions that ask it to demonstrate its 'impact' relative to fields in Science, Technology and Medicine (STM, sometimes also including Engineering to become STEM) that have closer ties to industry. As this chapter will discuss, Open Scholarship incorporates mechanisms such as e-Publishing, Open Access (OA) and Open Data, which lead to greater exposure, recognition and funding. But it is also much more than this – it is a culture of sharing, collaboration and efficiency among researchers that leads to more rapid advancement in knowledge.

The need to demonstrate greater impact for funding

In an environment of financial austerity the humanities must begin following developments in this direction within STM in order to remain competitive. The competition for resources in the UK is very real, acute and serious:

> the enormous achievements of non-STEM disciplines are often overlooked – even when these involve, as so often, vital interdisciplinary research spanning the natural and social sciences. These misconceptions are potentially very damaging, especially at a time of diminishing resources. As modern research has become more and more interdisciplinary, and we move increasingly beyond the sterile and outdated notion of a society of "two cultures", the mutual dependencies of "hard" science and the humanities and social sciences have become ever clearer (British Academy 2010: 5).

This misconception of the relative value of the humanities continues to exist even at a purely economic level, despite estimates from economists that for every £1 spent on humanities research, £10 of immediate benefit is derived, with another £15–£20 in the long term (AHRC 2009: 3). Archaeology contributes a significant share to this, especially through its integral support of the heritage and tourism industries, alone worth over £20.6 billion in GDP and supporting around 466,000 jobs (HLF 2010: 5). Despite this, when it comes to making budgetary decisions the humanities often come out on the losing side. A stark example of this is the announcement by London Metropolitan University that it plans to shut down 400 of its 577 courses, almost all of which are in the arts and humanities (Swain 2011). Archaeology has also been hit directly, with the Council for British Archaeology (CBA) set to lose all of its funding by 2015 (British Academy 2011).

In order to mitigate further cuts, and even reverse them if possible, it is therefore essential that all areas of the humanities including archaeology find ways to create and exhibit greater impact. This is especially important for university archaeology departments, who have to compete for funding by demonstrating impact in the Research Excellence Framework (REF) exercise. This can be done by embracing recent developments more prevalent in STM as well as the principles of Open Scholarship. In order to do this, it is important to note that there are significant differences in the way that research is both carried out and disseminated between the humanities and STM. Humanities researchers publish a far greater proportion of their work (around 50% compared to 20%) in monograph form for example (Huang and Chang 2008: 1820), and exhibit '… only limited uptake of even simple, freely available tools for data management and sharing' (RIN 2011: 7).

Open Scholarship

There is a general trend towards more open practices in science and technology, which has impacted both the scholarly process and publishing industry in several ways. Open source software has made it affordable for academic societies and smaller companies to enter the e-Publishing space. At the same time demand from researchers, Higher Education Institutions (HEIs) and funding bodies for more affordable access to research outputs has resulted in a rapidly increasing number of HEI research paper repositories ('Green' Open Access), Open Access journals ('Gold' Open Access), and more recently, Open Data repositories. A growing body of evidence is now accumulating that demonstrates that open practices lead to greater collaboration (e.g. Zhang and Chen 2010), increased efficiency of research (e.g. Houghton *et al*. 2009), and higher and wider impact (e.g. Evans and Reimer 2009). A great benefit of open systems having been designed to enable sharing is that, albeit imperfectly, they provide mechanisms for tracking the usage of scholarly outputs and providing statistical measures of their impact. This not only motivates individual researchers to take part by providing mechanisms for recognition and reward, it also has the potential to provide policy making and funding bodies with more accurate decision-making metrics when comparing the value and impact of various disciplines. All of this together can be termed Open Scholarship (**Figure 25**).

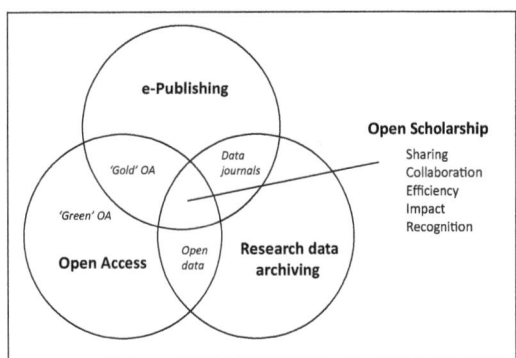

Figure 25. Venn diagram of Open Scholarship factors (see Plate 19).

There are many reasons for archaeology to make a cultural shift and embrace Open Scholarship, including the benefits of greater efficiency, impact and collaboration. The most pressing however is the need to be able to fully articulate its value and impact to government in order to receive a fair share of funding and protect its future. To do so it is necessary to keep apace with developments in other academic areas, especially STM, for which a funding bias currently exists and needs to be addressed. The following sections look at what embracing Open Scholarship will require in each of its main component areas – e-Publishing, Open Access and Open Data, from which a series of recommendations are then drawn.

e-Publishing

Along with conferences, publishing is the most prevalent means of disseminating research in the humanities. Publishing practices however are significantly behind those in the STM when it comes to wide distribution, tracking of impact, and rewarding of researchers. In order to reach as many readers as possible, it is essential to publish a paper electronically. Over 96.1% of STM journals have an electronic edition, but the humanities and social sciences are still trailing with 86.5% (RIN 2009: 14). The importance of this is highlighted by several studies that have shown that readership trends are strongly favouring e-journals. Tenopir *et al.* have found that electronic versions of articles now account for the majority of readings in the sciences (2008: 5), and a recent study titled *Information Behaviour of the Researcher of the Future* by the UCL CIBER group found that the younger the scholar, the stronger the preference for e-materials:

> The age differences are startling and they suggest that the shift away from the physical to the virtual library will accelerate very rapidly (CIBER 2008: 13).

What this means is that work published in print-only journals will not only be less likely to be read, but that in the near future it will hardly have any audience at all. The outlook is the same for monograph publishing, also of great importance to archaeologists. The CIBER study also mentions the 'inexorable rise of the e-book', predicting that they will soon be the 'primary format for educational textbooks and scholarly books and monographs' (CIBER 2008: 26). This is backed up by the JISC *National e-Books Observatory Project* report that found that nearly 65% of UK teaching staff and students have used an e-book, and recommends a 'major expansion of library provision' in this area (JISC 2009: 9). Paper-only monographs will have readers in the short-term, but in line with journals they will lose their primary position and have many less readers in future unless digitised.

In addition to being the main preference of readers for journals and the emerging one for books, electronic publications have other major benefits: they can more easily be found and citations to them can be tracked, which can in turn be used to help assess impact. Electronic articles are assigned a Digital Object Identifier (DOI) that is usually displayed at the top of the article (e.g. http://dx.doi.org/10.5334/bha.2114). Unlike a regular Web URL that is likely to stop working with time as webpages move, a DOI is a *persistent identifier* that is kept updated and should always point to the referenced article. If it is included in a bibliographic reference to the article, then readers will always be able to easily navigate to the article in future.

DOIs also enable citations of an article to be tracked, which helps to form an idea of the impact it has had. This is not a perfect measure, but it is the best quantitative measure currently available. Future improvements will include the ability to automatically assess the sentiment of a citation (i.e. positive or negative), but at the moment simply being able to rank articles from those with no citations to those with many is of great advantage. This is extremely useful for an assessor from a UK Research Excellence Framework (REF) panel or a US university's tenure review committee for example.

The use of DOIs is fundamental to unlocking the benefits of Open Scholarship, yet lacking in many archaeology journals. Readers perusing the references at the end of this chapter will notice that in stark contrast to the articles from STM journals, a reference (Richards 1997) from one of the leading archaeological journals, *Antiquity*, does not have a DOI. Authors who publish in journals that do not use such standards, no matter how prestigious, will find themselves disadvantaged in the longer term as article metrics become more established.

Citations using DOIs can also be aggregated to assess the impact of a journal overall, the most well known statistic being the Journal Impact Factor from Thomson Reuters. It is very common in the STM world to assess the quality of an article based on the Impact Factor of the journal it is published in, even though its accuracy is hotly contested (e.g. Rossner *et al.* 2007). This is something of a problem for the humanities as the Impact Factor is used primarily for journals in the sciences and social sciences (Hubbard and McVeigh 2011: 133). Not all humanities journals therefore are able to get an Impact Factor, and when they do it is often very low, as citations from the other humanities journals are not included in the calculations, and only citations for the last two years are taken into account (the typical timeframe of high-citation intensity for a sciences paper), but for humanities disciplines the majority of citations may be spread out to a much greater degree in the future. This is greatly compounded by the fact that at the present time citations in books, of great importance in the humanities, are also not counted. The presence, absence or value of a Journal Impact Factor is therefore not a good way of determining the impact of an article, with the number of citations of each article in isolation providing a much more accurate picture. This is something that researchers often misunderstand to their detriment in the UK's REF exercise, often submitting work from Impact Factor journals even though the Higher Education Funding Council for England (HEFCE) and the REF assessment panels explicitly tell them that this is not taken into consideration (SCST 2004, par. 209).

In order to counter the Impact Factor bias, publishers in the humanities and archaeology need to provide additional article level metrics such as those used in Public Library of Science (PLoS) journals (PLoS 2011) and recommended by the Alt-Metrics manifesto (Priem *et al.* 2010) and others (e.g. Neylon and Wu 2009). Citation data can be complemented with metrics on links to the article from social networking sites like Facebook and Twitter, social bookmarking services such as CiteULike and Connotea, reference tools such as Mendeley and Zotero, and in blogs and other media. This information provides a much wider context with which to judge the impact of research on both the academic and the wider community.

Fortunately for archaeology, with e-Publishing exactly the same solution as that described above can be applied to monographs. Social Sciences and Humanities researchers publish significantly less journal articles and more books than do their colleagues in STM (Huang and Chang 2008: 1820). By switching to e-book publishing (with the possibility of retaining print editions or using print on demand), publishers can treat books and book chapters exactly the same way as articles, with all of the same advantages. It is becoming standard practice to assign DOIs to book chapters, so that they can be easily found, cited, and tracked for impact as well.

The significance of this trend in publishing should not be underestimated. Many archaeologists publish as much as 50% of their research in book form, and if they do not publish these electronically they will find themselves at a significant disadvantage when their work is judged for impact against that of colleagues who do. Equally important in the UK, with print-only publications the overall impact of archaeology will not be assessed as highly as it might be, with a corresponding loss of government funding through the REF. In line with the principles of green OA, I have provided a reference[1] that points to an electronic preprint version of this chapter in the UCL institutional repository.

Open Access

The benefits to authors of publishing electronically are multiplied when this is Open Access (OA). OA refers to electronic papers that are published in proper academic journals and subject to full peer review as usual, but are also made freely available to anyone in the world with an Internet connection. Based on figures from the Directory of Open Access Journals (DOAJ), the number of OA titles is increasing at a rate more than three times

---

[1] Hole B., 2012. A Call for Open Scholarship in Archaeology. In Bonacchi C. ed., in press (2012). *Archaeology and Digital Communication: Towards Strategies of Public Engagement.* London: Archetype Publications. Available at: http://discovery.ucl.ac.uk/1326267/.

faster than for all journals on average (**Figure 26**, updated from Morrison 2011a). This indicates that OA is a major trend that will soon account for a significant amount of published journals.

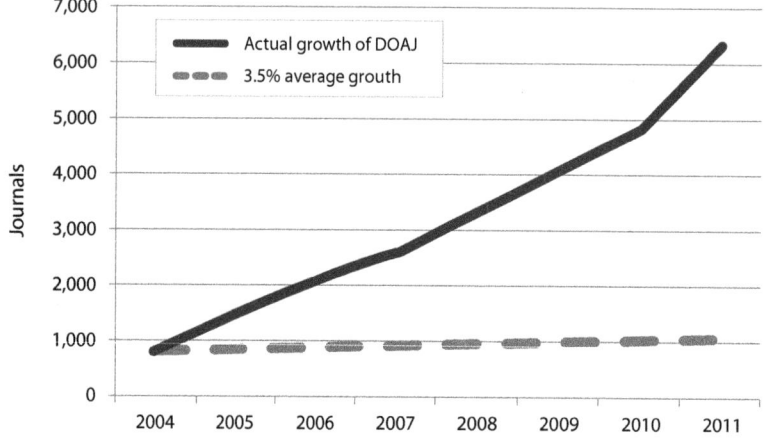

Figure 26. Chart of OA growth compared to the average for all journals, based on data collected by Morrison (2011b) detailing the growth of the Directory of Open Access Journals (DOAJ), and the estimate of 3.5% average growth from Ware and Mabe (2006: 5).

Table 1 Funding policies of UK research funders for peer-reviewed research outputs (derived from SHERPA-JULIET 2011).

Funding Agency	Article must be available free of charge without any access restrictions	It must be the final full version
Action on Hearing Loss	×	×
Arthritis Research UK	×	×
Arts and Humanities Research Council (AHRC)	×	
Biotechnology and Biological Sciences Research Council (BBSRC)	×	
British Heart Foundation (BHF)	×	×
Cancer Research UK	×	×
Chief Scientist Office, Scottish Executive (CSO)	×	×
Department of Health (DoH)	×	×
Dunhill Medical Trust (DMT)	×	×
Economic and Social Research Council (ESRC)	×	×
Engineering and Physical Sciences Research Council (EPSRC)	×	×
JISC (Joint Information Systems Committee)	×	×
Medical Research Council (MRC)	×	×
National Institute for Health Research (NIHR)	×	×
Natural Environment Research Council (NERC)	×	×
Parkinson's UK	×	×
Science and Technology Facilities Council (STFC)	×	×
Stroke Association		
Wellcome Trust	×	×

The humanities and archaeology in particular still lag significantly behind STM in OA publishing, and once more need to make up ground in order to remain competitive. OA articles have been shown to be downloaded 89% more frequently in the first year of publication than those from subscription journals (Davis *et al.* 2008: 1), thus reaching a wider audience more quickly and having a more immediate impact. This extra distribution subsequently results in significantly higher citation rates, e.g. 157% higher in computer science (Lawrence 2001), and up to 290% higher in the sciences in general (Eysenback 2006: 692).

This is not only important for increasing institutional funding by demonstrating greater impact, but also for the funding of individual researchers and projects. The Research Councils UK (RCUK) *Position Statement on Access to Research Outputs*, to which the Arts and Humanities Research Council (AHRC) is a signatory, states that:

> Ideas and knowledge derived from publicly-funded research must be made available, and accessible for public use, interrogation and scrutiny, as widely, rapidly and effectively as practicable (RCUK 2006).

Funders cannot force an author to use an open access publisher instead of another one, but their preference is reflected in their policies, which now overwhelmingly mandate OA archiving ('Green' OA) as a minimum (see **Table 1** for the UK). This is now also a requirement of the majority of UK HEIs (e.g. UCL 2010).

OA is above all an integral part of Open Scholarship because it prevents academic and economic exclusion. The OA funding model (for fully OA journals) involves charging an Article Processing Charge (APC) upon article acceptance, which is typically paid by the author's institution or funder. The article is then made freely available to anyone anywhere in the world, as opposed to the traditional model in which a reader or their institution must first either purchase a subscription or pay a relatively high fee to download it. The OA model is perfectly sustainable, as has been shown by highly successful publishers such as BioMed Central, and it has been estimated that its universal adoption in the UK could result in savings of £200 million per year (Houghton *et al.* 2009: xx).

The need for open access to scholarly resources in the developing world in particular is something that is widely recognised and supported in the academic community, and often this support is underestimated by non-OA publishers. This was demonstrated by the massive outcry against a leading group of publishers who chose to withdraw their journals from the World Health Organisation's (WHO) Health Internetwork for Access to Research Initiative (HINARI) in January of 2011 (Pérez Koehlmoos and Smith 2011). The argument that these countries could now afford to begin paying subscriptions to the most expensive medical journals in the world, despite having the highest levels of avoidable mortality caused outrage among the scientific community. An editorial in *The Lancet* (one of the journals that had been withdrawn by its publisher, Elsevier) summarised this, and presented something of an ultimatum:

> If publishers are genuine about their mission to improve health through partnerships with medical and research communities, they need to send a stronger signal of commitment to countries that most need the knowledge they control (The Lancet 2011: 272).

While archaeology journals cannot promise to help reduce mortality in poor countries, the arguments for providing free access to information are nonetheless strong. By withholding access to the research results of Western institutions, publishers are effectively ensuring the exclusion of researchers in developing countries from the global academic community. This is essentially a case of a privileged club protecting its own membership, despite outward claims to the contrary. As a telling example, as of 17th August 2011, the World Archaeological Congress (WAC) charges over £30 for a single 15 page article from its *Archaeologies* journal through Springer, and £81 for books in its *One World Archaeology* series. WAC claims that it aims '… to foster international academic interaction' and that it recognises 'the need to make archaeological studies relevant to the wider community', yet in the current economic climate these prices are already too much for researchers and libraries in the UK, and well beyond the reach of those in developing countries at any time.

Open Research Data

Research Data is any information collected and processed for the purposes of academic study. It can be in many sizes and formats, from large relational databases to small Microsoft Excel files. Some examples of archaeological research data are GIS data, geophysical survey data, image files and qualitative survey notes. The archiving of research data is another important aspect of Open Scholarship. As with electronic publishing and Open Access for research articles, there are major benefits, both to the originators of the data and to the wider community of this approach. Several open data repositories have appeared in STM such as GenBank, which specialises in gene sequencing data (Benson *et al.* 2007) and Dryad, which archives long-tail data in the biosciences (Vision 2010). While far fewer open data repositories exist in the humanities, archaeology is better served than most disciplines, with the Archaeological Data Service (ADS) in York for example (Richards 1997).

Despite the availability of these repositories, 80% of research data is not openly available (PARSE insight 2010: 19). Many reasons for this are cited by researchers, often including the lack of time to prepare data for archiving or to make it understandable to others, a problem that increases with time. The post doctoral researcher who collected the data may have left for example. Even after as little as a year those who produced the data files may no longer easily understand them, and within 2–5 years the file formats themselves may no longer be readable, while the disks or other media they are stored on may have decayed or become obsolete. Other scholars, particularly those who have assembled large datasets over a long period of time, often cite competitive advantage as a reason for not archiving. A recent study has shown that even in disciplines with a relatively strong culture of data archiving such as genetics, authors of only 25% of papers had placed the associated research data in appropriate repositories (Piwowar 2011). In another study, only 10% of researchers were willing to supply the data underlying their publications in medicine when requested (Savage and Vickery 2009). This is especially important as the data upon which a paper is based needs to be made available in order to validate its conclusions, including even the values used to make a simple chart (many graduate students know what it is like to have to extract such data from a graph with the help of a ruler, with all of the associated room for error). The data behind the charts and tables in this chapter are openly available in the UCL institutional repository (Hole 2011).

Besides validation, there are many compelling reasons to openly archive data. From a purely selfish point of view, researchers who do so can expect to be well rewarded in the near future. As with research articles, research datasets receive a DOI when archived. It is now becoming established as a best practice in STM to include the DOI to the archived data on which an article is based in the article itself, so that readers can navigate to it easily. Similarly datasets from other researchers that have been used should be cited in the reference section. This means that the data also becomes findable, citable and trackable, like any other e-publication. This is extremely important for archaeology in the UK, as from 2014 research data will be a recognised research output for the REF. The REF assessment panels will find it easiest to assess the impact of data if it has similar metrics to those for articles. It is highly probable that citation statistics for data are even more valuable. Where a research dataset and a research article each have ten citations for example, it can be argued that the dataset has had a greater impact due to the fact that it has been reused. This will only happen if both a culture of data archiving and data citation are established in archaeology, and if evidence from a recent study in the social sciences where only 29% of data used was found to be referenced (Mooney 2011) is any indication, then we still have some way to go. Overcoming the reluctance of some researchers to share data despite the above benefits could be achieved by offering an embargo period, through which they would retain sole access to the data for 2–5 years following deposition.

The incentives to openly archive and cite data are extremely compelling however. Not only do researchers get credit for having made the data available, but it has also been shown that this can lead to a significant increase in citations of associated research papers, found to be 69% higher in genetics (Piwowar *et al.* 2007). It is the actual reuse of archived data that has the greatest value. By providing their data as a platform for others to build upon, researchers can have a truly lasting impact. To borrow an extended analogy that Heather Piwowar from the University of British Colombia uses (see Cheng 2011 for a nice presentation of this), if you want others to see further by standing on your shoulders, then you need to have broad shoulders, and sharing your data is the most effective way to achieve this. This makes research more efficient overall, as researchers are able to reuse data instead of recreating it, effectively creating more output for less budget.

Data sharing not only means more citations and a greater legacy, it can also result in an increased number of opportunities for collaboration with others in the same field, research that in turn has been found to rank more highly than average for impact (Whitfield 2008: 721). Data repositories can also make datasets machine readable as 'linked data', resulting in new kinds of multidisciplinary research being done, which the creators of the data have not even envisaged (Van de Sompel and Lagoze 2009; Bizer *et al.* 2009). Examples could involve combining archaeological datasets with those from linguistics, genetics or environmental science.

In order to archive data effectively so that it will be available to other researchers in the long term, it is important to choose an appropriate repository. Making data available as supplementary files along with a research article is not archiving, and there is no guarantee that it will still be available on the publisher's website in future. One study on biomedical publications for example found that only 83% of links to supplemental material were still functional just one year after publication (Anderson *et al.* 2006), and another found that publishers only had preservation plans for 12% of supplemental files (PARSE insight 2010: 13). Repositories specialise in the care of data.

They curate it, add metadata, and index it with other services. They also keep back-ups, perform checks on its state over time to make sure that it hasn't changed, and migrate it to new file formats if the original ones become obsolete. Finally they provide the data with a permanent identifier such as a DOI so that it can be easily found and cited, and its usage tracked. It is also important that a repository is open, as it is of little benefit to the research community if simply used as a back-up, and will not attract any significant number of citations. The ADS is one such suitable repository for archaeology. Unfortunately specialised research data repositories hosted by HEIs are still several years away in most cases. Some institutional research article repositories may be extended to include data in the short term, important in the UK if datasets are to be archived in time to be assessed for the next REF. It is however essential that such a repository provides a DOI (not all currently do), and this should be checked before depositing data.

The kind of open license under which data is archived is also extremely important. Many open licenses such as 'share-alike' and 'copyleft' create legal obligations involving copyright and attribution that make sharing of data impractical, and their use is to be strongly discouraged (e.g. Science Commons 2011, par. 4.1). The potential of open and linked data is huge, but in some scenarios this may involve the creation of new datasets by federating data from anywhere from ten to 100,000 separate data sources. If each of those original datasets has a different license that a researcher is required to follow for their new dataset, then they are already lost. At the same time it may be very difficult to provide attribution for all of the source datasets in a myriad of different ways as requested under law. The solution is to choose a license that waives all rights to the data, and requests citation through scholarly norms, such as the Creative Commons Zero licence (CC0) (see Creative Commons 2011).

Finally, it is important to ensure that your data is in a sufficiently usable form that anyone downloading it can access and understand it. If they cannot then they are unlikely to reuse and cite it. This means that the data needs to be well formatted and described – for example a spreadsheet with ambiguous column headers will only cause confusion. The data should also be provided in an open format, which may mean exporting a Microsoft Excel file to CSV for example. This is important because you cannot guarantee that the recipient will have the same software, and a proprietary format is likely to be difficult to read 5–10 years down the line. This will also make it easier for the repository to automatically migrate your file to a new format later on if necessary. The deposited data must also be actionable, which means that if any unique software has been created to process and make sense of it, then this should also be deposited.

In summary, in order to broaden their shoulders and make their data open (and receive credit for it), researchers need to deposit it in an appropriate open repository that provides a DOI, make sure that it has a CC0 or equivalent license, and ensure that it is in usable form.

At the same time it is necessary to follow best practices in data citation. Once a dataset has been given a DOI, this should be cited in all publications associated with the data in the same way as a reference to a paper, in the references section. If placed elsewhere in the paper it is unlikely that the citation will be tracked and added to impact metrics. Ideally the DOI should be given with the 'http://dx.doi.org/' prefix, so that readers understand that it is usable as a Web link. For example:

Smith, J. 2011. ABC Project Osteological Data. *ADS Data Repository*. DOI: http://dx.doi.org/10.1234/98765.1

Table 2 Funding policies of UK research funders for data archiving (derived from SHERPA-JULIET 2011).

Funding Agency	Data archiving required	Data must be deposited within five years
Action on Hearing Loss		
Arthritis Research UK		
Arts and Humanities Research Council (AHRC)		
Biotechnology and Biological Sciences Research Council (BBSRC)	×	×
British Heart Foundation (BHF)		
Cancer Research UK	×	
Chief Scientist Office, Scottish Executive (CSO)		
Department of Health (DoH)		
Dunhill Medical Trust (DMT)		
Economic and Social Research Council (ESRC)	×	×
Engineering and Physical Sciences Research Council (EPSRC)	×	
JISC (Joint Information Systems Committee)		
Medical Research Council (MRC)	×	
National Institute for Health Research (NIHR)		
Natural Environment Research Council (NERC)	×	
Parkinson's UK		
Science and Technology Facilities Council (STFC)		
Stroke Association		
Wellcome Trust	×	

Although the benefits of these practices are substantial, it still takes time for them to be fully embraced, as seen in STM where adoption levels are still relatively low and increasing only slowly (Piwowar 2011). In the UK this is partly due to the absence of mandates from funding bodies (**Table 2**).

A good way to further encourage data archiving, sharing and citation is through the use of data journals, a relatively new concept in publishing. Ubiquity Press is launching a new platform of data journals in early 2012. This will include the *Journal of Open Archaeological Data* (*JOAD*)[2], among others in the humanities, social sciences and STM.

A data journal such as *JOAD* helps researchers to understand the value of archiving data by providing them with an additional citable publication in the form of an article, for which they are already used to gaining credit. This article, or data paper, is a concise description of the methodology by which the data was produced, and provides details of its reuse potential. The data paper and the dataset are submitted together to the journal and undergo peer review. In this case peer review is to ensure that the paper describes the dataset accurately, and that the data is in open form with an open license, well formatted and labelled, and is actionable. If the paper is accepted then user is given a provisional DOI for it, and asked to choose from a list of suitable repositories. The data is then deposited in the chosen archive, along with the DOI of the paper. In return the repository will assign a DOI to the dataset, which is then incorporated into the paper in the data journal, and this is published (along with any other DOIs for research papers based on the data). The metadata about the dataset is also exposed in the published paper as linked data, enhancing its chances of discovery and probability of reuse. This process is outlined in **Figure 27**.

As researchers are currently more likely to directly cite an article than a dataset, the data paper provides the author with a way to gain credit for open archiving. By engaging more readers with the data, the paper can be expected to also result in more citations of the dataset and the associated research articles, resulting in a more comprehensive demonstration of overall impact.

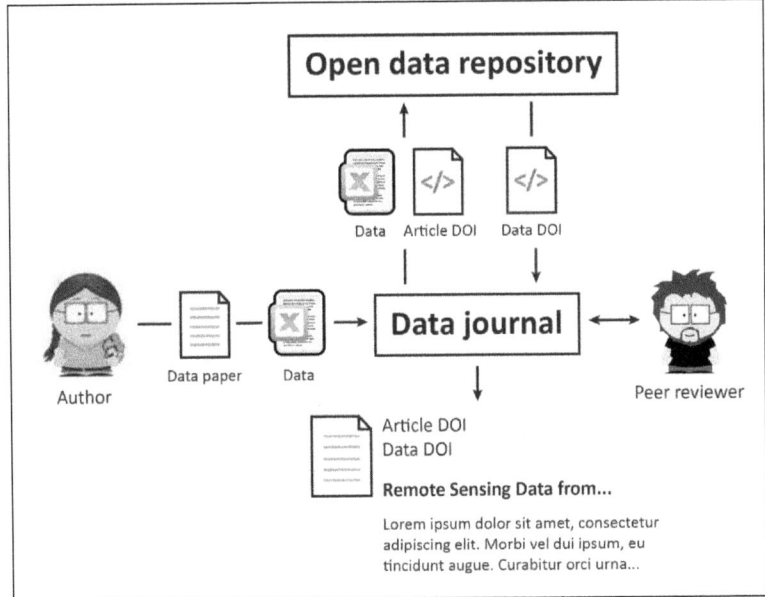

Figure 27. Proposed data journal workflow.

---

[2] http://openarchaeologydata.metajnl.com (accessed 31 January 2012).

Summary: recommendations for Open Scholarship in archaeology

1. Publish research articles electronically. The impact of work in print-only journals will not be apparent to anyone assessing it.
2. Publish books electronically too. If you are contributing a chapter encourage the editors to go with a publisher who can produce an electronic edition.
3. Ensure that your publisher gives you a DOI for your article, book or chapter. If they cannot then it is best to go elsewhere as your citations will not be tracked.
4. At minimum archive a copy of your article, book or chapter in your institutional repository ('Green' OA).
5. If you have a choice, publish your article in an Open Access journal or your chapter or book with a publisher who will release it as OA ('Gold' OA).
6. Archive your research data in an appropriate open repository, ensuring that it has a CC0 or similar licence and is in an open, usable form.
7. Ensure that the repository can give you a DOI or similar persistent identifier, otherwise consider another repository that can do so, so that use of the data can be tracked.
8. Cite the data in the reference section of any research articles based on it.
9. Publish a data paper if the option is available to you in order to ensure that the academic community are aware of its availability and reuse potential. This will also help you to achieve the widest dissemination of your work and the greatest overall impact.

Conclusion

This chapter has sought to demonstrate that practising Open Scholarship has important benefits for the advancement of knowledge, but also that doing so can greatly increase the visibility of research and benefit a researcher's career. Most importantly, these practices should improve the future prospects for the humanities and archaeology, enabling them to better assert their value and impact in a competitive world. It is hoped that the recommendations set out above can be of immediate and practical effect in moving towards this goal.

Acknowledgements

Many thanks to Heather Morrison for sharing her data on the growth of DOAJ (Morrison 2011b).

References

AHRC, 2009. *Leading the World: The Economic Impact of UK Arts and Humanities Research*. Bristol: Arts and Humanities Research Council [online]. Available at: http://www.ahrc.ac.uk/About/Policy/Documents/leadingtheworld.pdf (accessed 16 August 2011).

Anderson N. R., Tarczy-Hornoch P. and Bumgarner R. E., 2006. On the Persistence of Supplementary Resources in Biomedical Publications. *BMC Bioinformatics* 7, p. 260. DOI: http://dx.doi.org/10.1186/1471-2105-7-260.

Benson D. A., Karsch-Mizrachi I., Lipman D. J., Ostell J. and Wheeler D. L., 2007. GenBank. *Nucleic Acids Research* (2008) 36 (Database issue D25–D30). DOI: http://dx.doi.org/10.1093/nar/gkm929.

Bizer C., Heath T. and Berners-Lee T., 2009. Linked Data – The Story So Far. *International Journal on Semantic Web and Information Systems* 5 (3). DOI: http://dx.doi.org/10.4018/jswis.2009081901.

British Academy, 2010. Past Present and Future: The Public Value of the Humanities and Social Sciences. London: The British Academy, http://www.britac.ac.uk/templates/asset-relay.cfm?frmAssetFileID=9608 (accessed 15 October 2011).

British Academy, 2011. British Academy Funding for CBA. London: The British Academy [online]. Available at: http://www.britac.ac.uk/news/news.cfm/newsid/464 (accessed 16 August 2011).

Cheng C., 2011. Data Sharing Makes Our Shoulders Broader: A Prezi about Dryad for web visitors [online]. Available at: http://prezi.com/x0rcxhxqgtwf/dryad-data-sharing-makes-our-shoulders-broader/ (accessed 16 August 2011).

CIBER, 2008. *Information Behaviour of the Researcher of the Future: A CIBER Briefing Paper*. University College London.

Creative Commons, 2011. About CC0 — *'No Rights Reserved'* [online]. Available at: http://creativecommons.org/about/cc0 (accessed 16 August 2011).

Davis P. M., Lewenstein B. V., Simon D. H., Booth J. G. and Connolly M. J. L., 2008. Open Access Publishing,

Article Downloads, and Citations: Randomised Controlled Trial. *BMJ* 337:a568. DOI: http://dx.doi.org/10.1136/bmj.a568.

Evans J. A. and Reimer J., 2009. Open Access and Global Participation in Science. *Science* 323 (5917), p. 1025. DOI: http://dx.doi.org/10.1126/science.1154562.

Eysenbach G., 2006. Citation Advantage of Open Access Articles. *PLoS Biology* 4 (5):e157. DOI: http://dx.doi.org/10.1371/journal.pbio.0040157.

HLF, 2010. *Investing in Success: Heritage and the UK Tourism Economy.* London: Heritage Lottery Fund [online]. Available at: http://www.hlf.org.uk/aboutus/howwework/Documents/HLF_Tourism_Impact_single.pdf (accessed 16 August 2011).

Hole B., 2011. Data from 'A Call for Open Scholarship in Archaeology' fig. 2. UCL Discovery repository [online]. Available at: http://discovery.ucl.ac.uk/1325645/.

Hole B., 2012. A Call for Open Scholarship in Archaeology. In Bonacchi C. ed., in press (2012). *Archaeology and Digital Communication: Towards Strategies of Public Engagement.* London: Archetype Publications. Available at: http://discovery.ucl.ac.uk/1326267/.

Houghton J., Rasmussen B., Sheehan P., Oppenheim C., Morris A., Creaser C., Greenwood H., Summers M. and Gourlay A., 2009. *Economic Implications of Alternative Scholarly Publishing Models: Exploring the Costs and Benefits.* JISC [online]. Available at: http://www.jisc.ac.uk/media/documents/publications/rpteconomicoapublishing.pdf (accessed 15 October 2011).

Huang M. and Chang Y., 2008. Characteristics of Research Output in Social Sciences and Humanities: From a Research Evaluation Perspective. *Journal of the American Society for Information Science and Technology* 59 (11), pp. 1819–1828. DOI: http://dx.doi.org/10.1002/asi.20885.

Hubbard S. C. and McVeigh M. E., 2011. Casting a Wide Net: the Journal Impact Factor Numerator. *Learned Publishing* 24 (2), pp. 133–137. DOI: http://dx.doi.org/10.1087/20110208.

JISC, 2009. *National e-Books Observatory Project: Key Findings and Recommendations.* London: Joint Information Systems Council [online]. Available at: http://observatory.jiscebooks.org/files/2011/08/JISC-national-ebooks-observatory-project-final-report.pdf (accessed 15 October 2011).

The Lancet, 2011. Editorial: Bad decisions for global health. *The Lancet* 37 (9762), p. 272. DOI: http://dx.doi.org/10.1016/S0140-6736(11)60066-4.

Lawrence S., 2001. Free online availability substantially increases a paper's impact. *Nature – Web Debates* [online]. Available at: http://www.nature.com/nature/debates/e-access/Articles/lawrence.html (accessed 16 August 2011).

Mooney H., 2011. Citing Data Sources in the Social Sciences: Do Authors Do It? *Learned Publishing* 24, pp. 99–108. DOI: http://dx.doi.org/10.1087/20110204.

Morrison H., 2011a. Dramatic Growth of Open Access March 31 2011. *The Imaginary Journal of Poetic Economics* [online] 31 March 2011. Available at: http://poeticeconomics.blogspot.com/2011/03/dramatic-growth-of-open-access-march-31.html (accessed 16 August 2011).

Morrison H., 2011b. Dataset: 'Dramatic Growth of Open Access' [online]. Available at: http://hdl.handle.net/1902.1/14446 (accessed 16 August 2011).

Neylon C. and Wu S., 2009. Article-Level Metrics and the Evolution of Scientific Impact. *PLoS Biology* 7 (11): e1000242. DOI: http://dx.doi.org/1010.1371/journal.pbio.1000242.

PARSE insight, 2010. *Insight into Digital Preservation of Research Output in Europe: Insight Report* [online]. Available at: http://www.parse-insight.eu/downloads/PARSE-Insight_D3-6_InsightReport.pdf (accessed 16 August 2011).

Pérez Koehlmoos T. and Smith R., 2011. Big publishers cut access to journals in poor countries. *The Lancet* [online] 18 January 2011. DOI: http://dx.doi.org/10.1016/S0140-6736(11)60067-6.

Piwowar H. A., Day R. S. and Fridsma D. B., 2007. Sharing Detailed Research Data Is Associated with Increased Citation Rate. *PLoS ONE* 2 (3): e308. DOI: http://dx.doi.org/10.1371/journal.pone.0000308.

Piwowar H. A., 2011. Who Shares? Who Doesn't? Factors Associated with Openly Archiving Raw Research Data. *PLoS ONE* 6 (7): e18657. DOI: http://dx.doi.org/10.1371/.journal.pone.0018657.

PLoS, 2011. Article Level Metrics [online]. Available at: http://article-level-metrics.plos.org/ (accessed 16 August 2011).

Priem J., Taraborelli D., Groth P. and Neylon C., 2010. Alt-Metrics: A Manifesto. Version 1.0 – October 26, 2010 [online]. Available at: http://altmetrics.org/manifesto/ (accessed 16 August 2011).

RCUK, 2006. Research Councils UK publishes update of position statement on access to research outputs [online] 28 June 2006. Available at: http://www.rcuk.ac.uk/media/news/2006news/Pages/060628.aspx (accessed 30 October 2011).

Richards J. D., 1997. Preservation and Re-Use of Digital Data: The Role of the Archaeology Data Service. *Antiquity* 71 (274), p. 1057.

RIN, 2009. *E-Journals: Their Use, Value and Impact – Phase One Report.* London: The Research Information Network [online]. Available at: http://www.rin.ac.uk/system/files/attachments/E-journals-report.pdf (accessed 15 October 2011).

RIN, 2011. *Reinventing Research? Information Practices in the Humanities*. London: The Research Information Network [online]. Available at: http://www.rin.ac.uk/system/files/attachments/Humanities_Case_Studies_for_screen_2_0.pdf (accessed 15 October 2011).

Rossner M., Van Epps H. and Hill E., 2007. Show Me the Data. *Journal of Experimental Medicine* 204 (13), pp. 3052–3053. DOI: http://dx.doi.org/10.1084/jem.20072544.

Savage C. J. and Vickers A. J., 2009. Empirical Study of Data Sharing by Authors Publishing in PLoS Journals. *PLoS ONE* 4 (9): e7078. DOI: http://dx.doi.org/10.1371/journal.pone.0007078.

Science Commons, 2011. Protocol for Implementing Open Access Data [online]. Available at: http://sciencecommons.org/projects/publishing/open-access-data-protocol/ (accessed 17 August 2011).

SCST, 2004. *Tenth Report*. House of Commons Select Committee on Science and Technology [online]. Available at: http://www.publications.parliament.uk/pa/cm200304/cmselect/cmsctech/399/39902.htm (accessed 16 August 2011).

SHERPA-JULIET, 2011. Research Funders' Open Access Policies [online]. Available at: http://www.sherpa.ac.uk/juliet/ (accessed 16 August 2011).

Swain H., 2011. London Met VC Explains Why He is Cutting 400 Courses. *The Guardian* [online] 03 May 2011. Available at: http://www.guardian.co.uk/education/2011/may/03/london-metropolitan-gillies-course-cuts (accessed 16 August 2011).

Tenopir C., King D. W., Edwards S. and Wu L., 2009. Electronic Journals and Changes in Scholarly Article Seeking and Reading Patterns. *Aslib Proceedings: New Information Perspectives* 61 (1), pp. 5–32. DOI: http://dx.doi.org/10.1108/00012530910932267.

UCL, 2010. UCL Publications Policy 2010 [online]. Available at: http://www.ucl.ac.uk/library/publications-policy.shtml (accessed 16 August 2011).

Van de Sompel H. and Lagoze C., 2009. All Aboard: Toward a Machine-Friendly Scholarly Communication System. In Hey T., Tansley S. and Tolle K., 2009. *The Fourth Paradigm: Data-Intensive Scientific Discovery*. Redmond: Microsoft Research [online]. Available at: http://research.microsoft.com/en-us/collaboration/fourthparadigm/4th_paradigm_book_part4_sompel_lagoze.pdf (accessed 15 October 2011).

Vision T. J., 2010. Open Data and the Social Contract of Scientific Publishing. *BioScience* 60 (5), pp. 330–331. DOI: http://dx.doi.org/10.1525/bio.2010.60.5.2.

WAC, 2010. About WAC [online]. Available at: http://www.worldarchaeologicalcongress.org/about-wac/about-wac (accessed 17 August 2011).

Ware M. and Mabe M., 2009. *The STM Report: An Overview of Scientific and Scholarly Journal Publishing*. Oxford: STM: International Association of Scientific, Technical and Medical Publishers [online]. Available at: www.stm-assoc.org/2009_10_13_MWC_STM_Report.pdf (accessed 15 October 2011).

Whitfield J., 2008. Group Theory. *Nature* 455, pp. 720-723. DOI: http://dx.doi.org/10.1038/455720a.

Zhang J. and Chen C., 2010. Collaboration in an Open Data eScience: A Case Study of Sloan Digital Sky Survey. *ArXiv* [online]. Available at: http://arxiv.org/abs/1001.3663v1.

Conclusions

Daniel Pett, Chiara Bonacchi

The essays published in this volume provide a diverse and challenging discussion of potential strategies of public engagement for archaeology, with substantial conceptual synergies. They cover: the explosion of new forms of social media; the shift to open access publishing models; the use of the Internet via websites, knowledge resources and games; mobile platforms for integrating with a wider off-line offer and the digital evolution of television. The methods of engagement that are proposed have their own pros and cons. Some are easily imitable, sustainable and can be implemented at little or no cost, but with considerable effort (this is the case for social media, individually illustrated by Bevan, Pett, Richardson, Thornton, this volume); others require specialist knowledge, equipment and platforms for production and implementation (e.g. Bonacchi *et al.*, Goskar, and Jeater, this volume), or a fundamental 'ethical' change in the way in which intra- and inter-specialist communication is conducted within the archaeological research community (Hole, this volume). It is hoped that readers will find some of these strategies useful in their profession.

Papers all revolve around the ideological concept of Public Archaeology that was outlined in the introduction; ultimately, they deal with the production, communication, and public 'consumption' of archaeological resources (including the scientific results achieved, the material evidence that is interpreted, etc.), conceived as actions which (should) feed into and inform each other, as archaeological work is undertaken. Contributions highlight the importance of understanding the context of archaeology, its processes and diverse public audiences on solid theoretical grounds and through the collection of data, in order to improve public engagement and archaeological communication, more generally.

The revered Mortimer Wheeler, writing in his 1955 memoir, discusses an idea which we, the archaeological community, are still wrestling with: 'today the public has every right to its archaeology, palatably garnished; for the days of private patronage are over, and most field archaeology now comes directly out of our rates and taxes, whether we like it or not' (Wheeler 1955: 64). The discussions that took place at the workshop and which are collectively published within this volume underlined the topicality of this statement and indicated real ways in which such a concept can be implemented today, in a very much changed media context, which is increasingly dominated by the use of digital technologies. This pioneering archaeologist sets us on the route towards evaluating strategies of public engagement with archaeology more fully and this book is just the beginning. After a summative exploration of the concept of engagement, this brief, final piece will present the possible future steps that may be taken.

'Engagement': what does it mean?

'Engagement' is currently a cultural buzzword, often replacing the once popular term 'outreach', which was prevalent, for example, throughout sponsored projects administered by the erstwhile Museums, Libraries and Archives Council's (MLA) much maligned *Renaissance in the Regions* programme. In the September 2011 edition of the *Museums Journal*, Hedley Swain[1] wrote a commentary entitled 'Quality of experience and engagement is key' (Swain 2011), a piece primarily focused on museums and the arts, but conceptually applicable to archaeology. In this context, the term 'engagement' is confined to the extent to which individuals develop, or feel that they have a meaningful relationship or experience with the producing entity. Thus, within the realms of the discussions within, it is the public's relationship with the archaeological community (and associated bodies) that we are considering; an emphasis on raising the quality of such a relationship makes the bedrock throughout all the papers, and drives their proposed strategies, together with an attention towards attracting new audiences (younger and socially disadvantaged ones especially) and increasing the number and 'loyalty' of existing ones.[2]

However, in the archaeological sector, engagement is often seen as an ancillary activity that has a lesser role than research or fieldwork, and is therefore often neglected (BIS 2010: 34), when it should be one of the more pre-eminent aspects of publicly funded research. As recognised by the European Commission (2007: 12), existing obstacles to public engagement are serious and diverse: 'Systems of funding, processes of research assessment, and the softer structures of career advancement' – they say – 'do not provide many incentives for scientists to spend time engaging with the social and ethical dimensions of their work'. Such limitations must be overcome before high quality engagement can occur. Several institutions (including the academic host for the workshop[3]) now offer incentives and prizes for engagement activities, placing engagement higher up practitioners' agenda. At the time of writing, archaeology is embroiled in the turgid financial swamp that is encompassing most heritage sectors. Within his paper, Hole cites figures from Heritage Lottery Fund documents that show the economic benefits that heritage concerns bring to the UK's struggling economy, but demonstrating to our audience (the British public) the worth of our discipline is vital and it is here that coherent engagement can make the difference. Recent celebrated examples, such as the Fenland District Council debacle (Kennedy 2011), have shown that many are unaware of the need for archaeological investigation when housing developments are planned. Would archaeological engagement have been useful in this instance? Undoubtedly. The subsequent social media campaign and organised response via traditional media demonstrated that archaeologists could engage with a wider audience and influence political situations; probably this scenario will become more frequent as the recession bites deeper worldwide.

Are archaeologists prepared for how to react to these challenges? Perhaps the answer is not yet, and this is where strategy becomes all-important and the utility of guidance is more apparent. Projects raising awareness of the funding crisis in our sector are now starting to leverage social media (e.g. the Mortimer campaign[4]), and are learning rapidly about techniques that work. The Theoretical

---

[1] Hedley Swain is now Director of 'Museums and Renaissance' at Arts Council England.

[2] Yet, it seems that more research is still needed on the types and quality of audiences' experience of archaeology, in spite of the methodological difficulty of doing so. Counting the number of 'downloads' or of 'subscribers' is certainly easier (but not sufficient) than understanding who those users are, why they engage, with what motivations and expectations, and whether they are ultimately satisfied or truly engaged with the experience.

[3] The Institute of Archaeology (UCL).

[4] http://savearchaeology.co.uk/ (accessed 12 December 2011).

Archaeology Group conference 2011, for example, featured a session on the use of social media in archaeology[5], thus engagement methodologies are being discussed and implemented from grass roots right up to national high profile project level. The interest in and desire to access information on archaeology is not ubiquitous; the public want to do this on their own terms, for example when visiting an historic site, or they want to learn about their particular area or a specific discovery (e.g. the Staffordshire Hoard; Pett 2010: 51). Unless the archaeological sector can make itself an integral feature in the wider public's daily life, the situation will remain the same, with larger brands achieving greater exposure and the rest chasing the 'Long Tail' (a concept that is regularly cited throughout this volume; see Anderson 2006). The point is not to convince, persuade, or fill a hidden need for archaeology, but to guarantee open access to all those interested; also, it is a matter of proposing archaeology and make the public aware of its existence, meanings and value, so that they may (or may not) make the decision to engage with it. As underlined in the introduction, while more 'products', including cultural ones, are available online, audiences often discover new fondness for niche subjects, with which they could not easily engage in the previous prevalently off-line world of culture and entertainment.

Next steps on the path to engagement

The Internet is a powerful facilitator or catalyst for public engagement in archaeology; it is an enabler that can reach the widest audience (when thinking globally), and a technology that allows for the formation of social capital (on this concept see Bevan, and Pett, this volume) and for cultural ideological exchange that national bodies such as English Heritage or the Council for British Archaeology should be promoting vigorously. However, online engagement is not a catchall panacea for at least two main reasons. Firstly, many archaeological institutions are still sceptical about the potential of the Internet, as shown by Goskar (this volume), when describing his organisation. Secondly, the elderly and socio-economically deprived sectors of society often have marginalised access to digital resources (National Policing Improvement Agency 2010, House of Commons 2008: 3, 11–12); ten million people in the UK do not have online access, although, as cited by the ACE *et al.* report (2010: 4, 18), 53% of the online population have used the Internet to access information on arts and heritage based activities. This is a significant figure, but it is regular or repeated engagement which is desirable, and the challenge is to determine 'how' and 'why' such a result can be achieved and inclusivity guaranteed.

Papers within this volume also discuss a variety of audiences and sectors; for instance, museums, universities and academia, the private sector and the amateur enthusiast. Does one treat all of these as equals, or more emphasis is to be placed onto one over the other? Perhaps the desired path to follow would be to have an overarching engagement strategy, which addresses segmented audiences individually. Alternatively, one could follow a route whence each audience is a node that is given its own strategy that does not fit into the overall concept. The museum sector has made an adequate start to strategising; it has produced a report (Finnis *et al.* 2011) that presents case studies and methodologies for measuring or benchmarking online success, and which can be applied across diverse museum virtual estates.

It could also be of use to the archaeological community to look outside the discipline and study how others have developed their own 'strategies for engagement'. Cases such as the Ministry of Defence's social media presence[6], the Metropolitan Police *Community Engagement* document[7] and the successful *Science for All* campaign (BIS 2010) could be analysed and adapted for our

---

[5] http://centraltag.wordpress.com/call-for-papers/dr-web-love-or-how-i-learnt-to-stop-worrying-love-social-media/ (accessed 19 December 2011).

[6] The paucity of good quality websites to cite as exemplars, in the archaeological sector, has been debated on Twitter by participants in the workshop from both sides of the Atlantic.

[7] http://www.met.police.uk/dcf/files/ce_strategy.pdf (accessed 31 January 2012).

own circumstances, where opportune. The difficulty in the generation of social media strategies can frequently be seen on the Internet, evidenced by cross-sectorial search for exemplars (see, for example, Mulqueeny 2009, Pickard 2010, and the excellent article by Ide-Smith 2010) to follow or modify. Many of the ideas evangelised in these documents are common-sense: create a dialogue, learn about the network, choose the right tools for the problem or social network you want to engage, analyse and store your conversations for impact, be honest and accurate in your output, etc. Within this volume, Hole comprehensively demonstrates how the open accessing revolution is comfortable with emulation; it has been proactive in learning from the Science, Technology, Engineering and Medicine sectors, and also realised the need for 'impact' when trying to show relative worth to funding bodies.

Following on from these considerations and the publication as a whole, we would like to leave the reader with a few points on which ACRN[8] and CASPAR[9] will be working, on the route to defining and implementing coherent and measureable strategies of public engagement with archaeology.

- A three day conference and digital workshop will be held in late 2012 under the aegis of ACRN and CASPAR, which will allow speakers and delegates access to a platform for discussing and expanding the case study-led approach followed within this volume. Such conference will also encourage robust exploration of the proposed public engagement models, and improvements to be suggested. The speakers will be from a wider range of speciality fields (including museums, ICT, social media, etc.) and, perhaps most importantly, from funding bodies and potential partners for investment or knowledge sharing.
- It is also proposed that there is an urgent need to conduct extensive, national (and perhaps international) studies to determine how and why the public engage with archaeology, through all platforms.[10]
- There is a clear necessity of simple guidelines or 'terms of reference' on how to effectively communicate with online audiences and evaluate success. Information on how to produce high quality, engaging websites is particularly vital for allowing the public to access archaeological information easily via mobile and traditional means (as demonstrated in the closing discussion, at the workshop). The production of a social media toolkit would also provide organisations with the ability to professionally interact and engage with new audiences; indications on which platforms to adopt, how best to leverage them and potential risks to archaeological organisations would be welcomed. Finally, guidance on how to develop cultural content to be accessed via the mobile device has become paramount. Statistics cited in several papers demonstrate that this platform is now ubiquitous and grasping an increasing share of the way that people interact online (as mobile technology improves and devices get smaller and more powerful, we may see a shift away from the desktop era).
- Training on public engagement methods should be available and be an option for continuing personal development programmes (CPD), with a caveat that not all are suitable for participating in this activity. The BIS[11] (2010: 38) document raises concerns that natural ability has some impact on success in engagement and the Research Council UK (2010: 8) advocates 'flexible and responsive funding, training and best practice support to enable …

---

[8] The Archaeology and Communication Research Network (UCL).

[9] The Centre for Audio-Visual Study and Practice in Archaeology (UCL).

[10] Bonacchi's doctorate (*Communicating Archaeology: From Trends to Policy. Public Perceptions and Experience in the Changing Media Environment*) is a step in this direction.

[11] Department for Business, Innovations and Skills.

researchers to develop the capacity and capability to engage with the public effectively and sustainably'. A need has been identified especially for assistance in acquiring skills for the creation of audiovisuals; the dearth of those skills, in archaeology, remains a difficult divide to cross, even though the price of equipment is falling.

- Recognition should be forthcoming for the production of rich media from the sector. An extension of the Council for British Archaeology's British Archaeological Awards could encompass this with sub-categories including best website and/or best use of social media.
- Strategies of engagement are better driven from the top of the organisation (Econsultancy 2010: 8); having technologically minded management can make the difference when it comes to enabling engagement.

References

Anderson C., 2006. *The Long Tail. Why the Future of Business is Selling Less of More.* New York: Hyperion.

Arts Council England, Museums Libraries and Archives Council, and Arts and Business, 2010. *Digital Audiences: Engagement with Arts and Culture Online* [online]. Available at: http://www.artscouncil.org.uk/media/uploads/doc/Digital_audiences_final.pdf (accessed 08 June 2011).

BIS (Department for Business, Innovations and Skills), 2010. *Science for all. Report and action plan from the Science for All Expert Group* [online]. Available at: http://interactive.bis.gov.uk/scienceandsociety/site/all/files/2010/02/BIS-R8803-URN10-6262-1.pdf (accessed 01 November 2011).

European Commission, 2007. *Public engagement in Science* [online]. Available at: http://ec.europa.eu/research/science-society/document_library/pdf_06/public-engagement-081002_en.pdf (accessed 02 November 2011).

Econsultancy, 2010. *Digital Engagement in the Public Sector.* London: Farringdon.

Finnis J., Chan S. and Clements R., 2011. *Let's get real: How to evaluate online success.* Brighton: Culture24.

House of Commons, 2008. *Government on the Internet: Progress in delivering information and services online. Sixteenth Report of Session 2007–08.* London: The Stationary Office Ltd.

Ide-Smith M., 2010. *A digital engagement framework adapted for local government* [online]. Available at: http://www.ide-smith.co.uk/?p=474 (accessed 02 November 2011).

Kennedy M., 2011. Archaeologists furious over councillor's bunny huggers jibe. *The Guardian* [online] 27 June 2011. Available at: http://www.guardian.co.uk/science/2011/jun/27/archaeologists-furious-bunny-huggers (accessed 02 November 2011).

Mulqueeny E., 2009. Seven principles for digital engagement (please help me) [online]. Available at: http://mulqueeny.wordpress.com/2009/03/17/seven-principles-for-digital-engagement-help-me-please/ (accessed 02 November 2011).

National Policing Improvement Agency, 2010. *Digital Engagement – policy impact* [online]. Available at: http://www.neighbourhoodpolicing.co.uk/files/comms_digital_engagement_v3.pdf (accessed 01 November 2011).

Pett D. E. J., 2010. Meeting public interest in the hoard. *British Archaeology* 110, p. 51.

Pickard M., 2010. Open door. *The Guardian* [online] 01 November 2010. Available at: http://www.guardian.co.uk/commentisfree/2010/nov/01/digital-engagement-rules-of-participation (accessed 01 November 2011).

Swain H., 2011. Quality of experience and engagement is key. *Museums Journal* (September 2011), p. 16.

Research Council UK, 2009. *RCUK Public Engagement with Research Strategy* [online]. Available at: http://www.rcuk.ac.uk/documents/scisoc/RCUKPERStrategy.pdf (accessed 02 November 2011).

Wheeler R. E. M., 1955. *Still digging: interleaves from an antiquary's notebook.* Michael Joseph: London.

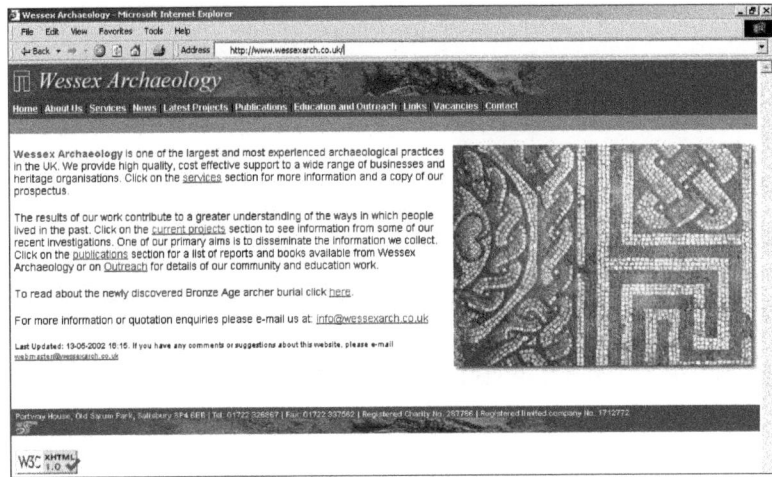

Plate 1. Wessex Archaeology website at the launch on 13 May 2002.

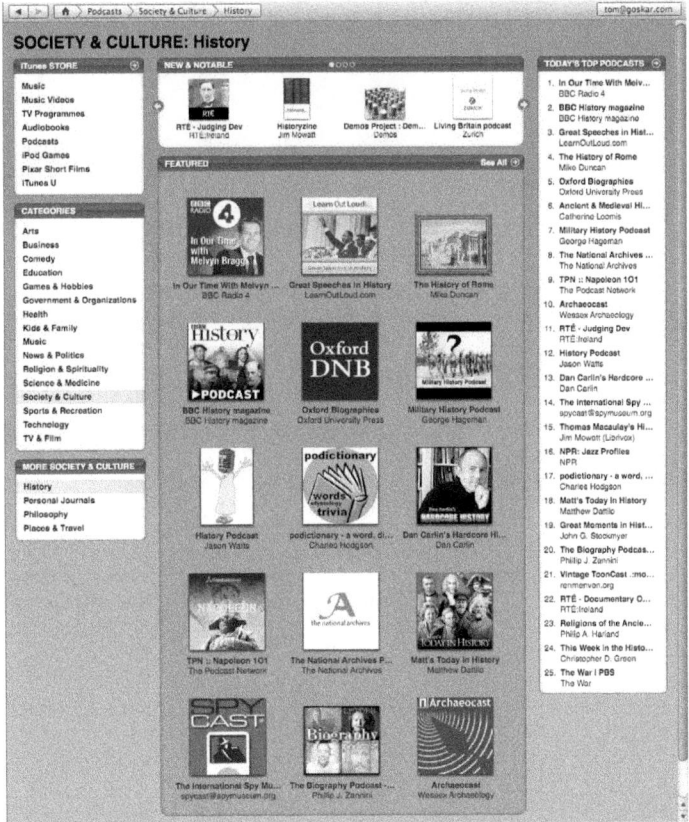

Plate 2. *Archaeocast* in the top 10 History podcasts in the iTunes podcast directory.

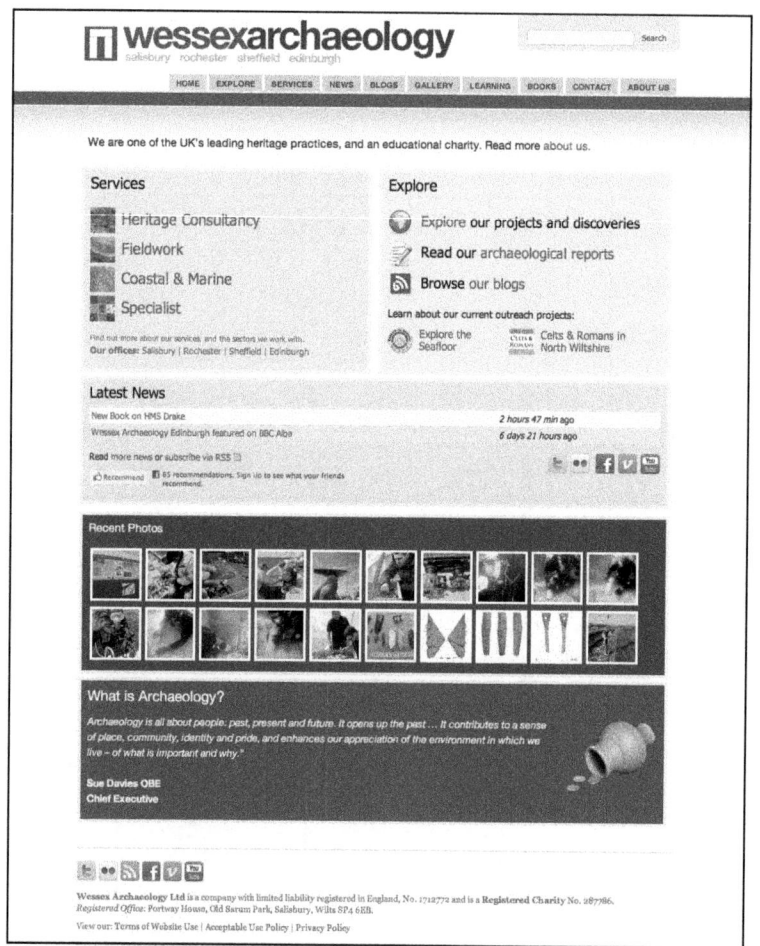

Plate 3. Wessex Archaeology's homepage in July 2011.

Plate 4. Introductory screen to a game of *Civilization V*, playing as the English (*Civilization V*: 2K Games/Firaxis Games).

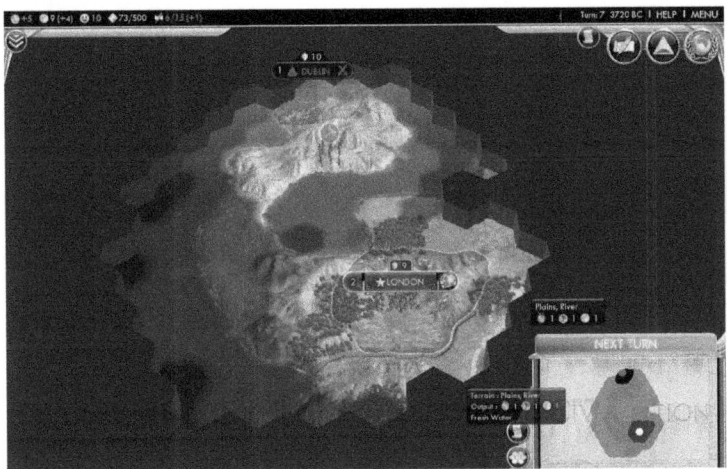

Plate 5. The English empire in 3720 BC, on a randomly-generated map (*Civilization V*: 2K Games/Firaxis Games).

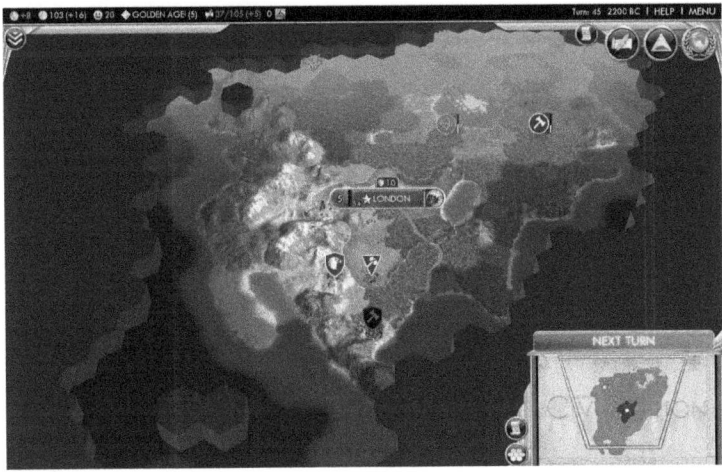

Plate 6. The English empire in 2200 BC, this time on a real-world map (but with randomised location!). The small icons on the map are different kinds of units (*Civilization V*: 2K Games/Firaxis Games).

Plate 7. The city-management screen for London, enabling control of production in the city and its hinterland (*Civilization V*: 2K Games/Firaxis Games).

Plate 8. In-game suggestions are provided by the Economic, Military, Foreign and Science advisors (*Civilization V*: 2K Games/Firaxis Games).

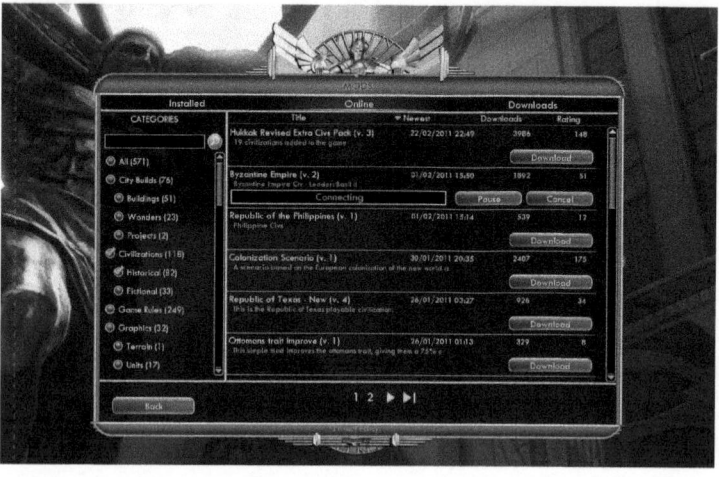

Plate 9. Access to player-created mods is facilitated within the main *Civilization V* programme (*Civilization V*: 2K Games/Firaxis Games).

Plate 10. Bomb damage at 21 Queen Victoria Street, 1941, © Museum of London/By Kind Permission of The Commissioner of the City of London Police.

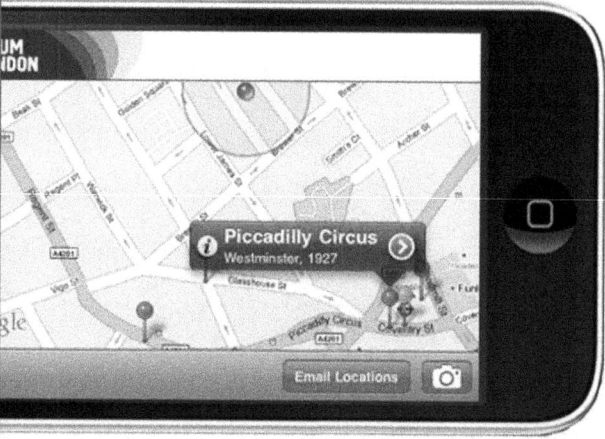

Plate 11. The finished *Streetmuseum* app © Museum of London.

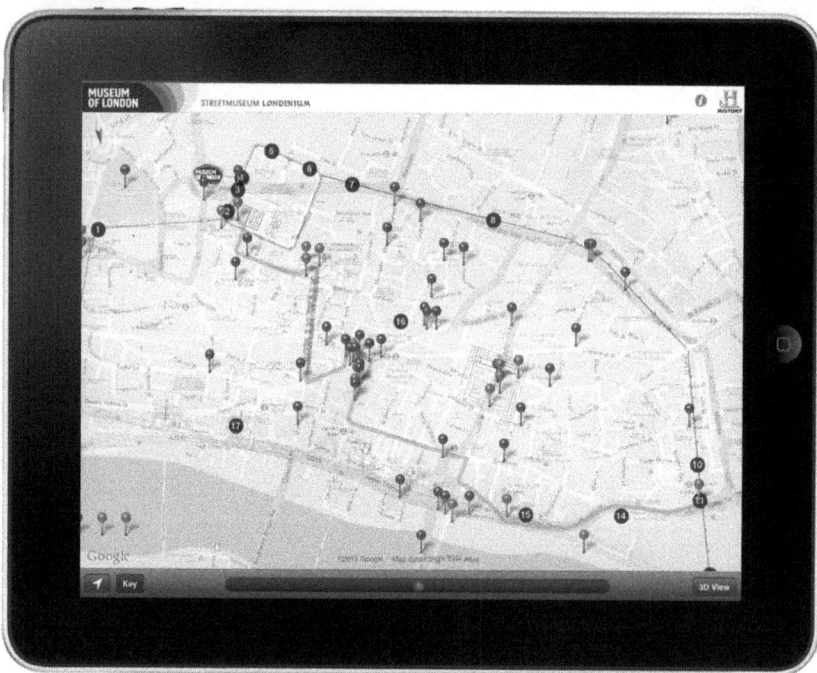

Plate 12. The map of Roman London overlaid on the modern Google map, viewed on an iPad screen © Museum of London.

Plate 13. An 'excavated' object, viewed on an iPad screen © Museum of London.

Plate 14. Video of gladiators fighting over a view of Guildhall Yard, viewed on an iPad screen © HISTORY.

Plate 15. One of Google's social Web adverts at Piccadilly Circus underground station.

Plate 16. A QR code in the BM *Australia Garden* exhibition on the West forecourt 2011. The QR code on the sign is shown on the right and when scanned goes to http://bit.ly/lHPhkB a short URL for a mobile webpage at: http://www.britishmuseum.org/mobile/australia_trail/australia_stop_1.aspx (Photo by author). This follows best practice for using the glyphs and mobile devices.

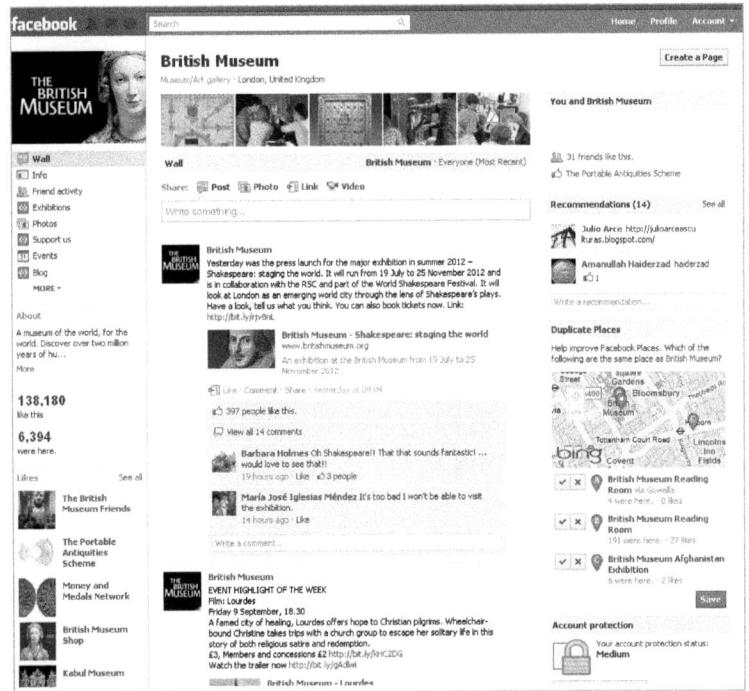

Plate 17. The British Museum's presence on Facebook.

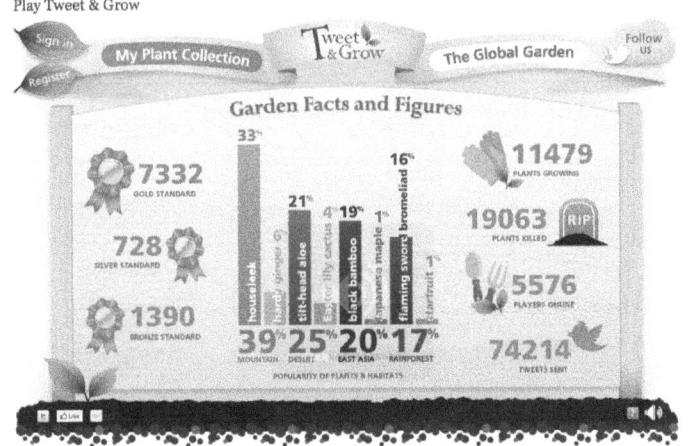

Plate 18. The *Tweet & Grow* 'Global Garden' screen.

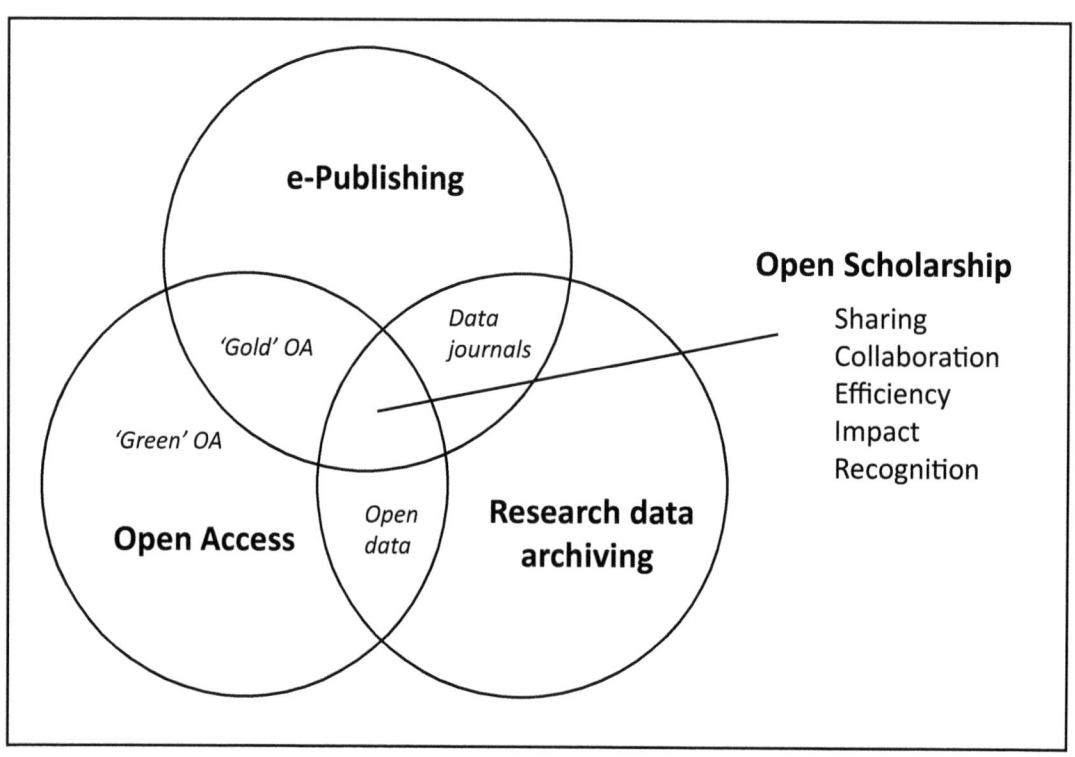

Plate 19. Venn diagram of Open Scholarship factors.

www.ingramcontent.com/pod-product-compliance
Ingram Content Group UK Ltd.
Pitfield, Milton Keynes, MK11 3LW, UK
UKHW050457150426
5217IPUK00025B/1731